THE ACCIDENTAL
HEADTEACHER

MARTIN DALE

The Accidental Headteacher is dedicated to the memory of the late Barry Hines whose novel 'A Kestrel for a Knave' provided the author with some much needed direction and realistic ambition sometime in the early 1970's and to genuine 'whistleblowers' everywhere, along with all those teachers and head teachers who go into teaching for all the right reasons, to make a difference to the lives of young people.

Most especially, it is dedicated to my daughter who is one of those described above and who, along with many others, has worked both tirelessly and selflessly throughout the Covid pandemic while others, who should have known better, appear to have done otherwise, 'twas ever thus.

Contents

Preface

From an inauspicious introduction, as a soon to be five year old in a late 1950's northern primary school, to an equally un-illustrious conclusion as a leader of a Midlands Special School half a century later, this book is a collection of tales, anecdotes and observations gathered together via an unlikely educational journey stopping off at northern Church of England Primary, Oxbridge Boarding School, Northern Grammar, 1970's College of Education (Teacher Training College) and three decades of teaching experience.

Many of the fictional characters encountered may, in some strange way, seem oddly familiar. Eleven or so years of education is, after all, something virtually all of us have in common, hence perhaps the almost universal popularity of school story settings from *Dotheboys Hall* and *'Tom Brown's School Days'* through to *Greyfriars*, *'Grange Hill'* and *'Waterloo Road'*.

To have over fifty years of such experience to call upon is not quite so common. The extensive variety of experiences allows the author, through the eyes of Lawrence, Loz, Utting, Lol, Lawrie, 'Sir' or Mr. Utting , to offer the reader an eye opening insight into the workings of the *'headucation'* (sic) system in all its various manifestations. In doing so we may also consider the impact that education, not least the characters encountered, including those fearsome headteachers (usually *headmasters*) and experiences we all remember, have on our very being, upon what goes on within our own heads both at the time and long after the formal conclusion of our education.

The included 'playlist' is just an additional piece of nostalgic fun. It is not intended as a definitive description of the greatest hits of the last half century, but simply a collection of forty songs, some more relevant than others, all selected from the years between 1959 and 2009, and aimed at providing a soundtrack to the landscape of Lawrie's educational odyssey.

Sitting here now I can well recall an English lecturer at College, one Harry Bowman to be precise, taking a break from discussion of *Willy Loman's* tragedy in Arthur Miller's *'Death of a Salesman'*, to momentarily and pertinently, given the context of the play, reflect on the fact that he (Harry) had never realised he was getting old until he caught sight of his own scarcely recognised reflection gazing maliciously back at him from a *Burton's* shop window.

This startling revelation was something we, as young men and women, all laughed *with* him about at the time. Only recently, having experienced such a disquieting event as an all too regular occurrence, have I discovered that our laughter would have been far more genuine than his. Indeed having fallen victim to my own malevolent, ageing image more times than I care to remember, I now realise it is such moments that contribute towards our need to produce something to prove that age can still lead to productivity, that the aging process need not be a wholly negative and degenerative one and that the experience acquired, as at least a by-product of age, can still leave us with something to offer.

In itself age is not synonymous with experience and

certainly not with wisdom. It should however provide at least a perspective, a looking glass even, through which our experiences may be made to serve some useful purpose. We are all said to learn from experience and in the same way we can teach by it too.

If this book is to have a purpose, other than to simply act as a collection of sometimes amusing, evocative, hopefully entertaining, nostalgic and, at times, downright disturbing and disconcerting observations, if it is to serve some greater didactic function, then one must hope that some illumination may be gained by the reader from the half a century's worth of educational experience and perspective which began in the shadow of an abandoned cotton mill at the foot of the Lancashire Pennines in September 1959.

Martin Dale. 2023.

PART I
FORMATIVE LESSONS

ONE

EDGEMOOR PRIMARY

IN THE BEGINNING

Track 1. 'Oh Carol!' Neil Sedaka.

Little Lawrence Utting's peculiar educational journey began, at the age of (very nearly) five with a first day at school that remains a curious fusion of vivid and murky memory, not least because it all came as such a shock. There had been no preparation, Lawrence would be 'starting school' and that was that.

Nowadays there would have been half days, whole days or an even longer period of something called 'induction', but back in the late fifties, especially as an only child with no experienced older siblings to call upon, Lawrence really didn't have the slightest notion of what 'school' actually was. Somewhere you went to or something that was done to you was far from clear. Little did he know that it was actually to become a curious mixture of both.

All Lawrence could gather from that first morning was that it involved getting up earlier than usual and walking about one and a half miles with his mother to an unfamiliar place filled with other equally unfamiliar children. What he was to do there, how long he was to stay there, or indeed if he was even ever to leave there at all, remained largely unanswered questions.

What else could he remember now? The smell! That scent of a new school year, which would become readily identifiable, and until relatively recently, surprisingly unchanged. A combination of floor polish, sawdust, ink, blackboard paint, lost P.T. kit, wax crayons, sweat and school milk (quite different from any other kind of milk, largely as a result of it usually being kept in cloakrooms adjacent to some unnecessarily and wastefully ferocious source of heat) and all mixed together with something more than just a soupcon of fear. Fear of the unknown, fear of being in the company of much older and larger children and fear, a quite unjustified fear as things would transpire, of the Headmaster, Mr. Failsworth, both the tallest and baldest man Lawrence had ever come across and his assistant, Miss Bolt, whose severe grey bun, lined face and wire rimmed glasses combined to make her the most elderly and sinister looking lady he had ever come across, apart from those within the institution his parents occasionally forced him into to attending to visit one of Lawrence's *'confused'* and elderly aunts.

The school itself was typical of the type which may still be found in use all over the North and Midlands even today. As a Church of England school it stood adjacent to the church and was separated from the local, even then derelict, cotton mill by the grave yard which served not only as the resting place of many poor souls but a similar number and variety of playground balls.

The only part of the school building not to qualify as archetypally Victorian was that known as the 'Institute', little more than a long shack situated on waste ground between

4

the 'backs' of two rows of terraced houses and opposite the school gates.

The 'institute' doubled as both a classroom and the school dining room. Although it didn't seem so at the time, after all this was the newest part of the school, this arrangement must have been enormously frustrating for poor Mr. Spindle, co-incidentally, or perhaps not, the youngest member of staff. Not only were all his lessons from mid morning onwards disrupted by the respective clatter and natter of pots, pans and dinner ladies operating in the kitchen at the far end of the building, but his room had then to be rearranged into a dining hall leaving it seemingly haunted by such penetrative aromatic delights as meat and (largely) potato pie, stewed cabbage, butter beans and tapioca throughout each and every afternoon. No wonder then that Mr. Spindle often seemed better tempered in the morning, but more of that later.

As for the main school building, the infants and younger juniors were housed on the ground floor where a hall, which was used for P.T. (P.E. had yet to be invented) and assemblies was also located. Upstairs was the domain of the 'seniors', or the 'big boys' as little Lawrence internally and, again fearfully, referred to them. Today they would be described as Years 5 and 6, little kids preparing for the potentially traumatic business of transfer to secondary school, but to a nearly five year old these ten and eleven year olds, who rampaged around the playground in a way Lawrence could only secretly aspire to, were never more aptly, or sinisterly, described than simply as 'the big boys'.

For now Lawrence's motto rapidly became *'keep your head down'* and it probably took him the best part of another two years to happily venture up the stairs to where those both physically and socially at the top of the school were kept under the firm control of Mrs. Bottomley, a large and formidable woman who, within ten minutes of the end of each school day, would be found alongside her husband, behind the counter of the nearby local post office. How times change.

Here it was then that Lawrence was abandoned, or so it felt at the time, along with twenty or so equally bewildered infants, into the 'care' of Miss Bolt. Still shocked at the apparent desertion by their mothers there was some degree of tearfulness, chiefly it has to be said amongst the girls and not, by this stage at least, from Lawrence.

Then came two introductions, the infants' to pencils and with it Miss Bolt's, to impassioned and unrivalled sobbing...from Lawrence! Quite why the sight of these admittedly somewhat clumsy looking and particularly dark leaded black pencils should have had this effect on Lawrence has never really been understood. The result however was spectacular. Lawrence howled, so much so that he had to be removed and placed alone in a separate room in the company of a large, supposedly cheerful and colourful model soldier made almost entirely of brightly painted wood save for its arms and hands which were made of...thick pencils and unsharpened pencil lead!

Why they should have been a source of such terror remains a mystery however Lawrence's subsequent tantrum was certainly spectacular. It was definitely all too much for Miss Bolt, who by this stage found little Lawrence's behaviour infinitely more menacing than anything she had to offer.

Stunned by such an outpouring of misery, Miss Bolt couldn't wait to hand the distraught infant over to her flame haired junior, Miss Clarke, a twenty something beauty probably in her first two or three years of teaching and with significantly more energy to spare. Miss Bolt had clearly seen enough and Miss Clarke was more than welcome to young Lawrence.

From his point of view things could not have worked out

better. The cold detachment of an elderly spinster was replaced by the warmth, care and enthusiasm of one of the new breed of teachers who, as an additional attraction, was what Lawrence's mother might then have described as '*bonnie*'.

Seldom can a little boy's tears and tantrums have been used to such good effect, or at least that would have been the case had the apparently terrified child had any idea what the source or purpose of this over dramatic display of distress actually was. Indeed so successful was the eventual, though quite unintended, outcome that it remains to Lawrence's eternal credit that he has managed to largely refrain from repeating the use of such a strategy ever since.

Track 2. '*Cathy's Clown*'. *The Everly Brothers*

For the next two years, until the time of her retirement, Miss Bolt and Lawrence gave each other a wide birth. Throughout this period he was to be found in Miss Clarke's class where he joyously learned the rudiments of education a significant part of which involved the very mixed blessing of what may now be recognised as having been a very first 'crush'. During this time Lawrence would barely shed another tear, well only when, at the end of afternoon play, he ran around a corner of the schoolyard straight into Gavin Grimes' head 'bursting' his nose and leaving a trail of blood the length of the playground. Even that was worth it, given the resulting attention provided by Miss Clarke, although Lawrence's mother may not have agreed when, having arrived to collect him, she spotted the very same crimson trail leading through the school doors at precisely the same time as Mr. Failsworth emerged to request, 'Could you come this way please Mrs. Utting!'

School had become a pleasure. Playtimes were spent in either endless buttock slapping games of 'Cowboys and Indi-

7

ans' or imagining that running around with their arms extended horizontally, making a peculiar nasal droning sound somehow turned all the boys into World War II fighter pilots.

Never great at arithmetic Lawrence did his best to impress Miss Clarke by learning his 'tables' and was at least reasonably competent at most other subjects, something new and supposedly innovative called 'Music and Movement' apart. Fighter pilot or Indian warrior...no problem, but who wanted to replicate a 'tree in autumn'?

He rapidly became an accomplished reader, inspired, like so many others, by the renowned *'Janet and John'* series or, to be more accurate, by an absolute desire to leave their monumentally dull world far behind and progress to a land of proper books where aspects that were to become known as *character* and *plot* were rumoured to feature.

Then, one day, Lawrence's contentment was suddenly shattered. Quietly preparing himself for the inevitable transition to Mr. Spindles' 'Institute' class the following September, Lawrence was totally unprepared for Mr. Failsworth's announcement at the end of term assembly.

'Those of you returning in six weeks time will have to get used to one or two changes for next year,' he sternly announced to the respectfully silent hall.

'The first of these changes' he went on 'concerns Miss. Clarke, who, I am delighted to inform you all, is to be married during the summer holiday meaning that when we return you will all have to get used to calling her Mrs. Dyson...'

Whatever came next Lawrence could claim no knowledge of. Congratulations, explanation, warning that the school was on fire...who cared? His world had just crumbled. Mr. Failsworth's mouth continued to move but no sound seemed to be uttered. Just seven years old and experiencing his first betrayal!

Lawrence went home for the summer and cried.

LOZ

Track 3. 'Stanger on the Shore' Acker Bilk

There were to be changes that holiday. As he spent the summer of 1961 riding imaginary horses across the now long gone surrounding fields, committing untold killings via the use of nothing more deadly than two, again horizontally pointed fingers or outstretched arms, and playing on bikes and homemade 'bogeys' around 'the backs', Lawrence's name, as part of that almost universal process of acceptance, had become abbreviated so that when he returned to school for the beginning of a new year, Lawrence had, much to his parents' disapproval, become 'Loz'.

Miss Clarke was not the only one who could change her name!

As part of the new 'Institute' class they were no longer regarded as 'babies'. 'Graduation' into Mr. Spindle's class provided some degree of kudos and there was the added benefit of Lawrence - or Loz - being unlikely to develop any sort of complicated 'crush' on him.

Loz now, quite astonishingly by today's standards, made the three mile return trip to and from school on his own. His mother, or 'MeMum', as she had now become known, had by now found work in a local mackintosh factory, turning Loz (although it didn't seem to provide the slightest source of concern at the time) into what would go on to become known as a *'latchkey kid'*.

As far as Loz was concerned he and his class were on the verge, or so they liked to think, of joining the 'big boys'. With that would come their acceptance into proper playground competition and that, for Loz, was all that mattered.

The local Rugby League side were still a force to be reckoned with following their crowning as Champions some five years earlier and despite the disappointment of England's Ashes defeat during the summer, cricket, rugby league, using a rolled up cap in the absence of a proper rugby ball, and football were the games of choice in the playground, played by those seeking to emulate not only local worthies but also the more distant and rarefied national heroes such as Blanchflower and Haynes, Dexter, May and, more locally, Brian Statham.

So impressive had been their performances during the summer, exceptions were even made for the likes of Richie Benaud and Fred Trueman. The former may have been England's chief tormentor from that terriers's head shaped island at the hot end of the world, but Trueman was an altogether different prospect. He hailed from Yorkshire, and while the border to this mysterious land may have been little more than a mile or two up the road, the Edgemoor children had been raised to regard their neighbouring county with a powerful mixture of hostility and suspicion.

'Only good thing to come out of Yorkshire is the road to Lancashire', seemed to sum up the politest form of local adult opinion, so for Trueman to assume even minor deity status in this little corner of Lancashire may, had he but known it, have ranked amongst his greatest achievements.

Entry into the newly available world of playground 'sport' became the be all and end all in terms of peer group acceptance. Unsatisfactory performance in the dreaded mental arithmetic or spelling tests, invariably the former in Loz's case, was not to be recommended, but such weakness paled into insignificance alongside identification as one of the playground 'softies' unable to run, kick, hit or catch.

Another change was that girls too became, for the first

time, a source of somewhat increased interest. Of course they'd always been there, in fact Loz had spent many a happy hour during the long days of summer playing in their company on, amongst other things, an old, dilapidated and long forgotten horse drawn milk cart or, as he perceived it, their 'stage coach' which he had bravely protected from a combination of vicious Indian and outlaw attack armed with nothing more than those same two fingers of his gun firing right hand, a broken cap gun and a slightly dubious fringed cowboy hat.

Now however, with the return to a new school year, playground ethos seemed to determine that girls were once again somehow excluded from the higher levels of schoolyard competition. Given such a situation they had little choice but to entertain themselves, and perhaps not so unknowingly the boys, by indulging in strikingly athletic and revealing handstands against the school wall. Certainly such exhibitions no longer went unnoticed, Carol McBride's lean lower limbs and navy blue knickers in particular proving every bit as appealing and inarticulately arousing to Loz as Susan Grimshaw's lumpy white thighs and grubby grey pants were oddly discomforting... *'headucation'* would take many forms.

A FIRST TASTE OF BRUTALITY

The transfer into Mr. Spindle's class, move over Miss Clarke...Mrs. Dyson... whoever you are, was every bit as Loz had imagined. Everyone looked up to him, partly because he could draw, and used this talent to produce the most spectacular and colourful blackboard illustrations imaginable, and partly because he ran the school football team and was thus in charge of who was to wear the much coveted red and white quartered school shirt.

Of course with those aged nine, ten and even eleven still well ahead in the pecking order selection was, to say the least, unlikely, but it never stopped the 'Institute boys' trying and desperately seeking to impress.

Loz had been doing exactly that when, one winter morning during the pre-school playground football kick about, he let fly with a particularly and, it has to be said, unusually well timed and perfectly hit half volley just guaranteed to find the 'net' or, to be completely accurate, the space between two jackets against the girls' toilet wall. This was Loz's moment! Ian Greaves, the (nearly eleven year old!) school goal keeper had no chance…or wouldn't have had, had it not been for the involvement of Mrs. Grimshaw's more than ample backside as she walked her younger daughter across the 'pitch' towards the main school door.

'Bloody 'ell!' groaned Loz, entirely uncharacteristically.

There followed a pause, as Mrs. Grimshaw turned to face her unlikely adversary, during which everyone else seemed to turn to stone and suddenly little Loz's whole world began to revolve in slow motion.

'Bloody 'ell?' shrieked Mrs. Grimshaw shattering the silence… 'Bloody 'ell?… I'll give ya bloody 'ell! I don't walk all this way at this time of the day to be spoken to like that by some cheeky little bugger like thee!'

'Gimme that flamin' ball…we'll see what Mr. Failsworth 'as to say about this' and with that she snatched the ball from Derek Jackson's rapidly weakening grasp and stormed in through the school doors.

Masterstroke! Whatever status may have been temporarily achieved through Loz's initial and truly unintentional bravado had now been almost instantly replaced by the alienation of his peers following the confiscation of their treasured football.

'Aahhh… yer gonna get done you are!' seemed the common concensus.

'Failsworth's gonna bloody strap thee Loz!' was another helpful suggestion.

'Strap? You're in for t'cane you are'…

Any further advice was abruptly silenced by the sight of a russet necked Mrs. Grimshaw waddling out of the main entrance followed by a ramrod straight and particularly severe looking Mr. Failsworth striding behind her.

Loz watched, trying desperately to disappear within the depths of his winter coat, as Mrs. Grimshaw lurched back across the playground, her backside wobbling in perfect synchronicity with his own trembling bottom lip.

'Lawrence Utting…go and wait outside my office.'

'As for the rest of you, you're going to have to manage the rest of the day without a football', and with that Mr. Failsworth strode back into school, Loz following mournfully, eyes pricked with, as yet, unshed tears, wondering just what was to come and how much it was going to hurt.

Loz had heard tales of both Mr. Failsworth's strap which was delivered across the hand, and his cane, which unfortunate recipients felt across their backside. He was rumoured to be a skilled practitioner of both methods of punishment but until now Loz had mercifully avoided coming even close to receiving either.

Standing in his office the headmaster seemed even taller, more rigidly upright and sterner than ever. Separated from him only by his desk Loz wondered where he kept his cane. Was he about to open a cupboard and produce his infamous stick or would the thick and allegedly studded leather strap suddenly materialise from within his desk drawer?

Mr. Failsworth's silence probably lasted seconds, but Loz was still in the grip of both that childlike and seemingly endless slow motion terror, along with the tallest and baldest man in the world's unrelenting eye contact, when he eventually broke the stillness.

'Now then Lawrence…' began the bald giant of a man… will you explain what all that was about?'

'Please Sir', spluttered Loz as the tears began to silently spill.

'Please Sir... it just slipped out Sir... I didn't mean to say it, Sir. Just slipped out Sir... 'onest Sir...it just slipped out. Never meant it, Sir'.

As defences go one has to admit it wasn't the best, although it actually was quite genuine and, possibly as all wise judges do, taking 'previous' into consideration and perhaps realising that if this went on much longer there might be something much more ominous to 'slip out', Mr. Failsworth relented.

Of course Loz still got the stern words, and deservedly so, and he still suffered the indignity of returning to class with a tear stained face but no swollen, reddened hand to justify it. He was still shunned for the remainder of the day as a result of being blamed for the absence of any playtime football. Worst of all though was the skilful and quietly menacing delivery of his headmaster's final question...'What would your mother and father have to say if they knew you'd been using such language?'

Such a thought was worse than the strap, the cane and peer group humiliation all rolled into one.

Did Mr. Failsworth know his charges well? Did he under-stand the need to treat each case on its merits and recognise the impact his chosen course of action might have? Of course he did, but others would not always be so rational.

Track 5. 'I Wanna Hold Your Hand.' The Beatles.

In retrospect it is sad to recall that Loz's first experience of corporal punishment, other than that quite routinely dished out under the guise of 'parental guidance' by *'MeMum'* and *'MeDad'* came, quite unjustifiably, from the otherwise invariably reasonable Mr. Spindle.

Perhaps he had some personal problem, or perhaps he

was, more understandably, consumed by nausea at the all embracing stench of cheese and onion pie, mashed potato and white sauce that lingered in his room throughout that particular afternoon. Either way he was not himself and became distinctly irritable when, because he had not been paying attention, Loz offered a particularly foolish and inappropriate answer to his question.

Moments later Mr Spindle became uncharacteristically enraged when he caught Loz talking, and despite hearing the words, 'Lawrence Utting, how many times do I have to tell you not to talk in lessons? Come here lad.' Loz was entirely unprepared for what to happen next.

No sooner had he reached the front of the class, now all stunned into absolute silence, than Loz heard the previously revered young teacher say, 'Hold out your left hand!'

The moment Loz held out his hand Mr. Spindle immediately raised his strap and delivered not just one, but two stinging blows seemingly with all his not inconsiderable might.

Loz felt his face redden and, after an all too brief initial numbness, his hand stung as never before. On the long, silent walk back to his seat the other pupils averted their eyes in that way children do, suspicious of the possibility that eye contact might somehow lead to some sort of contagious pain. Still at least the tears didn't come and Loz just about clung onto his dignity, something that perhaps Mr. Spindle had failed to manage that afternoon. Loz had, after all, only been talking in class. He'd deserved a telling off, possibly more, but not a punishment on this scale. Still, even then, at just nine years of age, Loz somehow recognised it to be completely out of character. Disappointment was his strongest emotion and yet, in these early years of the 1960's, it was, oddly, as if nothing had happened by the following morning.

Did Loz tell his parents? Not a chance! He could already

hear his mother's ill considered and instant verdict of, 'Well you must have done something to deserve it!' Worse would have followed and indeed much worse was yet to come!

VOICE TRIALS

By the time he was eight Loz's father had seen fit to introduce his young son to the 'delights' of the local Church choir. While 'MeDad' took his place at the back amongst the basses, Loz joined the four other unfortunate trebles in performing on Sunday morning at Matins and then again later in the day at Evensong. There was a commitment to a long practice session every Wednesday evening and although Loz never displayed any huge enthusiasm, if indeed any at all, for the business of choral singing it wasn't long before the organist and choir master, a man who held something approaching hero status amongst the aspirational middle class churchgoers, had identified Loz as a potentially gifted singer who might well benefit from proper training.

Exactly how many times Loz wished that the same might have been said about his sporting expertise rather than his singing, is difficult to overestimate but of course 'MeDad' couldn't have been prouder and immediately arranged for attendance at singing and piano lessons with an elderly lady called Annie Egerton who lived some distance away in one of the many terraced streets at the top side of town.

Twice a week Loz took, first a bus and then a long steep walk to Miss. Egerton's tiny terraced house where he was zealously put through his paces. She had a reputation to maintain did Annie Egerton, after getting a similarly 'talented' boy a place in the choir at Westminster Abbey, and before long, after taking delivery of a kindly donated second hand piano which totally dominated the 'front room', Loz was adjudged ready to be entered for voice trials at a variety of choirs across the country.

Never one to hold back, 'MeDad' soon had Loz booked in for scrutiny at, not just any old place but at supposedly the leading choir school in the country, at Kings College, Cambridge.

The whole experience of visiting Cambridge, let alone Kings itself, was an intimidating one. MeDad, whose own experience of Cambridge amounted to little more than a vague notion of its whereabouts, had booked bed and breakfast in one of the city's terraced streets. This though was nothing like the terraced houses whose 'backs' Loz spent so much time playing amongst at home. This house was, including the cellar, four storeys high, set elegantly and imposingly behind immaculately painted black railings, with half a dozen steps up off the street just to reach the front door.

By the time the somewhat overwhelmed family of three arrived at Kings the following morning Loz was already in awe, and when he was introduced into the 'custody' of four fully fledged choristers, all dramatically dressed in top hats and Marlborough suits, for the remainder of the 'trial', his feelings of inferiority were complete.

It perhaps goes without saying that Loz failed, probably dismally, but MeDad's philosophy was one of *'if at first you don't succeed...'* and with that he was soon investigating other avenues through which his son's apparent vocal talents might be recognised.

A fortuitous attack of chicken pox enabled Loz to avoid any potential pitfalls presented by Lichfield Cathedral and there then followed entry into a singing competition nearer home at the Buxton Pavilion.

Standing alone on a vast stage to sing his 'party piece', Bach's *'Come Let Us All This Day'*, to an audience consisting largely of other competitors and seemingly somewhat self important judges, Loz was overcome by nerves and finished a dismal seventh out of a cast of ten other unfortunates.

MeDad barely spoke on the train back from Buxton to Manchester, but still he wasn't done.

Just two weeks short of his tenth birthday, Loz was invited for a second voice trial at one of the University Colleges in Oxford. If Kings was the most prestigious choir in the country and thus self evidently in Cambridge, then this particular establishment must surely have been its Oxford equivalent.

In a dry and dusty practice room off the College cloisters and in the shadow of its iconic tower, Bach's popular anthem was performed yet again and Loz somehow managed a perfect piano rendition, albeit in the wrong octave, of a piece called *'March from Rob Roy'*. There then followed a series of vocal challenges whereby Dr. Wood, the imposing choir master, or *Informator Choristarum* to give him his seldom used but full and most ancient title, would play a series of three adjacent notes simultaneously and Loz would have to sing the middle, top, or bottom one as instructed.

Unlike Kings there was no academic test on this occasion and amazingly, in his own opinion at least, Loz passed. Even more astonishingly he was offered unconditional acceptance, even though the main 'trials' weren't due to take place for another week.

MeDad was absolutely beside himself with pride and delight, MeMum too, although her pleasure at this turn of events did appear a touch more measured.

Old Annie Egerton had worked her magic again. Her reputation for identifying the town's next *Ernest Lough* remained intact, but for Loz the transformation, along with its many implications had only just begun.

THE CALM BEFORE THE STORM

Within the church community Loz's 'success' led to him and MeDad being treated, for a little while at least, not unlike minor celebrities. The ambitious upper working/lower middle class families, that both the church choir and congregation seemed to be almost largely made up of, loved nothing more than to be able to identify with what they regarded as their very own child protégé.

The local evening Chronicle even requested an interview and featured a photograph of Loz all dressed up in cassock and surplice mouthing the words to 'Angel Voices Ever Singing' in their 'Lancashire Scrapbook' section. He'd felt quite proud for an hour or so until, on the way to Cubs that same evening, a familiar bus conductor brought him firmly down to earth.

'Saw your picture in the paper last night, lad', he smiled. 'Put me off me bloody tea!'

Other embarrassing moments followed when Loz was regularly stopped in the street or approached on buses, usually by ladies of a certain age, and interrogated at full volume with questions like, "Ere aren't you the one what's goin' to that posh University place?'

In the meantime life at Edgemoor carried on largely unchanged. The adult obsession with minor celebrity did not, Loz disappointedly noted, appear to extend to his peers, and he plodded along in the redoubtable Mrs. Bottomley's class for what had suddenly been transformed from his penultimate year to now become his final two terms of primary education.

Amongst all the other things Loz had to come to terms was the sad realisation that he would now be unlikely to pull on that object of desire, the coveted red and white quartered school football shirt, and he contented himself instead with taking every opportunity to practice his new obsession, rugby league.

'MeDad' had taken Loz to his first match a couple of years earlier, having been wisely and firmly forbidden by 'MeMum' from visiting the *'pictures'* owing to the frankly terrifying implications of an epidemic of polio.

The trip, although no more than half a mile or so from home, had led to the most spectacular afternoon of Loz's young life and although a variety of cowboys, Indians and assorted other celluloid warriors still held an enormous degree of fondness within Loz's heart, they were rapidly finding themselves completely superseded by his new found heroes in the red and white hoops . Not only were they strong, skilful and brave, but you could also touch them, pat them on the back even, as they made their way from the pitch to their changing rooms in the incongruously named Pavilion. They were like gods or, at the very least, real and rather sweaty live gladiators, and one or two even walked past Loz's house on their way to the match!

These were real, totally tangible, heroes and their absence, from September of that same year, would be just one of the many things Loz was going to have to adjust to during life after Edgemooor.

LESSONS FROM EDGEMOOR

1. Even the sternest and most severe of adults are capable of fairness. Tales of Mr. Failsworth's expertise with both strap and cane were legendary at Edgemoor and yet, in Loz's case, he had shown both compassion and wisdom in dealing with Loz's 'misdemeanour'. He had affected a more subtle type of 'punishment' and earned Loz's respect, not to mention gratitude, without recourse to assault.

2. Conversely, adults can be inconsistent and act out of character. Mr. Spindle was invariably kind and

encouraging but even he had proved capable of brutality. To thrash the hand of a nine year old child with a leather strap was simply wrong. It doesn't matter that at the time it wasn't actually a criminal act, it was just plain wrong and to receive such a punishment merely for not paying attention and talking, simply unjust.

3. Tears, along with 'genuine' displays of remorse, can be a very effective way of altering adult behaviour. Correspondingly, unless accompanied by copious amounts of blood or appropriate trauma, they don't work at all well with other children. Sometimes older girls could be moved by the genuine tears of a younger boy but even then an additional visible source of pain was to be recommended, egg, or at least marble, sized lumps on the head and nose bleeds proving particularly advantageous.

4. Isolation is painful. Throughout Loz's Edgemoor years his home was one of the very few without a T.V. meaning that he was regularly excluded from the enthusiastic dinner time debates centred around such essential viewing as *Bonanza, Rawhide and Juke Box Jury*. He'd tried to join in but was quickly found out and subsequently ostracised until a kindly dinner lady, who lived close by, recognised Loz's discomfort and provided ready access to at least the earlier evening delights of *'Ivanhoe'*, *'The Range Rider'*, Dale Robertson in *'Wells Fargo'*, and best of all Clint Walker as the greatest of all pre-Rugby League 'Gods', *'Cheyanne Brodie.'*

5. Keep your mouth shut when confronted by bigger boys and grumpy mothers whilst also always avoiding the label of playground 'softie'.

6. Don't run round corners into Gavin Grimes' head, or deliberately thump his toes, mistakenly believing it to be someone younger and smaller, while getting to your feet at the rugby 'play the ball'. Both actions are likely to lead to considerable pain!

7. Such agonies are as nothing compared with the pain of female 'rejection'...thanks Miss Clarke.

8. Girls, or at least those with the attributes of Carol McBride, can have a confusing and mysterious effect upon a young boy, but they can soon be forgotten and anyway girls were useless at war games and rugby in the 1960's

9. Real life heroes, those you can reach out to touch and who actually walk down your street, are much more exciting than the 'movie version'.

10. If you're going to excel at something make sure it's something 'cooler' than being a choirboy! 'Private tuition' with a guitar, cricket bat or rugby ball would have been far more welcome and, as we shall see, infinitely less complicated.

TWO

BOARDING SCHOOL

A DIFFERENT WORLD

Track 6. 'The House of the Rising Sun'. The Animals.

Perhaps surprisingly, between 'success' at his voice trial in January and the day Loz began at his new school, on Friday 18th September 1964, he was never invited to visit again.

The voice trial had taken place within the College itself, meaning that, even in the intervening eight months, Loz had yet to see anything of his future school let alone the 'Boarding House' which was to become his *home* for the majority of the next four years.

Of course Loz's parents had received plenty of written communication and although all tuition and a large proportion of the boarding fees were to be provided as a result of Loz having earned what was known as a 'choral scholarship', MeDad in particular still appeared occasionally overwhelmed by the financial demands involved with the belongings list alone, which included a blazer and three suits (two charcoal grey and one Marlborough to be worn on Sundays) just for starters!

With the benefit of hindsight any belongings list for a ten year old boy that requested a greater number of suits than it did underpants or socks (two pairs...unspecified and grey!) should have been treated with the greatest suspicion. The list went on and on, shirts (two white), shoes (black), rugby shirts (1 red/ 1 black), shorts, socks and boots, gym shirts (1 white/ 1 house colours), shorts, socks and pumps, black chorister tie, separate school tie, bath towel, toothpaste, toothbrush, tuck box (?), 'outdoor play' clothes etc. and lest anyone had forgotten that he'd be staying, not for one night but for virtually every night until Christmas, slippers, dressing gown and pyjamas (two pairs)!

Exactly how Loz's parents managed to collect all these belongings together is difficult to imagine. MeDad worked as a Youth Employment Officer while MeMum now held a number of positions as a shorthand typist in a variety of local mills and factories. They'd had the foresight to try and buy their own house which had already meant sacrificing the purchase of items now increasingly synonymous with the symbols of lower middle class convenience and aspiration in the mid sixties. As a result, between bonfire night and Easter the house frequently resembled an igloo. There was no central heating, no fitted carpets, no TV and any notion of ownership of even the most basic family car would have been fanciful in the extreme

Loz hadn't even owned a proper football shirt before now and yet here they were gathering together this endless list where the 'tuck box' itself, a handsome large lockable wooden box with steel framing and a hinged lid that had *L. Utting* neatly inlaid into it, probably cost more than a week of 'MeMum's' wages. They were meant to provide a trunk too, but fell short on that count, all Loz's belongings having to be crammed into a huge, ancient and consequently somewhat battered brown leather suitcase that 'MeMum' had to sit on while 'MeDad' forced the locks shut and tightened the stout leather 'security belt' through the handle and around its bulging girth in readiness for collection by the BRS (British Road Services) lorry.

Not a great deal had been said between January and September about what to expect at Oxford, probably because neither of Loz's parents had any clue at all about what boarding school life would involve. 'MeDad' remained proud as punch though, declaring to anyone who would listen that it would be 'the making of him', whatever that meant. While 'MeMum', who'd left school herself aged fourteen, had discovered that Loz would be doing subjects called Latin and French which she thought he'd be good at, though goodness only knows what she based that horribly misplaced theory upon.

In that way that only young children seem to be able to manage, Loz had never really concerned himself with what was actually about to happen until his parents had left. 'MeMum' and 'MeDad', who'd been there almost every day and night of his ten and a half year life were leaving him, and not just for the night, or even a whole day, as had been the case at Edgemoor, but for what seemed like forever. He wouldn't see them again until half term, towards the end of October, and that even by Loz's not entirely reliable reckoning was at least six weeks...and two hundred miles...away!

They'd stayed with him as he'd entered the Boarding House, that separate part of the school that housed the approximately sixty 'boarders' whose experience of school would be so utterly different from that known to the four hundred or so 'day-boys'. They'd stayed with him as they all ventured down the unfamiliar trunk (and one conspicuously scruffy battered brown leather suitcase) lined corridors and were introduced to 'Matron', who was to become a kind of shared surrogate mother for the forseeable future . They'd even stayed with him to climb the three flights of stone stairs to see for themselves the dormitory that Loz would be sleeping in for at least the first year of his life in the Boarding House and then they were gone!

Just like that, with 'MeMum' probably obeying 'MeDad's' pre-planned maxim of, 'best to just get off and not look back, duck'...that was that...a few words of encouragement, a moist eyed kiss from 'MeMum', a firm handshake from 'MeDad', a brisk, conversation less walk to the station and back home on the train to Manchester, two hundred miles and a thousand light years away, leaving Loz in the calm but, quite frankly, bewildering, company of Matron.

One of those particularly neat, elegant and relatively elderly ladies (through the cloudy lens of an emotional ten year old's eyes) Matron was not altogether unlike Miss Bolt in appearance, although Loz was pleased to note a twinkle of what he imagined, and certainly hoped, to be kindness in her eyes, as opposed to the steely glint that had inhabited Miss Bolt's.

She was clearly well used to the company of emotionally confused 'new boys' although one must doubt that, even with her years of experience, Matron could completely identify with the feelings of despair, dismay and sheer abandonment which Loz felt at that precise moment.

Everything was so utterly unfamiliar.

At Edgemoor they'd all enjoyed an adequate sized playground and the steeply sloping vicarage field for summer games. All the buildings were of darkened red brick, impregnated with the soot of over a hundred cotton mill and thousands more coal fed house fire chimneys. Here the buildings were golden, built of Cotswold stone and clad in spectacular and rapidly reddening Virginia Creeper. There was no longer just one set of church bells that rang twice on a Sunday, but a whole array, all of which seemed determined to acknowledge the passing of every quarter hour and enter into the most astonishing symphony of campanology to celebrate what was merely the turning of the hour.

The Boarding House stood proudly above a beautifully maintained garden devoted entirely to manicured lawns and roses, and beyond which lay the river and two wooden 'willow pattern' footbridges, giving access to the plateau like and tree shrouded four acre island which provided the school with its picturesque but notoriously flood prone playing fields. Along with its own cricket pavilion the island provided three full size rugby pitches along with plenty of extra space, some of it still recovering from the scarring which had resulted from the previous summer's siting of cricket nets and lawn tennis courts.

For many it would have seemed idyllic. To Loz it was hugely overwhelming and he longed for the safety and security of his far off Lancashire homeland in a world where, every other Saturday, 'heroes' walked down his street, where Gav was 'cock o'the school', where the limit of Carol's McBride's childhood ambition was to achieve the perfect handstand and where people knew their place, which, as far as Loz was concerned just then, was back home amongst the red brick streets with MeMum and MeDad.

In this new and horribly unfamiliar environment Loz had no idea who he was. Even the name identifying occupancy at the end of his bed seemed alien. *Utting. L.* had been neatly written in capitals on a piece of paper, encased in sellotape and stuck onto the bottom of the tubular black metal bed frame. In a dormitory accommodating eleven others Loz noticed that he would be sleeping between *Petersfield S.N.A.* and *Waterstone J.E.* Even then the surfeit of initials, that would prove useful in pursuing the public school practice of creating such acronym based lifelong nicknames as, 'SNAP' and 'Rab' (short for Rabbi), left Loz's own name looking curiously inadequate and oddly unrecognisable.

UTTING!

He had left Lancashire as *Loz*, or at the worst, in the adult-speak world of Mr. Failsworth and his parents, as *Lawrence*. At the Boarding House, as had become almost immediately obvious, he was now entering a different world, and one in which he would be known just as *'Utting'*.

Those first twenty four hours at his new school were, without any shadow of a doubt, to be amongst the most lonely and baffling of Utting's young life. As an only child, albeit never one of the stereotypically spoiled variety, he'd had little experience of being away from home, let alone of sharing meal times and a bedroom. Yet here he was, less than twelve hours after leaving the 'sanctuary' of his northern roots and just a short time after bidding farewell to the previously ever present 'MeMum and MeDad', dressed in a black tie and charcoal grey suit, being led into a huge room, the 'dining hall', with around sixty others for something called 'supper' and an 'Introduction Assembly' prior to going to bed in a room he would apparently be about to share with eleven others.

Back at home 'supper' had seldom been anything more than a cup of hot chocolate and a biscuit, two, if he was lucky. In the 'Boarding House it transpired to be a hot meal, served at eight o'clock each evening. On that first evening all the boys had to wait outside the hall while the prefects, who appeared to Utting as huge and intimidating young men, which is indeed what most of them were, ensured that their minions entered the hall in an appropriate fashion in readiness for the arrival of the Headmaster, his wife and the other Housemasters.

The hall itself was furnished with two rows of long,

highly polished, trestle tables with chairs on either side, which ran along its length leaving a space through the middle and a 'top' table at the far end of the hall, set at right angles to the rest, where the elite collection of teachers, senior prefects and any other guests would be seated.

The emergence of the aforementioned hierarchy from a door at the top end of the hall led to the noise of much scraping and grating of chair legs on freshly waxed floorboards, as the whole hall rose to acknowledge their arrival. Grace was said by the Headmaster, Mr. Beaumont, who was much shorter and had rather more hair than Mr. Failsworth, before a second similar din preceded the rapid demolition of huge trays of sausages, bowls of baked beans and mountains of toast.

At the conclusion of supper, it being the first night of term, the Headmaster rose to briefly address the Hall. He welcomed the new boys, of which there were ten, four of them choristers who were already identifiably different owing to their faintly ridiculous suits. He reminded older pupils of the need to be supportive and recall how difficult some of them had once found starting at a new school, before handing over to the Senior Housemaster, Mr. Burt, unsurprisingly known amongst the boys as 'Herb'.

A tired looking, balding and somewhat overweight man, dressed in grey flannel trousers, a cream jacket, pink shirt and his old college tie, an unheard of combination in faraway Lancashire, Herb wearily read through a list of reminders and notices before dismissing everyone except the 'new boys' who he told to remain in order that they should, slightly ominously, 'understand what was expected of them'.

Gathered round him now at the 'top' table, Herb introduced two older boys, Hadleigh and Coverdale, also choristers, who, he informed the newcomers, would take it in turn to act as the seniors in the dormitory. They 'knew the ropes' and would be able to help everyone 'settle in' added Mr. Burt, in a not entirely successful attempt at reassuring his increasingly anxious new charges.

Mr. Burt went on to explain that, as the youngest in the Boarding House, the new occupants of what was apparently known as *'Baby Dorm'* were expected to be ready for bed at 8.25 each evening. All they would need that first night, advised the housemaster, would be their over-night cases which they had now to collect from Matron's office, before going quietly upstairs to complete their ablutions...'clean your teeth, wash your hands and have a piss', explained Coverdale later...and get ready for bed, whereupon Herb had promised to return and, assuming all had been completed to his satisfaction, deliver a bedtime story.

Sure enough, about fifteen minutes later, by which time all the boys had, more than a little self consciously in Utting's case, climbed out of their clothes and into their pyjamas, Mr. Burt arrived complete with a well thumbed copy of *'King Solomon's Mines'*.

To Utting the idea of being read a 'bedtime story' was something which he felt he had left behind long ago. It must have been a year or more since MeDad had read to him and the suggestion did appear a surprisingly childish one.

Utting, or at least 'Loz', had grown used to playing out until the very last moments of daylight. He'd made a habit, a skill even, of 'stretching' the daylight hours until they were fully and finally used up. The idea of now being tucked up in bed and listening quietly to a story seemed like a totally unforeseen backward step and the name of the author, *H.Ryder Haggard*, appeared as yet another confusion in a world which was rapidly filling with increasingly eccentric and, had he known the word then, slightly pretentious names.

Having little if any choice other than to listen, Utting had to secretly concede that Mr. Burt read well and, if truth be told, that this introduction to the unfamiliar world of Victorian hero *Alan Quartermain* was a decent enough way to try and diffuse any first night nerves.

It was also a 'world' which Utting and the other new boys would rapidly become used to as old Herb seemed to have something of an obsession with nineteenth century adventure yarns and went on to read from the likes of *Robert Louis Stevenson* and *Conan Doyle* before returning to the '*Alan Quartermain*' sequel and the strangely mystifying, to a dormitory full of ten and eleven year old boys at least, story of '*She*'.

Throughout that first year in '*Baby Dorm*', Herb would either read from his vast collection of Victorian novels or invite the boys, all dressed in pyjamas, dressing gowns and slippers, down to his study where he would toast crumpets over his gas fire and arrange evening readings of plays, *Arnold Ridley's 'The Ghost Train'* being a particular favourite, which he would record on his reel to reel tape recorder before indulging in, sometimes quite hurtful and stinging critical appraisal of the boys various performances during the process of play back.

Herb also used to take pairs of the youngest boys out for Sunday afternoon jaunts in his sports car, an obsessively well maintained white, wire-wheeled Triumph TR4 with bright red leather upholstery. They would sometimes stop for afternoon tea in some of the idyllic nearby Oxfordshire villages and while such activities may, in today's more suspicious world, provoke 'raised eyebrows' or even calls for the immediate intervention of social services, Utting never felt there to be anything disturbing about Mr. Burt. Indeed, rumours of some sort of unlikely flirtation with Matron aside, there was never any evidence to suggest that he was anything other than just an avuncular and slightly lonely, asexual old academic. The type who, years later, might have been best described as 'never entirely comfortable in his own skin'.

The fact though that Herb did prove to have a quite alarming temper was something Utting would find to his cost, on more than one occasion, much later, but whatever the appropriateness or otherwise of his later ill tempered actions, the new boys of *'Baby Dorm'* were grateful that first night for the distraction provided by Mr. Burt's bedtime introduction to the tale of *'King Solomon's Mines'*. What Utting and the rest were less well prepared for though was Herb's closing comment about it being 'time to stop now as we all have school in the morning.'

SCHOOL? ON SATURDAY MORNING!

'But tomorrow is Saturday…no one goes to school on a Saturday!' were Utting's thankfully unspoken thoughts.

He was quite wrong of course but then this was, as he was very quickly discovering, the altogether different world of the Boarding School.

After a fitful night's sleep, made all the harder by the regular chiming of numerous bells, Utting was wrenched from the sanctuary of eventual slumber that first morning by the completely unanticipated most claxon like sound he had ever heard. It went off, like some sort of explosive device, at 7.30 in the morning, and again ten minutes later, just to persuade any sluggards of the necessity to be up, dressed and ready for breakfast at eight o'clock. Only on Sundays were the boys spared this infernal racket and even then only until 8.00.

Having little real idea of what to do next, Loz followed the example set by Coverdale, gathered up his wash bag and towel and followed him through to the washroom. Here the ten sinks, comfortably shared amongst the new occupants of 'Baby Dorm' the previous evening, now had to provide for the needs of an additional twenty boys, the twelve to fourteen year old residents of 'Junior Dorm'. These older and significantly larger boys were 'privileged' to not have to get ready for bed until thirty five minutes later, thus avoiding any evening congestion. Now however the stridency of the second bell was only matched by the urgency of the older and more powerful boys' reaction as a 'survival of the fittest' mentality, which didn't auger at all well for the 'new-boys', totally over came any more rational concept of 'first come first serve'.

So it was, after the quickest and least effective of washes, interspersed by a first experience of stinging 'rat's tail' wet towel attacks from the indignant *'Junior Dormers'* who objected to any 'new boy's' occupancy of a sink ahead of them, that Utting miserably struggled into yesterday's clothes and dragged himself along the still unfamiliar dingy passageways and back down the three flights of stairs to the dining hall.

There they were 'greeted' by the Head Prefect, a boy, or fully grown man if you'd asked Utting, by the name of Bridge-Collins.

'Why would anyone call a boy Bridge?' Utting later remembered thinking, totally unaware, prior to his arrival within the alien confines of the Boarding House, of the concept of double barrelled names.

Showing all the empathy to be expected from someone who had himself been rudely awakened at half past seven in the morning for the first time in almost two months, Bridge-Collins explained that the 'new-boys' were expected to serve the older, and thus clearly superior, boys their breakfast. That each morning for the next year (!) they were to collect bowls of dry cereal from the kitchen (huge aluminium jugs of milk and bowls of sugar were already on the tables) and place them in front of each and every older boy. Then, once the cereal had been finished these same new innocents were to take the empty bowls back to the kitchen and serve up the cooked element of breakfast in a similar fashion, before finally ensuring that all the crockery and cutlery had been returned to the kitchen and all the tables wiped clean.

Needless to say the bemused new recruits were treated by many as the most servile of servants, in that way that children have truly mastered, whereby those with the lowest self esteem so frequently become the most vociferous and determined of bullies. Cutlery was deliberately dropped or hidden, milk intentionally spilt and a large hot steel tea-pot brought into contact with the young servers' hands on so many occasions that the excuse of it being in any way 'accidental' rapidly ceased to hold even the faintest degree of credibility.

This though was only the latest of what seemed to be so many hurdles. After the ordeal of that initial breakfast, or 'new boy baiting' session as it may have been more accurately described, it was now time for Utting to leave the Boarding House and cross the road, the very same street where those now distant 'carers', MeMum and MeDad, had last been seen *abandoning* their only child, to venture into the school itself.

Here the real enormity of the changes which were so rapidly impacting on Utting's reality became instantly and more intimidatingly evident. The School, and everything about it was huge compared to Edgemoor. The playground seemed at least five times the size and was inhabited by hundreds of pupils many of whom, in terms of sheer size and hirsuteness, seemed already to have assumed the appearance of 'young men'.

The number of classrooms was immeasurably greater, indeed the newest part of the school reminded Utting of the new sixties three storey glass and aluminium housing developments that had been gradually colonising his home town in the now faraway North West. As for the teachers, there must have been at least thirty of them, all male and known alarmingly as 'masters', many of whom were clad in odd flat topped skull caps and somewhat sinister looking black robes, or 'mortar boards' and 'gowns' as Utting would soon learn that they were called.

It was only when the new boys were dispatched to their

classrooms and 'form tutors', Utting's as yet unidentified but ominously named Mr. Butcher, that he began to fully acknowledge how not only was he now one of the youngest pupils in school but, as a chorister, one of the youngest of the young.

Effectively, in order to make the most of their unbroken voices and in attempt to gain at least four years of choral service the choristers had begun secondary school at least a whole school year early and Utting was now, to his dismay, one of the ten year old parts of an environment that taught over four hundred other pupils up to the comparatively ancient age of eighteen!

Along with Coverdale and Hadley and two other older and even more confident boys, Utting and the other three new choristers, who he had now come to recognise as Dickinson, Drinkwater and Greene, found their way across the vast playground and up a flight of stairs where, at the end of a short corridor they located their classroom, appropriately labelled 2C.

Standing outside the classroom door was Mr. Butcher, a short, trim little man, probably in his early fifties, with a thick head of wiry black hair and a pale, creased face within which seemed to burn dark, fierce eyes. He greeted those already known to him warmly and shook hands enthusiastically with each of the new boys, whilst simultaneously welcoming them to school and revealing himself, from both the tobacco infused smell of his black gown and the nicotine stained fingers of his right hand, to be a particularly heavy smoker.

The welcoming process complete, Mr. Butcher proceeded to explain how things worked for choristers at the Choir School and exactly what his role would be. He had nothing to do with the Boarding House, he explained, but as far as the main school was concerned he would act as form 'master' for the first two years. The 'C' in 2C apparently denoted 'Choristers' and unlike the rest of the school, who did not start until the age of eleven, the new choristers would remain in the same class for their first two years before then joining normal classes, which explained why, in this otherwise huge new institution, the class of 2C contained just eight grey suited pupils, four new boys and a further four who were in the process of beginning their second year.

Mr. Butcher went on to speak of the commitment involved in being a chorister and explained that, 'unlike all the other boys' at school, as the College itself would be 'meeting the cost of all fees' it was they who had first call upon the boys' 'services'. In other words, 'he who pays the piper calls the tune' and in return for the public school education the boys were to receive, the demands of choir practice and performance would be rigorous, indeed seldom was the saying 'singing for one's supper' ever to prove quite so fitting.

Such 'choral duties' Mr Butcher continued, in his gravelly but well spoken tones, could however be 'forgotten for a little while' as, he explained, all choral activities had to coincide with the University (as distinct from the School) term. This meant that for the first ten days within their new environment the new boys would be able to 'take the opportunity to familiarise themselves with the ways of the school and the Boarding House and not concern themselves with the business of being a chorister' which, Mr. Butcher concluded, 'would arrive all in good time'.

Already young Utting was feeling more than a little overcome by a combination of something approaching his earlier terror, tiredness and the apparent need to assimilate quite so much information at what his Timex watch, a treasured Christmas present from his grandparents and as such some sort of tangible connection to a much happier past life, told him was still only 9.20 in the morning.

Mr. Butcher however was far from finished and rapidly

moved on to introduce the boys to the concept of a 'time table', the first peculiarity of which they were already experiencing, school on a Saturday morning, although this, they were all quick to notice appeared to be compensated for by there apparently being no school on a Tuesday afternoon.

The time table included completely new and unfamiliar subjects, not only Latin and French, which Utting now vaguely remembered MeMum saying she thought he'd be good at, but also Chemistry and Biology, and it also became clear that Mr. Butcher would only be actually teaching them English, Latin and Maths (called 'Sums' or occasionally, 'Arithmetic' at Edgemoor) meaning that they would have to encounter other teachers and even other classrooms for their remaining subjects. Still at least there was no 'Music and Movement' thought Utting, dejectedly searching for any proverbial 'port in a storm'.

Once the timetables had been copied down Mr. Butcher decided that, as an initial activity, it would be a good, if unoriginal, idea for the four new-boys to introduce themselves, both to each other and their four older classmates', by giving a brief talk about themselves including what they had done during the summer holidays.

As seemed to be the unimaginative case in virtually all institutions, this activity was to take place in alphabetical order which provided the mixed blessing for Utting of going last, but he wasn't too concerned after hearing how both Dickinson and Drinkwater, who came from places called Henley and Dorchester respectively, both appeared to have spent their summer at something called their 'holiday homes' and how Greene, a postman's son from Ipswich, didn't appear to have done very much at all.

When Utting's turn came, he walked nervously to the front of the classroom and, following the same format as those who had already 'performed', introduced himself as Lawrence Utting, even at this stage he'd instinctively thought it best to drop the 'Loz', before embarking on an enthusiastic description of how MeDad had taken him to his first Test Match at Old Trafford and how he'd then spent two weeks of the summer at 'MeGrandad's' house in Wales where he'd gone on the train with 'MeMum' and 'MeDad' and where he'd had a fantastic time catching crabs, exploring rock pools, playing cricket on the beach and even catching a small flat fish which 'MeAnty' had cooked for 'MeTea'.

So caught up was Utting in these happy reminiscences, that he had completely failed to notice everyone else in the class clutching their mouths or sides in a vain attempt to stifle their laughter.

Utting was aghast. Nobody else had been laughed at and he really hadn't tried to be funny. His summer in Wales had been his best ever, and that was exactly what he'd told them. So why was he suddenly an apparent object of ridicule?

'Something wrong Coverdale?' asked Mr. Butcher.

'No Sir, nothing Sir,' spluttered Coverdale.

'And you Faulks ?' queried Mr. Butcher of an unpleasant looking pinched faced boy who continued to smirk.

'Sorry Sir', replied Faulks... 'but what's 'MeAnty'? ...is Utting talking about his 'aunt', he asked, placing heavy emphasis on the initial *'are'* sound, or is he related to insects Sir?'

At this the whole class collapsed in guffaws, calling to each other in gleeful imitation, 'MeAnty cooked MeTea' and 'A went with MeMumanMeDad'.

'Alright, alright', shouted Mr. Butcher. 'That's quite enough!'

'I think we all understand that Utting comes from the North... and there's absolutely nothing wrong with that...', but it was all too late and Mr. Butcher's admittedly patronising attempt to pacify the class fell on deaf ears. He'd been at his new school for less than twenty four hours. Just one night and two meals later and already he'd been found out, his weakness...their target, already horribly exposed. Unfamiliarity was already turning to exile!

Things didn't improve over that first dinner (make that lunch) time. The food was good and at least Utting didn't have to serve it as the prefects now took responsibility for groups of ten pupils, ladling out food from great steaming steel bowls and employing a totally incomprehensible 'Quis? Ego!' system of deciding who was most deserving of 'seconds'. Unfortunately however Utting's fame, or notoriety, had spread, largely he suspected, thanks to the delighted and thoroughly malicious efforts of Faulks and quite probably Coverdale, who were rapidly proving to be anything but the protective influence initially suggested.

Throughout lunch time and on into the afternoon Loz found himself repeatedly asked by older boys who were otherwise total strangers, 'Are you the boy from the North?' or 'Are you the Northern oik'?

This having been ascertained, although Utting didn't really know what an 'oik' was, they then sought to mock him by getting him to say words such as *'grass'*, *'glass'* and *'fast'* which apparently should be pronounced in a way which rhymes with 'arse' but which by pronouncing them, quite correctly he believed, in a way which rhymed with 'ass' , provoked howls of amusement and led to further chants of 'here comes MeAnty' and the like.

During the afternoon Utting found temporary respite by taking himself off to the school playing field with Dickinson, Greene and another new-boy who wasn't a chorister, called Elton. At first they just mooched around on the edge of the island field, thrashing the dying nettles with sticks, disturbing mallards and moorhens and watching with fascination as the large shoals of small silver fish, called, quite appropriately given Utting's mood, 'bleak', suddenly changed direction, as if with just one swarm like instinct, in response to a thrown pebble or stick.

Then, after Dickinson had come across a long lost rugby ball which had clearly been lying hidden in the undergrowth for some time, they passed the remainder of the afternoon using either side of a set of rugby posts for a two aside kicking and catching contest which, in the absence of any games kit, not only succeeded in making four brand new pairs of black leather shoes look rather prematurely 'worn in' but also provided an activity in which Utting could, at last, earn some positive acknowledgement.

During that first long, lonely week at the Choir School, Utting only ever came close to being happy when in the company of a rugby ball. Virtually all his spare time was spent practising catching and kicking by the rugby posts and he proved more than useful during a first games lesson, when the members of 2C joined an older class in order to have the necessary numbers, and where, despite his initial lack of familiarity with the rules of 'Union', the 'lessons' he'd learned back on the Vicarage Field back at Edgemoor still stood him in good stead.

Otherwise things just seemed to go from bad to worse. Utting's battered suitcase became another object of derision as it sat apologetically in the passageway amongst the other boy's trunks.

An older boy called Meenan, two years Utting's senior and one of the small but vicious variety who would probably go on to be recognised as suffering from some sort of 'little man syndrome', seemed particularly determined to make Utting's life a misery.

Answering to the nick name 'A.J.' he took every opportunity to make capital out of Utting's northern speech 'impediment' - especially at breakfast when he was guaranteed an audience - and began to make, what he imagined to be, derogatory allegations about 'MeDad'.

'Suppose coming from the North he votes for Wilson and reads *The Guardian*' taunted Meenan. Utting hadn't the slightest idea who 'Wilson' was or what he was getting at, but, as 'MeDad' did indeed read *The Guardian*, the confused ten year old was convinced that the obnoxious little bully possessed some sort of second sight.

Then came the final straw when, towards the end of the week in what was only his second ever French lesson, Utting committed yet another faux pas, or *'fox-pass'* as he would almost certainly have innocently pronounced it. Asked by the French Teacher, Monsieur Bellou, to explain how one might make a request in French, Utting's peculiarly phonic Lancastrian rendition left the teacher quite unreasonably appalled.

Living up to his name and much to the delight of others in the group, he rose from his chair and roared, 'It's s'il vous plait...S'IL VOUS PLAIT!... not *'silver plate'* you stupid, stupid boy!'

For the rest of that evening in the Boarding House a chastened Utting heard nothing other than references to *'silver plate'* or the now resurrected *'MeAnty'*. In comparison to other examples of bullying it may have seemed trivial, but to that particular ten year old at that particular moment, suddenly finding himself two hundred miles from home in an alien environment where he seemed completely unable to escape the ridicule of his tormentors, it was the final straw.

Just a short time ago, as *'Loz'*, he had been contented and happy. Now he was *'Utting!'*, lost in a world where everything felt 'wrong'.

He felt as if he had entered some sort of parallel reality where he had to spend every day dressed in the same absurd grey suit and where he was repeatedly ridiculed, for the first time ever in his life, simply for speaking in the only way he knew. Where he had to serve older boys their breakfast, and had to learn other languages like Latin and French, when suddenly he no longer appeared to even have mastered English, and where he was constantly unable to escape the mockery and torment or take overnight refuge in the advice and home comforts normally provided by 'MeMum'and 'MeDad'.

It was as if, although he couldn't articulate it at the time, someone had plucked a character from one of Mr Lowry's landscapes and, as a result of some dreadful mistake, then carelessly dropped it into Monet's Garden. Utting felt hopelessly misplaced and utterly lost. He needed to do something about it. The time had come to run away!

BID FOR FREEDOM

That night Utting lay awake hatching a plan which the following morning would be put into operation.

After the usual ordeal of northern new boy baiting at breakfast, he carried on as normal until it was time to go to school. Then instead of crossing the road and entering the school by a side entrance, as the boarders usually did, he hid at the front of the Boarding House, until everyone had left for school, before surreptitiously slipping through the front gate to begin his bid for freedom.

Reckoning that keeping away from the city centre would be the best idea, Utting crossed the bridge, turned right up Longwall Street and on into Holywell Street. Here, still using his all too limited knowledge of how to avoid the centre and constantly glancing back over his shoulder, he turned right into Parks Road. The sense of 'escape', fuelled by the longer term possibility of freedom, was exhilarating, but the only 'route' he had worked out to get home was by aiming for the names of stations he had passed through on the train south just a week earlier.

He knew that the nearest of these was at a place called

Banbury and was relieved when, having walked the length of Parks Road, he found himself at a junction where the main road ahead was marked with a black and white sign reading *'Banbury Road'* and which even Utting's limited logic suggested should, in all probability, lead towards Banbury.

Another anxious glance behind reassured the young escapee that there was still no sign of any pursuers and, mentally running through the hopelessly unrealistic order of station destinations...Banbury...Leamington...Birmingham... Wellington...he set off up the Banbury Road and away from the 'City of Dreaming Spires'.

Just over two hours and fortunately no proffered lifts later, Utting had reached the village of Kidlington. All of six miles from the hated Boarding House, by now even Utting had begun to recognise the recklessness of his venture. He had no money, he was ten years old and after more than two hours of walking, the mileage signs back to Oxford remained in single figures.

Wondering what to do next Utting noticed that coincidentally he had stopped outside the local police station.

Actually it didn't look like a police station at all. It appeared just like any normal modern detached house only with an very visible *'Thames Valley Police'* sign situated on the hard standing area where normally there would have been a front lawn. It took Utting just a few seconds to formulate yet another plan, this one even more brainless and desperate than the first.

'Hello, I'm from Greyfriars School', uttered Utting, hoping against hope that, given the grey suit, reference to *Billy Bunter's* alma mater might provide his tale with some bizarre degree of credibility.

'Erm, it's in Oxford...' he continued, increasingly hopelessly, '...and it's er...really important that I get back to Manchester today. I wondered if you could lend me some money or...give me a lift?'

Barely even bothering to look up, the desk sergeant gave a resigned sigh before glancing away from his paperwork and saying calmly,

'I see young sir...right well if you'd like to come through we'll get you a cup of tea and a biscuit and see what we can do.'

Liking the sound of being called 'Sir', and believing blissfully that he was now as good as home, Utting followed the officer to a kitchen area at the back of the building where he sat contentedly with his very welcome mug of tea and plain digestive biscuit...and waited.

After no more than a quarter of an hour Utting heard a car pull up outside followed by the sound of voices coming from the desk area where he had recently arrived. He was just in the process of delusionally convincing himself that 'perhaps that will be my lift' when the door opened and in walked an all too familiar shock of Einstein like white hair attached to his headmaster.

'Utting', said Mr. Beaumont, not angrily, but with just with a hint of resignation in his voice.

'We all wondered where you'd got to...I think you'd better come with me'.

And so, it seemed, the game was up. No point in running. No point in attempting any further form of flight...and with that the inept escapee reluctantly climbed into the front seat of Mr. Beaumont's saloon and unhappily endured the pitifully short and silent fifteen minute journey back to captivity.

By the time they arrived back at the Boarding House, so pathetic had been the attempted escape, that morning school was still in progress. Mr. Beaumont, still showing nothing more than the slightest hint of irritation, delivered the boy into Matron's care suggesting, rather like a kindly doctor intimating to a psychiatric patient's carer of the need for treatment, that perhaps a spell in something called 'Sick Bay' would be appropriate.

Only having ever heard of 'Cardigan Bay' before, Utting had no idea what to expect but after leaving him in no doubt as to precisely how 'silly' he'd been , *'desperate'* was the word Utting might have preferred, Matron led the way to what was in effect a small and slightly isolated dormitory with just four crisply made up beds, all of them unoccupied, where Utting was to have his lunch and wait for Mr. Beaumont's return.

Sick Bay represented an entirely different form of isolation, where the hubbub of boy's voices was vaguely present but too far away to seem remotely threatening.

A pleasant boy of about fourteen wearing round horn rimmed glasses, who Utting had noticed never gave the new boys any grief when serving breakfast and who he thought he'd heard referred to as *Peewee*, arrived carrying a plate of fish in parsley sauce, mashed potato and peas and actually seemed quietly concerned about the younger boy's welfare.

Then not long after he'd finished his pudding of sponge and custard, the result of a second visit from the seemingly amiable *Peewee*, Mr. Beaumont arrived again.

Taking his place gently on the edge of the bed, Mr. Beaumont spoke more softly than Utting would ever have imagined possible given the circumstances. The traces of irritation he had shown earlier were now all gone and there was a genuine note of sympathy in his voice.

He seemed to understand how difficult it often was for boys to have to 'adjust' to being away from home at such a young age, especially he added when 'home was so far away'. He brightened Utting's mood slightly by suggesting that, 'If I'd had half a crown for all the new boys who've tried to run away during my years here I'd be a rich man by now', before gently but firmly reminding his pupil of both the time he had wasted and the danger he had put himself in.

45

Without ever truly giving Utting the opportunity to voice his own feelings, which would probably have been impossible anyway without recourse to the always unforgiveable folly of 'sneaking', Mr. Beaumont went on to suggest that Utting had 'still to give the school a chance'. The real purpose of him being there, performing as a chorister, was still to begin and anyway 'surely' he'd heard of 'Lancashire Grit?'

Actually Utting hadn't, the only grit he'd ever come across in Lancashire had either been picked out of a graze on his knees or spread on the road to combat the snow in winter. However the headmaster seemed to sense the boy's confusion and proceeded to speak quietly but firmly of the need to 'pluck up courage', to realise that sometimes 'we all have to show that extra bit of determination' and of how important it was to 'reward all the effort and sacrifice' made by MeMum and MeDad in sending him to Boarding School.

To be completely honest, Utting wasn't so sure about the last bit and he wasn't totally convinced that even Mr. Beaumont, with all his apparent powers of gentle empathy, was truly capable of imagining quite how difficult it was to be new, northern and aged just ten at an Oxbridge boarding school.

He had however provided a second example of a Headmaster proving himself capable of showing patience and understanding. Perhaps, Utting pondered, he did owe it to 'MeMum' and 'MeDad' to do his best to settle down, after all, he had a dim recollection of hating Edgemoor on that very first morning, and with that thought in mind he took himself off to afternoon lessons almost as if nothing had happened.

A FRESH START

Curiously, little attention was paid to Utting upon his return to Mr. Butcher and 2C. Of course he remained self conscious about his northern accent, of course this only reinforced his terrible home sickness and of course the unpleasant *A.J.* made every effort to be predictably objectionable the next morning.

'Ah, did you try and run off to 'MeMum', he mimicked, before the intervention of *Peewee's*, 'Oh for Christ's sake, just shut up Meenan!', which for once, earned the support of others in the immediate vicinity and convinced the odious little persecutor that, on this occasion at least, it might be better to let things go.

Letters from home, the first of which arrived that morning, proved a mixed blessing. Thoughtfully accompanied by a Monday night edition of the local evening paper, and including a report of the weekend match between his home town heroes and Huddersfield, the mention of names such as *Smethurst*, *Warburton* and *Pycroft* seemed only to reinforce the other worldliness of Utting's situation. Such definitively Northern names, together with the grainy black and white image of action from the match, which he alone could translate into the technicolor battle of red and white hoops against the famous claret and gold, appeared completely alien in this new and foreign environment. It felt painfully odd to learn, from both 'MeDad's' spidery handwriting and the local paper, that life back home remained so utterly unchanged at a time when Utting's own had been so correspondingly transformed, and though grateful for reports of life back in Lancashire, they actually did nothing to combat his feelings of homesickness.

In other ways however he began to settle. The novelty of the northern new boy had begun to wear off. Serving at breakfast had begun to seem almost routine, especially now those beginning their second year had got over their own delight at no longer having to perform this ritualistic chore. Even Meenan seemed to have become bored with his tiresome jibes and Utting had at least won some plaudits for his performances on the rugby pitch.

Another change arrived with the introduction to choral performance. Other than having to wear grey suits, a white shirt and black tie as an alternative to the red edged black blazer and similarly coloured striped tie worn by the vast majority, there had been little else to distinguish the choristers from the remainder of the school during those first ten days. That though was all to change quite spectacularly with the onset of choir duties.

There were sixteen choristers all together, aged between ten and approaching fifteen. Of these twelve were established within the choir, the other twelve adult male voices being provided by under graduates, while the youngest four, Utting included, were known as *probationers*. That is to say that, while they had to attend all the choir practices, of which there were at least eight each week, and all the sung services, performed on all but one evening of each week, they would not actually be expected to participate in any of the choir's performances prior to successful completion of their probationary year.

Another difference became immediately apparent when the choristers gathered together for the first time as, with the exception of the probationers, all the other boys emerged from the boarding house having suddenly assumed the appearance of 'mini-masters' by all wearing, rather preposterously in Utting's opinion, albeit one he chose not to articulate, mortar boards and gowns.

At the call of '*Chorrers*' this collection of sixteen children, all by definition still with unbroken voices but now transformed into something resembling pigmy academics, gathered together outside the Boarding House where order was rapidly established by Chandler, the Head Chorister.

Charged with responsibility for, amongst other things,

ensuring the ten minute walk from Boarding House to College cloisters was completed safely, Chandler and his assistant (Deputy Head Chorister Jervis) quickly and confidently sorted the younger choristers into some sort of paired 'crocodile' with probationers at the front followed, from front to rear, in ascending order of age and seniority.

Appropriately ordered, they then set off, gaining access to the other side of the road via an ancient and un-illuminated riverside gated tunnel, before climbing back to street level, crossing the river by bridge, and covering the quarter mile journey, in step all the way, before, much to the frustration of the numerous camera clicking Japanese and American tourists, disappearing via an abrupt right turn into the privacy of the cloistered heart of the college where the practice room was located.

This was the first time Utting had entered the antiquated and still dusty room since his voice trial nine months earlier, but just walking, again in step of course, through the echoing fifteenth century cloisters that first time provided a taste of what was to come, this being a return journey that the choristers would make at least eight times each week.

Six evenings a week, throughout each University term, they would sing that particular evening's psalms together with a different service (Magnificat and Nunc Dimittis), and concluded by a separate Anthem on each occasion.

They also had to learn an additional Introit for performance in the Anti-Chapel one night a week and while the choir master, Dr. Wood, could project himself as a kindly and generous man, he was a skilled musician and a tough taskmaster and one who was acutely aware that each evening represented not simply a chapel service, but a *performance* upon which both his and his choir's reputation rested. At least as important as any Headmaster in the lives of the choristers, he was not a man to disappoint and while he never resorted to any form of cruelty or violence, his dissatisfaction with any aspect of the boy's performance or behaviour would lead to stern words and the almost certain likelihood of extra practice.

Neither was Dr. Wood the only senior figure to avoid disappointing. Vaughan Chandler, the Head Chorister, could also have an enormous impact on the lives of the choristers. All of fourteen years old and unlikely to last the whole year in the choir, owing to the onset of adolescence and with it a gradually 'breaking' voice, 'V.C.' was confident to the point of being arrogant.

Within the context of the school as a whole Chandler did not possess any great significance and was very much a figure of secondary importance when set alongside those, three or four years his senior, who held the prestigious and powerful positions of prefects. As far as the choristers were concerned however, *VC's* confidence knew no bounds and he ruled with a rod of iron.

Still trying to work out whether Vaughan was a Christian name (it was) or another of the peculiar double barrelled affectations that remain so abundant throughout the English Public School system, Utting was pleasantly surprised when, in the days shortly after choral duties had begun, Chandler began to take what seemed a positive interest in him.

It was in the ambitiously named 'games room', in truth nothing more than a scruffy basement area of the boarding house which housed a table tennis table and a collection of antique board games, that Chandler's interest took on a new dimension.

Finding himself alone with such a senior and high ranking figure, Utting was surprised when the Head Chorister suggested that they ventured through a hitherto mysterious and ill fitting door linking the games room with the bottom of a long abandoned lift-shaft. Pleased with the attention and neither wishing, nor daring, to rebuff such an authority figure, Utting followed Chandler's tall figure into the dank and musty blackness where, within moments, the senior boy's practised hand produced a box of matches and lit two well used candles that had been placed in a pair of ancient and grimy jam jars.

Before leaving home, when he wasn't holding up stage-coaches or trying to emulate his sporting heroes, Utting had often indulged in the excitingly mysterious, formative and almost obligatorily furtive game of 'doctors and nurses' with the girl next door. What followed next then could hardly be considered his first introduction to 'sex education'. It was however to play a very significant part, and although never frightened or even truly alarmed, Utting's reaction was one of complete astonishment as, within the dank stale air and flick-ering candlelit semi darkness of the lift shaft, Chandler proceeded to undo his trousers and release probably the biggest, and for that matter only, erect penis Utting had ever seen.

Now, as any etymologist or historian who concerns them-selves with the specific area of ancestry will confirm, the origins of the name *Vaughan* are said to have their roots in Wales and mean 'little one'. Hence Vaughan Chandler may be 'translated' as 'little candle maker'. If that is the case then never has someone been more inappropriately named than this particular head chorister. Just fourteen years old and still some months away from his voice 'breaking', he was hung like a horse. The 'rod of iron' concept took on a whole new meaning as Chandler began to stroke and rub his cock (Utting had always referred to them as willies or dicks beforehand but Chandler's was definitely a 'cock'!) before producing an eruption of white liquid that spattered onto the wall and litter strewn floor narrowly avoiding extinguishing one of the candles.

The look on the younger boy's face must have betrayed both his innocence and amazement.

'What's the matter Utting? Never seen anyone ejaculate before?'

Utting said nothing. His eyes had widened in direct proportion to the size of Chandler's penis. In all truthfulness Utting had never even heard the word 'ejaculate' before and until that moment he'd not had the slightest inkling of what was involved. He'd certainly never seen a willy or a cock, whatever the hell it was, that big before and it definitely crossed his mind that Chandler had actually 'done himself some sort of mischief' as the white liquid began to spurt forth and land heavily in glistening globules all over the floor. In short, the ten year old child had been shocked into silence.

There had been no touching involved, although Chandler all too obviously derived pleasure and excitement from being watched. The whole scenario would be worked out again, either at the bottom of the stagnant lift shaft, amongst the overgrown foliage which skirted the school playing fields or in the outside toilet at the back of the cricket pavilion. Utting wouldn't have dared resist, but he never felt in any way violated and to an extent his role, in this peculiarly juvenile fusion of voyeurism and exhibitionism, was even to prove useful. Being in the influential head chorister's 'favour', however discreet, was no bad thing, especially as Chandler was more than a match for Meehan whose own particular 'interest' in Utting was far more unwanted and malicious than anything Chandler proposed. A lesson had been learned in the 'facts of life', and not just in a sexual sense.

SETTLING DOWN

Although those first few weeks at the Boarding House were at times both immeasurably miserable and bewilderingly different and eye opening, Utting did eventually begin to settle down into the routine of the place.

The whole day seemed to be dictated by bells. Bells told them when to get up, when to eat, when to go to school, when to change lessons and even, in the case of the youngest boys, when to go to bed.

The other instruction, which the choristers at least could never ignore, was the Head Chorister's ritualistic cry of *'Chorrers'* indicating that they had five minutes to be appropriately dressed and gathered ready for the route march to the cloisters. No one ever dared be late or inappropriately dressed, although there remain a great many tourists who remain blissfully unaware that their photographs of *'the cute little choir boys'* frequently contained a two finger 'salute', or worse, hidden behind a strategically held mortar-board.

When not overwhelmed by a combination of homesickness and desperate feelings of alienation, Utting recognised that aspects of the facilities he was now surrounded by could, in any other circumstances, have been described as idyllic. For a child with sporting inclinations, where else could one have had such easy access to a surfeit of rugby posts, hockey goals or cricket nets and tennis courts, all depending on which term they were in? Not only was the four acre field equipped with such 'essentials' it was also both a haven for wildlife and a natural playground. Completely encircled, and occasionally overwhelmed, by two deep rivers, the field and its tree lined banks were home to tree creepers, nuthatches, woodpeckers, squirrels, swans and a whole array of other water fowl. The rivers teemed with a variety of coarse fish. Bleak, roach, perch and less frequently, pike and chubb were easily caught and a little poking around in the muddy banks with the end of a fishing rod would often expose crayfish whose irritation was only matched by Utting's own astonishment when, on the first occasion at least, he truly believed he was about to be attacked by a miniature lobster.

In addition to the opportunities offered by access to these exclusive school grounds, life within the Boarding House, quite paradoxically, also provided a huge degree of freedom. As long as the boys attended school, conformed to the times set for meals, bed and homework and most importantly of all, answered the call of *'Chorrers'*, they were largely free to do as they liked. Trips to the city centre and to the more local shops, including the nearby tobacconist were common place, all made in their 'play clothes' of course rather than the give-away grey suit or blazer.

AN IMPORTANT LESSON LEARNED

Despite appearing on the time table as some sort of free afternoon, Tuesdays actually turned out to be anything but. There may not have been any lessons to attend, but they were actually devoted to either inter house rugby matches, cross country running or opportunities for the schools CCF (Combined Cadet Force) to practice such vital 'skills' as marching, boot 'blacking', badge polishing and rifle main-tenance.

Although still too young to join, Utting had absolutely no intention of ever becoming involved with the preposterous boy soldiers but he was delighted to be given opportunities in the sporting activities and it was through rugby in partic-ular that Utting attracted the interest, entirely dissimilar and thankfully far more wholesome in nature to that shown by Chandler, of 'Pip' Gilbert.

Gilbert held a position as one of the House prefects and, presumably as a means of providing the teaching staff with what would go on to be known as 'non-contact' time, one of his prefect's duties involved coaching and refereeing the under- twelve rugby players.

During the course of the match Gilbert was impressed by young Utting's performance, especially as he had been playing largely in the company of boys who were a year older. To receive such compliments and acknowledgement from such a source, a seventeen year old prefect and member of the first XV no less, was to both prove a turning point in Utting's school life and provide a lesson in the power of approval and praise, one significant incident apart, that he would never forget.

Using Gilbert as the healthiest and most appropriate of role models Utting began to thrive, at least as far as sport was concerned. He became captain, at both under twelve and, later, under fourteen level, of both his House rugby and hockey teams, and the only thing that prevented him achieving a similar feat with the cricket team was that the duties synonymous with the all important and immovable business of 'Chorrers' prevented him, or in fact any of the choristers, from becoming involved in the lengthier hours demanded by that particular sport.

Being a chorister also involved compulsory tutelage in the playing of two musical instruments. The first of these was the piano, which he had already gained a limited proficiency in from his days back in Annie Egerton's terraced home, and the second was the trumpet which Utting had chosen in error during his first school music lesson.

Confronted with as wide and varied a choice of string, wind and brass instruments as it was possible to imagine, he had actually intended to choose the trombone, largely because he liked the look of the lengthy sliding instrument's capacity for making mischief. Upon realising his mistake however, Utting possessed insufficient confidence to admit it, and thus became stuck with the trumpet and the interminable practice sessions that went with it. Four half hour lessons a week, two for each instrument, were expected of all the choristers and, short sightedly gaining absolutely no joy from the attempted mastery of either, Utting rapidly began to resent the way in which these difficult and tedious sessions ate into time which he would much rather have spent indulging his obsessions with sport.

Commitment to the choir however had become something of a different matter. Having satisfactorily completed his probationary year, Utting's self esteem had been further boosted by words of praise from Dr. Wood (the 'paymaster general' as far as school fees were concerned) and by the beginning of his second year Utting had become entitled to wear both the mortar board and gown, en route to the College, and the cassock and surplice within it.

By this time the likes of Chandler and Jervis had of course departed from the choir, their voices having reached that stage of adolescence which certain other aspects of the former's anatomy appeared to have surpassed some time earlier.

No longer a mere probationer and now at the beginning of his first year as a fully fledged chorister, Utting was, surprisingly as far as he was concerned, beginning to make something of a name for himself within the choir, but as is so often the case, pride was to come, quite justifiably in this case, before the inevitable fall.

Track 7. 'Mr Tambourine Man'. Bob Dylan.

A combination of the arrival of a fresh intake of probationers, the relief of no longer being one of the servile breakfast 'waiters', together with the esteem he had achieved both on the games field and within the acoustically perfect Chapel walls, had begun to make Utting rather too big for his boots.

Remembering his own excruciating experience of twelve months earlier, Utting reached the odd, but sadly not unusual, conclusion that it was 'his turn now' and, having identified his 'target' amongst the new probationers, a rather plump miner's son from South Wales called Price, Utting set about the task of gaining his perverse and wholly unjustified retribution.

Poor young Price ticked all the boxes as far as Utting's incarnation as a bully was concerned. He was overweight and unathletic. He'd proved, during his first few lessons in 2C, to be not especially bright and, although he may have had the singing voice of an angel, he also had a very distinct and pronounced Welsh accent.

Throughout Price's first two weeks in the Boarding House Utting did his best to make himself feel better about his own remaining insecurities, by tormenting and harassing the miserable young new boy at every opportunity. Price's waist-line, his inability to spell, his lack of any physical co-ordina-tion and, above all of course...his accent, all rapidly became the target of daily persecution from Utting.

Then one day, having dropped a simple pass, that should have led to a match winning try, a tearful Price found himself on the receiving end of yet another tirade.

'You fucking fat Welsh spastic...' shouted Utting...but even before the final angry and distorted syllable had even left his mouth, Pip Gilbert had grabbed the astonished Utting by the back of the collar, spun him round and now held him, with both hands clutching the stunned bully's shirt front, firmly against the changing room wall, his feet dangling all of five inches from the floor.

'What did you just say?' demanded Gilbert, of a suddenly dumbstruck Utting. 'Just who the hell do you think you are anyway?' he continued. 'Have you forgotten what things were like for you when you were new here? Forgotten how you ran away when people picked on you...forgotten how you tried to run back home to mummy when things got tough? Bet he never told you that did he Price?' asked Gilbert in the direction of the no longer tearful but clearly speechless and utterly flabbergasted little probationer.

'Oh yes', continued Gilbert. 'Quite the runner', was our

young Utting. 'Scared to death of Meenan weren't you? But you seem to have conveniently forgotten all that now...' went on the prefect, letting his grip slacken so that Utting slithered down the wall to sit in an undignified heap at the senior boy's feet. 'What have you got to say to Price now then?' continued Gilbert contemptuously.

'Sorry', stuttered Utting.

'Louder...' demanded the prefect..

'I'm sorry Price'...reaffirmed Utting.

'I should damn well think you are...' replied Gilbert '...and if I ever catch you behaving like that again...'

'You won't...' interrupted Utting, both genuinely ashamed at the realisation of what he had become and completely mortified at having earned the contemptuous disapproval from a role model he had always held in such high regard.

'Well we'll let that be the end of it then...' answered Gilbert, '...but don't you *ever* forget how tough things were for you and don't *ever* let me see you acting like that again.'

Utting didn't, it was a lesson...quite probably more than just one...well learned and he would never ever bully anyone again, quite the reverse in fact.

Placed in the middle of the *Decani* side of the choir Utting was regularly outperforming older boys in the solo stakes and although he still dreaded the idea of having to perform in front of family or friends, never more so than when his Grandmother would suggest, usually at Christmas...'wouldn't it be grand if our Lawrence were to sing for us?', the notion of his moment in the spotlight in front of a packed Chapel began, slightly paradoxically, to hold ever greater appeal.

At first the major solos continued to go to the more senior thirteen and fourteen year old boys but before long, and certainly by the time of his second summer in the choir,

Utting was beginning to monopolise such opportunities and his performances were no longer confined to the 'home territory' of the Chapel.

There were recordings of Evensong for the BBC's Home Service and a Japanese T.V. crew recorded a live performance of madrigals from the top of the college's ever so slightly swaying tower at 6.00 a.m on May Day morning.

Concerts were given in both Warwick and St. Albans Cathedrals while, reporting on a performance of Christmas Music at St. Clement Danes in The Strand, *The Daily Telegraph* reporter referred to the *'Pure Tone of this fine Chapel choir'* and eagerly described how the choristers, particularly the main soloist, had delivered a *'neatness and clarity of enunciation and sweet purity of tone so characteristic of the English Cathedral and Chapel choirs'*.

Three recordings followed but perhaps the highpoint arrived with the choir's appearance at Westminster Abbey where Utting, still consumed with nerves when asked to sing at family gatherings, allowed his, by now unrivalled, treble tones to soar through the vaulted ceilings during the introductory solo to John Gould's *'Sans Day Carol'*.

Within weeks, following Drinkwater's untimely entrance into somewhat premature adolescence, Utting was made Head Chorister, a position he may have achieved earlier given better behaviour elsewhere in the school, and he went on to wear the precious diamond shaped silver medallion with pride throughout his final two terms as a chorister.

CRIMES AND PUNISHMENT

Track 8.'Dead End Street'. The Kinks.

Given the eminently reasonable Gilbert's reaction to his equally unreasonable earlier behaviour Utting should probably have been thankful that prefects had lost the 'right' to inflict the cane on wrongdoers just a term prior to his arrival. They were still empowered to mete out significant punishments, but the matter of caning, or beatings as they were perhaps more fittingly referred to, was now considered, much to the frustration and disappointment of the more sadistic senior boys, a matter best left to the Masters.

On the first two occasions that Utting had been beaten it had been by a junior House Master, Mr. Ainscow, who, having identified the culprits during some typically rumbustious evening dormitory escapades, had angrily ordered the miscreants to 'attend his study after breakfast' the following morning. On both occasions Utting, along with his 'partners in crime', received three strokes of the cane however the efforts of the Master could not in any way be described as wholehearted and in any case, the intended impact was dramatically weakened by the fact that any subsequent tears were, rather puzzlingly, to be found in the eyes of the assailant rather than those of his victims.

Beatings from Herb were however an altogether different matter. As Senior House Master he regarded himself as having a position to maintain and while he could often potray himself in the light of a kindly and benevolent uncle, Herb would not tolerate cheek at any price and his good humour would rapidly disappear, with almost schizophrenic readiness, should he ever imagine himself to be the butt of any misguided schoolboy humour.

The first time Utting felt the wrath of Herb was the result

of a complete accident. In his second year and following another afternoon games lesson, Utting had been getting showered and changed when some perfectly good natured tomfoolery resulted in his school scarf being left hanging, beyond reach, from one of the horizontal ceiling supports above the changing area.

Alerted by the subsequent commotion caused by a group of small boys delightedly aiming a selection of shoes skyward in an effort to release the scarf, Herb marched through the shower block into the changing room only to be hit squarely on his receding hairline by one of the aforesaid missiles.

There could be little doubt, even in Herb's increasingly agitated state, that the incident was entirely unintentional but, while everyone else in the room seemed to freeze, Utting couldn't contain a slight snigger.

More nervous than disrespectful it was all that was required to send Herb over the edge. Veins pumping in his already reddened forehead and eyes popping as if they were about to evacuate their sockets, Herb roared at the boy, 'How dare you? Get to my study this instant!' and as a stunned Utting started to unhesitatingly conform to the enraged House master's demand he heard Herb yell at the remaining boys, 'and the rest of you… get this damned mess tidied up now if you have any idea at all of what's good for you!'

Utting arrived outside Herb's study only seconds before the enraged Housemaster who, having used the separate staff staircase, had only half the distance to travel and, unfortunately for Utting, barely anytime to calm down.

Still incensed by what he perceived as *'total disrespect and gross insubordination'* Herb manhandled the boy roughly into his study before angrily pulling his high wing backed armchair into the centre of the room and ordering Utting to bend forward with his outstretched hands holding the two uppermost corners of the leather backed chair.

Then, with barely a moment's hesitation, Herb reached

for his cane and, allowing himself ample space for maximum power, brought down, with practised accuracy, the first of four savagely stinging strikes onto the eleven year old's backside.

If Utting had remained relatively unaffected by his previous faintly half hearted beatings, from the somewhat over emotional Mr. Ainscow, this was certainly no longer the case. On this occasion there could be no doubting whose eyes were filled with tears. Appearing strangely appeased by the energy involved in the delivery of the blows and now believing his 'authority' to have been fully restored, Herb dismissed the boy with no further word of explanation other than a departing comment of, 'and let that be a lesson to you!'

Had Utting learned a lesson it was probably not the one intended by Herb. It took five days for the marks from his caning, badges of honour amongst his peers, to completely disappear, and while it would not be the last of his beatings, the whole incident only actually served to reinforce the lesson learned back in the institute with Mr. Spindle. Even the most otherwise agreeable of adults could, in certain circumstances, be complete bastards!

Perhaps then it was with this thought in mind that prefects had, mercifully, had the power to cane removed. If middle aged and otherwise allegedly professional adults were incapable of showing self restraint then it was quite startling to imagine what damage a vindictive seventeen or eighteen year old might have managed.

Deprived of the power to legally inflict pain, certain prefects would still however go out of their way to make life as uncomfortable as possible. Time consuming punishments were commonplace for such comparatively trifling offences as talking after lights out or during the communal homework sessions known as 'Prep'. Such 'crimes' would result in having to clean and polish the particular prefects rugby boots, sand down a desk or complete a four page essay on such instructive subjects as *'The Inside of a Table Tennis Ball'*.

Indeed Utting himself, having been caught harmlessly but illicitly listening to Radio Luxembourg on a small borrowed transistor radio beneath his pillow, had been given three days to complete a five page essay on the subject of *'Euthanasia'* .

Unfortunately, at the time Utting had no awareness whatsoever of the concept of mercy killings and delivered a carefully crafted dissertation on the problems posed for young people by poverty and starvation within the Indian sub-continent or, as he had genuinely misunderstood the topic to be, *'Youth in Asia'*.

Possessing a sense of humour which was apparently only matched by his sense of justice the prefect concerned ripped up the offending words, all one thousand of them, patronisingly explained what was required and gave Utting a further three days to complete the task properly, at which moment, as Utting would always recall, he secretly wished his antagonist the least merciful of deaths.

Track 9. 'Itchycoo Park'. The Small Faces.

Another beating from Herb was to follow in Utting's third year.

Finding the unholy trinity of Utting, Greene and Drinkwater together on the school's tennis courts one summer Sunday afternoon and realising that he had forgotten his glasses, Herb provided Greene with his keys and dispatched him back to the Boarding House with instructions to 'go through my drawers until you find them'.

Utting of course should have known better, but he all too often spoke before fully engaging his brain and he simply couldn't resist the temptation to venture into the increasingly popular culture of innuendo by querying with affected innocence, 'Go through your drawers Sir?'

No sooner had he uttered the words than he knew he had gone too far. Herb's brow darkened and his eyes bulged as rapidly as Greene's mission became redundant. Gripping Utting forcefully by the ear Herb marched the boy over the bridge, along the drive and up the stairs to his study where Utting was forced to bend over the very same chest of drawers and receive four more strokes of the cane for what Herb simultaneously described, his mouth actually frothing with anger, as *'his downright insolence'*.

Nothing though compared to the beating Utting was to receive from what he considered the unlikeliest of sources.

As ever during half term, while the remainder of the school basked in the luxury of a whole week off, the choristers only benefited from a two day break and had to spend the remainder of the week fulfilling their choral responsibilities and otherwise kicking their heels.

Time hung heavy and with so little to do and the long summer evenings providing so much time to do it, it was only a matter of time before the opportunity for mischief took over.

Having completed their Evensong performance and returned the probationers to the security of supper and 'Baby Dorm', Utting and four of the other Junior Dormers crept out of the otherwise seemingly deserted Boarding House in search of fun.

They'd already acquired a couple of bottles of cider and, camouflaged only by the cunning disguise of abandoning their school uniform, had found the local newsagent only too willing to exchange two packets of twenty cigarettes, including one of *Consulate* for Utting, who as Head Chorister now also harboured heady delusions of the new menthol cigarettes representing the height of fashion, in return for ready cash. Now all they needed was a punt, one of the long narrow flat bottomed boats synonymous with sophisticated student fun in both Oxford and Cambridge.

There was a whole flotilla of them moored just the other side of the bridge and although the poles were all separately locked up, Dickinson managed to find two rather battered paddles so that within moments of untying one vessel, the infamous five slid not so gracefully away from the mooring, back under the bridge and on to the planned circumnavigation of their four acre field.

Seeking to emulate the frequently witnessed behaviour of their undergraduate counterparts it wasn't long before the bottles were opened and the cigarettes lit. With no one else out on the river at this hour of the evening and the company only of a few startled mallards and swans, the boys proceeded on their Bacchanalian journey around the school field, pausing only to try and peer, more in hope than expectation, into the windows of St. Hilda's (all female) College which lay opposite their own island playing field.

An excess of the unfamiliar and sickly sweet cider, together with the aroma of tobacco and the sheer exhilaration of being out on the river alone in the gathering dusk, was to prove a truly intoxicating mixture and it was during one of the boys more raucous moments that the inevitable happened. Concentration having now completely given way to laughter and alcohol they collided heavily with a submerged willow root, whereupon the punt rolled and capsized, flinging the crew of five into the deep, dark and murky water.

Fortunately for Utting who, despite his other areas of sporting prowess had remained a hopeless swimmer, he fell out on the shallower side and managed to grope his way to the river bank, hastened by the combined sobering effect of cold river water and the memory of the pike and 'lobsters' that lurked beneath the surface.

Dickinson too had been able to almost stride ashore but the other three, who had been catapulted into the deeper water in the middle of the river had had to swim for their lives and now, having struggled to the opposite bank, still within the school grounds, lay breathlessly panting in a bedraggled heap staring forlornly at the vacant vessel which, lying largely submerged at a forty five degree angle beneath the surface of the river, now swayed gently and accusingly in the current.

'Shit...what the fuck do we do now', gasped a shocked and soaking Dickinson.

Before any of his fellow conspirators had a chance to reply however a familiar and, it must be noted, ominously calm adult voice answered...

'I'll tell you exactly what you do now Mr. Dickinson. You get inside, you get out of those wet clothes, get showered and get to your dormitory...and you do it right this minute!'

Mr. Beaumont, pipe aglow, had made his way down from the Boarding House, using the wisdom acquired by years of acquaintance with the behaviour of bored school boys, so that he now stood in the centre of the willow pattern bridge which linked the two banks of the river.

He watched silently as Utting and Dickinson warily dragged their dripping and sodden selves past him and across the wooden timbers of the bridge to join the three swimmers as they walked silently and forlornly up the gravelled path back to the Boarding House.

Such can be the misplaced and misguided optimism of thirteen and fourteen year old boys that, by the time they had showered, left their saturated clothes with a clearly un-amused Matron and climbed into bed in their pyjamas, the boys had begun to convince themselves that the worst was over.

'Maybe he thinks we've suffered enough...'

'Probably just glad we didn't drown...would have taken some explaining,' appeared to reflect the consensus of wishful thinking.

That though was indeed all it was. No sooner had they

turned the dormitory light out than the door at the far end, which accessed the Headmaster's living quarters, opened and there, framed in the illuminated doorway stood the unmistakable figure of Mr. Beaumont.

'I think it's time to see you five foolish young men in my study now', came the stern, but still menacingly calm, tones of the Headmaster.

Realising at last what was likely to lie ahead, the five miscreants climbed out of bed and padded reluctantly across the bare floorboards after their headmaster, down the contrastingly comfortable and carpeted stairs to his study.

There followed a totally logical lecture and explanation as to what they had done wrong. They had taken it upon themselves to sneak out of the building, steal a punt and put their lives in danger.

'Thank fuck he doesn't know about the cider and the fags,' thought Utting.

'And, as if that wasn't enough, I believe you've all been smoking and drinking too'.

'Oh shit!', though Utting, who right at that moment felt as far removed from being, in the words of the iconic *Consulate* advert, *'as cool as a mountain stream'* as it was possible to be.

'You are all lucky not to be expelled, and as for you Utting...as Head Chorister I hold you above all as being responsible for this incident...this debacle!'

Utting actually had little idea of what a 'debacle' was. He doubted it was good but right at that moment he was far more concerned with the thought that he might well be about to become the first Head Chorister ever to be stripped of his 'title', and worse, much worse, was the fact that, if that was the case all this would unavoidably get back to 'MeMum' and 'MeDad', or 'my mother and father' as almost four years at boarding school had taught him to describe them.

The caning that followed came, initially at least, almost as a relief. Expulsion or demotion was rarely used in conjunction with a beating, the former being regarded as far more serious. Standing there in his pyjamas, no longer with the benefit of any protection which may have been provided by his abandoned and soaking wet underpants, Utting, having been identified as the most culpable, had to wait at the end of the line as his partners in crime all bent forward in turn to receive their four strokes of the cane.

The 'whoosh' and gunshot 'thwack' of contact was witnessed sixteen times before Utting, now left alone with the Headmaster, stepped forward to receive his punishment.

As he bent forward Utting rather doubted Mr. Beaumont's suggestion that, 'this is going to hurt me a lot more than it hurts you', but as he started to stand after the fourth stinging blow, he was surprised to find the Headmaster's restraining hand between his shoulders as a fifth and then a sixth swipe of the cane made increasingly painful contact with his pyjama clad back side.

Six of the best! He'd never imagined he was to get six strokes. Never imagined that the previously benevolent old Headmaster, who was never seen without a CND lapel badge and who exhibited none of Herb's uninhibited anger, could deliver such blows with so much calm and controlled efficiency. Moreover, as he climbed slowly back up the carpeted stairs to the bare boards of the dormitory, Utting knew that this time, by the standards of 1968, he'd thoroughly deserved it.

MOVING ON...

Whatever happened as far as the conspicuously semi-submerged punt was concerned Utting had no idea. Such matters had a habit of being 'taken care' of by those within the adult world, and the capsized boat had 'disappeared' within a couple of days, the whole sorry business never to be spoken of again.

Just a few weeks later the time had arrived for Utting to move back home.

At this point one must understand that the 'life' of a University or Cathedral chorister is a short one. Situated between the constraints of the watching brief performed during the unavoidable probationary year, and the inevitable termination brought about by the move into adolescence with its timely removal of any further capacity to display the desired angelic tones, it is rare for the 'Singing Time', the actual performance days, to amount to anything more than three years. Indeed such is the social pressure from peers and so strong is the desire not to be one of those 'unfortunates' who attain the age of fifteen with their voice still childishly unbroken, that many choristers of the time ended up willing and often 'smoking' their voices to break.

In Utting's case he had mixed feelings. During the Easter holidays his acquaintance with the girl next door had progressed well beyond the juvenile experimentation days of 'doctors and nurses'.

With both parents out at work all day, he and Kay, his somewhat older 'girl next door' *companion* had ample opportunity to enter into a brave new world of bra-straps, breasts and other emergent adolescent fumblings. To Utting, the unwanted attention once offered by Chandler paled into complete significance compared with Kay's infinitely more desireable attractions.

Here then, to this particular fourteen year olds not enormously forward thinking mind, was at least one good reason for wishing to return north, and although he also longed to spend more time on the sports field and would miss the kudos and personal prestige brought to him by his performances within the choir, Utting recognised the ultimate reality of the situation. His voice was breaking, the highest notes had been on the edge of his vocal range and reach for months. Now, with his parents hopelessly unable to afford the considerable fees demanded once he was no longer of any service to his College Choir benefactors, the journey into late puberty and early adolescence was also to coincide with the end of his own personal 'Singing Time' and the beginning of a one way journey back North.

LESSONS 2

Some of what was learned at Boarding School perhaps falls into the category of reinforcement, but the main lessons of those four years may be found below.

1. However hard they may try, Matrons are no substitute for mothers.
2. The gap between North and South transcends mere physical distance.
3. Alienation and being made to feel different is enormously painful, particularly at the age of ten.
4. Entirely male environments can produce some real little sods.
5. Adults, even seemingly caring ones, can be even bigger ones and do hit harder.
6. Double barrelled names are a peculiar public school affectation and an invariably unnecessary complication.
7. Running away seldom achieves very much but if you're ever contemplating it then make sure any necessary plans and lies are properly thought through beforehand.
8. Success is empowering. Everyone needs to succeed at something.
9. There are worse things to contend with at Boarding School than the *juvenile* and *harmless* sexual

advances of an older pupil. (Note the emphasis on the words *'juvenile'* and *'harmless'*.)

10. Make the most of whatever charms you may possess.

11. There are no such things as freshwater lobsters in the rivers of Oxford.

12. Winding up occasionally psychopathic house masters is not to be recommended.

13. The cane can hurt...a lot.

14. Unfair punishment equals lasting resentment. Fair punishment, even when it hurts a lot more, does not.

15. Rivers, punts and alcohol are a dangerous combination, most especially for people who cannot swim.

16. Smoking regularly, even *Consulate*, can encourage your voice to 'break'.

17. As previously suspected, approval is hugely important. Along with food, shelter and warmth it is an essential requirement of the human condition.

18. Bullying is always a bad thing and bullies are invariably compensating for some inadequacy of their own. Never participate in it and never accept it.

THREE

GRAMMAR SCHOOL

NO WOMAN. NO CHOIR!

Track 10. All Along the Watchtower. Jimi Hendrix.

Utting's return to the North didn't start well.

Fondly and, in his misplaced opinion at least, not unreasonably imagining that he was about to pick up where he had left off, some two and a half months earlier, with the girl next door, Utting, who had now gratefully reverted to either Lol or Loz, was dismayed at his mother's revelation that, 'I see that young Kay next door has got herself a new boyfriend'.

'She can't have! Can't be true,' thought Lol, but it undoubtedly was. More to the point, having reached the age of almost sixteen it seemed that the lovely Kay now had little difficulty in attracting the sort of older boy who, unlike Utting, had already managed to grow into his face, had the ability to frame that face with proper adult sideboards and was also the proud owner of those two objects most coveted by teenage girls at the time, a motorbike and a leather jacket.

'Probably hung like fucking Chandler too', thought Lol

bitterly, as Kay and her new young Lothario cruised past him one day, the object of his affection now scarcely able, or willing, to release her grip on the leather clad hips of her seducer for long enough to offer Utting even the slightest acknowledgment.

So it was that Utting, in this fresh and all too familiar state of emotional turmoil, if indeed teenage *lust* and *jealousy* can be described as emotions, prepared himself for entry into the Grammar School.

Moves to any new environment often bring with them some degree of anxiety. This latest move however held none of the complexity and bewilderment that had accompanied the upheaval from Edgemoor to the 'Boarding House' four years earlier.

Lol, already knew a good number of those he would be attending school with and had easily adapted over the summer holiday. Four years in Oxford had taught him the need to heavily disguise his more natural Lancastrian accent and in the same way as 'my mother and father' rapidly returned to being 'MeMum' and 'MeDad', Lol had experienced no great difficulty in reacquainting himself with the hard northern vowels and dropped 'h's in order to avoid being once more identified as the dreaded *'l'etranger'*.

'MeDad' had experienced little difficulty in convincing the Grammar School to accept his son. A boy from Oxford and a former head chorister to boot had appealed to the rampant snobbery of the headmaster, one Mr. S.J. Bennett B.Sc (Hons Cantab) known as either Sam or 'Bendover Bennett' by his pupils.

Indeed the whole Oxford connection provided a legacy which Lol quickly had to live down. One or two of the less welcoming pupils had already scathingly referred to him as the 'little Oxford queer boy' and, having had quite enough of choirs, the music teacher was the first to be disappointed when, evidently believing he was to be the recipient of some new musical mentee, Lol promptly, and not entirely politely, made it abundantly clear that he had no interest at all in spending his lunchtimes in the company of either the school choir or orchestra.

Now also faced with making his 'O' level choices, Lol was already resentful of the fact that he had been forced to give up Art, the only subject he had ever 'come top' in, and made to replace that 'option' with the hated and dreaded Chemistry.

There was, he soon discovered, infinitely more esteem to be gained from making his presence felt in the break and lunchtime playground football games and the teachers unfortunate enough to deliver the subjects that Lol had difficulty with, and therefore absolutely no interest in, quickly found the former 'Oxford boy' to be awkward, uncooperative and quite the 'class clown'.

Two exceptions to this situation were Lol's English and History teachers, both of whom he respected and got on well with.

The latter of these two was a young Yorkshire man from nearby Halifax called Jeff Stone. Coincidentally arriving at the grammar school as an Oxford graduate at exactly the same time as Lol, Mr. Stone was perhaps too pleasant a man to make classroom control easy.

His lessons were often disrupted by pupils for whom the intricacies of the French Revolution held little interest but Lol was never one of them. Indeed he had, quite uncharacteristically, 'floored' one of Mr. Stone's tormentors when, fearful of attack from the compass wielding pupil himself, he had, as the saying goes, 'got his retaliation in first' and stopped the charging would be assailant in his tracks with one perfectly timed punch to the face earning the welcome admiration of his classmates and, perhaps more covertly, his long suffering History teacher too. The incident went unreported.

Hopelessly deprived of his adolescent 'love interest', Lol had sought succour again in his beloved rugby team. After the success of the fifties and early sixties, the side were now in a sad state of decline, but to Lol they were all still heroes and he used to love the atmosphere at games which were now largely played on Sunday afternoons or under the atmosphere enhancing floodlights on invariably dank and damp Tuesday evenings.

It was on just such a typically chilly, misty and coal fire smoke infused October evening that Lol made a surprising discovery, when, there amongst the relatively sparse crowd at the front of the terraces, he spotted the familiar face of Jeff Stone.

Lol had never thought of Mr. Stone as sharing his own interest in rugby league and, originating from the 'wrong' side of the Pennines he would, in any case, have expected his history teacher to have followed a Yorkshire team.

Come to that, again in the way that youngsters so often do, Lol had never really contemplated the fact that any of his teachers had any sort of existence beyond school, but here his teacher undoubtedly was and, more to the point, Mr. Stone had recognised Lol and raised a gloved hand in acknowledgement.

'Recognition!'...more than he ever got from Kay these days...and from a teacher too!

Suitably encouraged, Lol snaked his way through the plentiful gaps in the crowd until he was standing alongside his teacher.

'Sir'...began Lol, attempting to sound suitably respectful and adult...'never expected to see you here'.

'Nor I, you Utting', replied Mr. Stone, retaining the teacher-pupil convention of observing only the surname.

'Come every match Sir...nowt better to do...could do with

a try before half time though...gettin' a bit close for my liking'.

Just then there was a huge groan of disappointment as the home team's winger, a black player from South Wales, dropped a pass which, had he clung on to it, would have led to a certain try.

'All the bloody same that lot...' began a truculent and pugnacious looking loud mouthed fan. All the bloody same...soft as bloody grease them blackies...soft as grease...no bloody use to anyone!'

'That'll be why he's the leading try scorer then will it?' said Mr. Stone, turning to look the accuser in his eyes.

'Leading bloody try scorer...I could have scored half o' them', continued the fat man, leading Lol to rapidly conclude that this seemed unlikely seeing as, on the one hand stood a lithe, fast, brave and skilful athlete, whereas on the other, was a fat, morose, loudmouth who looked barely capable of anything more than waddling to and from the nearest bar. Lol was in no doubt which of the two he aspired to be.

Moments later the half time whistle sounded and as the players began to leave the pitch, the home side holding a slender three point advantage, the self opinionated windbag began again, holding forth ostensibly to his two friends but loudly enough to engage the attention of anyone who would listen.

'Never get anywhere with darkies in't side I tell ya. Too ruddy soft...no ruddy guts...can't tek a tackle, see...we'd be well ahead now if he'd kept his bloody eye on the ball.'

Resisting, in all probability, the urge to take matters into his own hands Mr. Stone looked away and shook his head. Looking down at Utting he raised his eyes discreetly to the skies, as the belligerent fool continued his diatribe.

'Take no notice...there's always one Utting...always one,' said Mr. Stone resignedly.

'Aye Sir...but he's a big fat stupid one that one in't he?'

77

replied Lol, glancing up, to see just the hint of an approving smile briefly brighten his history teacher's face.

That feeling of tacit approval, of being treated as some kind of kindred spirit, was to prove something of a turning point as far as Lol's relationship with and perception of teachers was concerned. Simply being spoken to with respect and sharing in the covert adult condemnation of the outspoken bigot was to signal the beginning of an association with his history teacher that would have fortunate and far reaching consequences for Lol.

'BENDOVER' BENNET

Track 11. 'I Talk to the Wind'. King Crimson.

The same could, most emphatically not be said for Lol's relationship with his new headmaster, Mr. Bennett.

Prior to his arrival at the Grammar School, Lol had never had a problem with his headmasters. Contrary to rumour, the initially intimidating Mr. Failsworth had proved himself to be nothing if not fair and, despite the beating handed out by Mr. Beaumont, Lol had always accepted his undisputed guilt, and still believed the most fitting adjectives, as far as his Boarding School headmaster was concerned, to be patient, tolerant and understanding.

'Bendover' however was a wholly different matter and the complete antithesis of patience, tolerance or any semblance of empathy and understanding, at least where teenage boys were concerned.

Unlike Mr. Beaumont, who was only ever found wearing his 'gown' for school 'functions', and Mr. Failsworth, to whom the nonsensical and impractical idea would have never even occurred, 'Sam' Bennett was never without his. Indeed he was never seen in one of the school assemblies without his accompanying university hood, made from light blue silk and ermine which should, in the circumstances, have provided an early warning of some sort of narcissistic personality disorder, had Lol only been worldly enough to recognise it.

Sam Bennett stalked the school corridors like some sort of hideous outsized bat, ready to pounce on any poor and unsuspecting pupil whose own developing 'image' failed in some trivial way to conform to the Headmaster's view of the world.

Unfortunately for Lol, Bendover had quickly become exasperated by repeated reports of the new boy's 'impertinence' and 'stupidity' from his Maths, French and Chemistry teachers. The almost tearful Music master, wearing some sort of quasi military uniform, also hadn't helped when he'd referred to Lol's 'disrespectful disinterest' in having anything at all to do with his beloved school choir and even less in the CCF.

Only his English, History, Geography and Games teachers seemed to have anything genuinely positive to say about him and the result was that 'Bendover' felt affronted. He'd believed he'd picked up a worthy addition to *his* school. An 'Oxford Public School boy', a 'former Head Chorister of one of the country's most famous choirs' no less, a pupil full of the 'moral fibre' that Bennett repeatedly and meaninglessly blathered on about, at least twice a week in assembly.

Perhaps most importantly, the Headmaster had believed, given all the evidence of the boy's past achievements that, in Lol, he had acquired a definite 'university material' boy (hence the insistence that he swapped Art for Chemistry), when, in reality, it now seemed that the Headmaster had actually misguidedly admitted some sort of 'dullard', and an 'insolent' one at that.

The inevitable result was conflict and although the Headmaster appeared to hold all the 'aces' he wasn't to have things entirely his own way.

Time and again 'Bendover' would leap out into the corridor, black gown flapping, like a huge badly coordinated bird, ready to accost Lol over such trivia as, his hair being too long, his tie knot too small or his shoes the 'wrong' style.

One of Bennett's favourite tricks was to wait in his study doorway only to emerge, in perfectly timed synchronicity just as Lol or his friends were passing, where upon he would withdraw his pen and release the carefully concealed 'side boards' from behind the boys' ears before judging them 'entirely inappropriate' and threatening expulsion if they hadn't been suitably cut off by the next morning.

Track 12.'Let it Be'. The Beatles.

Neither was the question of hair length the only thing to get under 'Bendover's' skin. Winters in that area of the southern Pennines were notoriously cold and Lol, together with his best friend Mark Ripley, had invested in the current fashion for wearing army surplus greatcoats as a means of both combating the bitter winter weather and simultaneously cultivating the 'hippy' image they both craved.

Incandescent with rage, Bendover insisted that the two boys, complete with greatcoats, one RAF grey, the other khaki, accompanied him to the stage during assembly where he sought to heap further public humiliation by ranting angrily about boys coming to school dressed like something from a *'bally hippy colony'* and how he would have *'no brass buttons'* in *his* school.

There followed further furious and predictable accusation about such clothes somehow again representing a 'complete lack of moral fibre', before the Headmaster began to angrily conclude a process which, had he been wise enough to understand, had achieved nothing other than to make him look completely ridiculous and provide *Utting* and *Ripley*, as they'd been sneeringly referred to for the last ten minutes, with precisely the type of subversive esteem they both thrived off.

Had he left it there, Lol would have undoubtedly achieved the first of many minor victories but, showing far greater awareness of what was actually going on than 'Bendover', and having been made to feel like some sort of parading mannequin in front of the whole school, Lol couldn't resist opening his great coat wide and giving the whole school a twirl as he left the stage.

Hitherto subdued sniggers turned into unrestrained hilarity as the whole assembly hall collapsed into fits of raucous laughter leading to Lol being immediately marched to Bennett's study by one of his 'henchmen', where he was soon to painfully learn that the origin of the headmaster's nickname was certainly not purely alliterative, in conditions that involved absolutely no protection from his greatcoat.

SAVIOURS

Given such an environment of misbehaviour and malice it should come as no great surprise that Lol was to make hard work of his 'O' Levels. 'MeMum' and 'MeDad' were of course disappointed but the only real surprise was that Lol had somehow contrived to fail History and as such let down his unofficial mentor, Jeff Stone.

It is difficult to imagine exactly what 'Bendover' felt. There had been a couple more canings and one fully fledged 'assault', all for perceived 'insubordination' of one sort or another. Pupils acquiring a proper and acceptable number of 'passes' represented the headmaster's whole 'raison d'etre' and although he doubtless wished to retain his all important 6th form numbers, it seemed likely that he would have happily traded Lol's failures for an excuse to rid himself of the recalcitrant *Utting*.

Here however was where the 'fortunate and far reaching'

implications of Lol's rapport with Jeff Stone were to truly begin. Already accepted for access to 'A' level courses in English and Geography, Lol needed a third subject if he was to be admitted to the school's sixth form.

Failure to pass a subject at 'O' level inevitably, and not unreasonably, prohibited access to the same subject at a higher level, but Mr. Stone somehow managed to present a case for Lol to sit his exam again in the autumn while in the meantime beginning work on his other 'A' levels.

Ultimately the deal was that, so long as Lol passed his 'O' level at the end of October 'Bendover' would allow him to remain. If he failed he'd be out and looking for work. No pressure then!

Around the middle of November it was confirmed, much to the relief of all, with the possible exception of 'Bendover', that Lol had passed, albeit with another in his collection of mediocre 'C' grades.

Track 13. 'Famous Blue Raincoat'. Leonard Cohen

Survival in the 6th Form was not the only thing that Lol had to be grateful to his young History teacher for. At the beginning of the school year Lol and a couple of like minded friends had asked Jeff Stone if it would be possible for him to organise a rugby match between the sixth formers and the staff.

In the otherwise strictly football playing school, the match attracted a small crowd of interested onlookers to the one remaining non *'red-gra'* facility at the bottom of the school's playing fields. Only finally managing to attract two teams of ten, rather than the more conventional thirteen, the game would have been of little consequence had it not been for the appearance on the staff side of the hitherto little known biology teacher, Bob Lord.

Lord, an energetic little scrum half for the town's Rugby

Union team, was sufficiently impressed by three of the sixth formers, Lol included, to invite them down for a 'trial'. While one of the chosen trinity declined, claiming to have 'only played for a laugh Sir', Lol and his mate 'Jacko' duly turned up the following Saturday afternoon and were surprised to, within half an hour of their arrival, find themselves pulling on the red, amber and black jerseys in readiness for a third team debut against Manchester YMCA.

Whether the teenagers' debut appearances in the 3rds first victory of the season was entirely coincidental remains debatable, but with Lol, at centre, sending his winger over for his first two tries, and actually quite possibly his first two passes, of the season, and 'Jacko' notching an impressive personal tally of one try and three conversions, the two sixteen year olds most certainly not only dramatically increased the 'mobility'of the side but also brought about a significant decrease in the team's average age so that it now hovered just below the *'late thirties'* mark.

From the Autumn to the Spring of their two 'A' level years the two boys continued to represent the team and the town. Lol enjoyed hearing his selection card drop through the letter box each Wednesday morning and took pride from seeing his name posted in the 'teams for the weekend' section of the local evening paper every Friday evening.

With all the facilities of a proper club house, including changing rooms, communal baths, post match pie and peas, a fully stocked bar (where they could actually get served!) and a little old man (aka 'loyal club servant') who dispensed hot sweet tea to the muddied and bruised participants on their return from the frequently wind blasted and frozen pitches, Lol wished for nothing more.

He was mixing with adults, but not the sort exemplified by 'Bendover' Bennet. These were 'proper' men, hard and full of yarn and humour, who had either come down from the 'firsts' together or were rugby 'refusniks', now playing under an alias, from the never to be acknowledged professional code of League.

These thirty five to forty something year old men valued the boys' comparative speed and determination and ferried them all over an area the shape of a rough cut diamond bordered by Wigan to the west, Matlock to the East, Leek in the south and Halifax in the north. They taught them the protocols of drinking, offering approval and occasional rebuke along with praise and protection in equal measure.

Indeed never was Lol more appreciative of such protection than when, on a frozen pitch at Huddersfield, he had been grabbed and maliciously 'buried' into the bone hard dirt by an opposition forward who could best be described as resembling some sort of mutant cross between *Magwitch* and the *Incredible Hulk*.

Pulling all of Lol's barely conscious ten and a half stone back to a roughly vertical position , George, the boys' 'driver' and team captain simply said...'don't worry about him lad...I saw that...he'll not be trying it again'. Sure enough, after the very next ruck, *Magwitch* was to be found lying in a crumpled heap. He had to be helped from a match he was to play no further part in, while an angelic looking George gave Lol the the subtlest of winks, leaving what went on at the bottom of that ruck as a complete mystery and making George another example of an adult role model that Lol would have happily walked over hot coals for.

Despite Lol's complete rejection of anything to do with organised and 'approved' music in the form of choirs and school orchestras, another form of music was to play a vital part in his complex journey through adolescence.

Lol had missed the access to records and record players that the Boarding House had provided. There, under the occasionally patient guidance of much older and more knowledgeable pupils, his liking for such groups, the term *'band'* was still some years away, as *The Troggs*, *The Bee Gees* and *Dave Dee, Dozy, Beaky, Mick and Titch* had been 'challenged' to say the least. *The Kinks*, *The Small Faces*, *The Rolling Stones* and of course *The Beatles* were all amongst those still recognised as deserving of acknowledgement and respect, but in place of those considered less worthy, Lol, or Utting as he still was then, had been introduced to the likes of *Bob Dylan*, *John Mayall*, *Cream* and the fittingly named *Long John Baldry*, whose credibility would perhaps end just as his *'Heartaches'* began.

Back at 'MeMum and MeDad's' there was no record player, not until he was approaching seventeen anyway, and Lol had to be satisfied with a small transistor radio, which frequently grew increasingly unreliable as the night drew on and through which he gained access to such diverse and lonely delights as *'Savile's Travels'* and a rather crackly version of John Peel's altogether more worthwhile *'Night Ride'*.

What Lol had discovered though, with entry into the sixth form, was the availability of live music and, having convinced 'MeMum', who had in turn, eventually persuaded 'MeDad' that their son was now old enough to be permitted to venture into the comparative metropolis of Manchester, Lol, along with a group of four of his sixth form friends, made their first trip to the University Students' Union in Oxford Road.

They'd had to stand around patiently, waiting for benevolent students to 'sign in' each of them individually in order to see *'Deep Purple'* but what followed was to become a seminal moment in Lol's life and one which he had been utterly unprepared for.

He knew all about record players with the volume knob turned to a distorted maximum volume but Roger Glover's bass, which seemed to actually hit Lol somewhere in the chest, Ritchie Blackmore's guitar and the raw power of Ian

Gillan's vocals, along with a combination of the tightly packed hall, and his first experience of both stroboscopic lighting and the sweet scent of second hand cannabis smoke, left Lol reeling. By the time the band returned for an encore and the long awaited rendition of *'Black Night'*, Lol had to stagger out onto the steps of the Union Building in search of fresh air.

Sitting on the typically drizzle dampened steps outside it was all Lol could do to avoid throwing up, but equally he was completely hooked and that Deep Purple concert was to be the first of many trips back to the University, the Polytechnic, nearby Salford University, Belle Vue and of course the City's top venue, The Free Trade Hall.

It is probably no exaggeration to suggest that if there was one single moment when the scales were lifted from Lol's eyes, allowing him to recognise the desirability of entering into 'Higher Education', it was that night.

Lol had never seen such excitement, such rampant hedonism. Equally he was sufficiently self aware to recognise that acceptance into University was looking unlikely. The not so proud owner of just four - although soon to be five - 'O' levels and a far from outstanding 'A' level candidate he, not entirely unrealistically, didn't regard himself as University material.

Help however was to arrive from two unlikely sources.... 'MeDad' and the local library!

'MeDad' was something of an aficionado of the library service, from where he obtained his endless supply of thrillers and historical novels as well as, somewhat more confusingly, framed pictures from artists as diverse as Constable and Jackson Pollock which he borrowed to hang on the chimney breast for a period of three or four months at a time.

He'd set great store by introducing young Lawrence to the pleasures of the written word from as early an age as possible, but Lol no longer found the place sufficiently 'trendy' and certainly, at a time when he was approaching seventeen, not in the company of 'MeDad'.

Never one to give up, 'MeDad' arrived home from one of his now solitary Saturday morning literary reconnaissance missions with a copy of a book which he hoped might be of interest to his son.

It was the fact that the book appeared to tell the story of a kestrel that had initially attracted 'MeDad' into thinking that it might appeal to Lol, who remained something of a closet ornithologist. That book however 'A Kestrel For A Knave', was to have much more significant implications for Lol's future than even 'MeDad' could have ever realised.

For those who aren't familiar with it, 'A Kestrel for a Knave' probably provides one of the bleakest yet finest accounts of adolescent angst to ever emerge from the great tradition of English literature. Written by Barry Hines in the late sixties it centres upon the downtrodden character of teenager Billy Casper who, as the book describes, is *'part of the limbo generation of school leavers, too old for lessons and too young to know anything about the outside world'*.

It wasn't that Lol identified with the novel's main protagonist. His own life had been far too comfortable for that and, quite unlike Billy, he'd been blessed with perhaps the greatest 'advantage' of all, wholly adequate, loving and caring parents.

It was the world that Casper inhabited, particularly within the confines of his dreadful secondary school, which resonated with Lol.

Mr. Gryce, the bitter and loathsome Headmaster, is portrayed as appearing to despise his pupils. He is a character completely devoid of any understanding of anything approaching a more 'modern world' and as such, in Lol's opinion, provided the perfect 'blueprint' for his own experiences with 'Bendover' Bennett.

Likewise, Lol had come across plenty of other bullies amongst the teachers at the Grammar School. Many whose ridicule and acerbic words would wound far more deeply than the all too frequently heavy handed clips around the ear, and although he had never actually been on the wrong side of any games teachers, Hines' portrayal of Mr. Sugden, the boorish and brutal games master, again provided Lol with a stereotype he could easily identify with.

Above all though, was the character of Mr. Farthing, one of the new brand of younger and more compassionate teachers. A character who, although always firm and authoritative, was respected by his pupils not least because, unlike all the other staff, he displays both an actual interest in and compassion towards them. If 'Bendover' could be based on Gryce then Mr. Farthing and Jeff Stone equally had much in common and when Lol was provided with the opportunity to see the subsequent film of the book, simply called 'Kes', the die was surely cast as far as a Lol's future career was concerned.

It is perhaps ironic that a book so concerned with Billy Casper's hopeless lack of direction should in turn play such a momentous part in providing Lol with precisely the ambition he had previously lacked. Realisation had dawned, Lol wanted to be a teacher, and not just any old teacher, he wanted to be Mr. Farthing, albeit a slightly cooler, more 'rock'n'roll', version than that brought to life by the excellent Colin Welland in 'Kes'.

Further investigation revealed, surprisingly to Lol given the apparent arrogance of some within the teaching profession, that with as few as five 'O' levels and two 'A' levels he had every chance of being accepted into a 'College of Education' (Teacher Training College), and so it was that, driven by the collective aims of emulating Mr. Farthing and Jeff Stone, attending as much live music as possible and spending at least three years enjoying the hedonistic excess involved in being a full time student, that Lol began his unlikely journey towards becoming a teacher and, in case you were wondering, he did repay Jeff Stone's loyalty and pass his History 'A' Level. The 'Physical Geography' 'A' level paper however proved totally beyond him, although 'Bendover' hadn't helped by ordering Lol to return home and shave off his emerging embryonic beard before he was to be allowed to sit the exam!

LESSONS 3

Between the ages of fourteen and eighteen Lol was to learn many lessons, the main ones being;

1. It is quite true that there are few things more painful than sexual rejection but fourteen year old boys are in no position to compete with more mature owners of facial hair and leather jackets.
2. Grammar Schools of the sixties were far more concerned with 'box ticking' subjects of appropriate 'status' than education of the whole individual. Now you know where Michael Gove and Gavin Williamson got it from.
3. The teaching profession was thoroughly confusing in that it appeared to include a mixture of some of the most objectionable adults and yet some of the finest role models Lol would ever encounter.

4. Adult approval and acceptance from those who have won respect as 'significant others' was even more important than he had already been taught to realise.

5. Racists are stupid and repugnant human beings who, like bullies, invariably carry a huge chip on their shoulders.

6. Adult individuals who cannot identify with the developing needs of young people have no place in schools.

7. Making people laugh is a whole lot better than being laughed at.

8. When confronted by a hard man and the prospect of pain the benefit of protection from someone even 'harder' can be particularly welcome.

9. Libraries are good things as books can provide the answer to many of life's mysteries.

10. Loyalty begets loyalty.

11. Few things were more exciting than gaining successful access to the world of young adulthood.

12. Becoming a full time student looked likely to be a lot of fun.

FOUR

COLLEGE DAZE

AWAKENING

Track 14. 'Heart of Gold'. Neil Young.

Having scraped together sufficient qualifications to make application for a place at a 'College of Education', as they had recently become known, a reasonably realistic proposition, Lol set to work.

Being sufficiently bright to recognise that *first impressions* do actually matter', Lol went about the application form with care and although his three 'D' grade 'A' levels (including General Studies) meant that he had to go through the *'Clearing House'* procedure he was soon rewarded by being invited for interview at two Midland colleges, one which came under the auspices of Warwick, and the other, Nottingham University.

Knowing only that he wanted to go to College amongst the bright lights of a City and that the latter of the two options was, at the time, home to the current League Champions, Lol opted for the slightly more northern of the two sites.

Borrowing the family's green Renault 6 and having now adopted something of the look of Jesus, albeit, at his mother's insistence, the son of God dressed in a decidedly dodgy C&A suit, Lol drove across the Derbyshire Peak District and on into the unfamiliar East Midlands conurbation, finally arriving at his destination with only minutes to spare.

Entering the College's 'Great Hall' Lol was somewhat concerned to find himself in the company of at least thirty other 'candidates' who, almost by definition, shared with him the same label of 'A' level 'also rans'. Even more alarming was the fact that the Hall appeared to be laid out in a way that was all too reminiscent of an 'A' level examination room.

Sure enough, having been welcomed by the Dean, it was explained that there would now follow two forty minute tests of literacy and numeracy, satisfactory completion of which was essential, followed by lunch and afternoon interviews.

Neither of the two tests would actually have proved particularly troubling for the average eleven year old however, although Lol found the literacy test almost embarrassingly easy, the huge gaps in his mathematical knowledge, did leave him feeling that the outcome of the numeracy 'exam' was hanging a little more in the balance.

After lunch, half a dozen or so of the no longer expectant candidates, presumably those who could neither count nor spell, having now disappeared, Lol had to wait around for about an hour before his interview with the Dean, a friendly giant of a man with uncommonly big hands and facial features to match. Having read quickly through Lol's application, the Dean conversed enthusiastically with Lol about rugby but appeared to have little knowledge or interest in his previously prepared spiel about the works of Graham Greene and Mrs. Gaskell, or the role of Charles Dickens as a form of social commentator. As for the question of teaching...it basically never arose.

Within a week Lol received an A4 envelope marked by the giveaway postmark. He'd earned himself a place at College, and virtually eight years to the day after beginning at the 'Boarding House', Lol was to embark upon this altogether less daunting journey to becoming a teacher.

Finding his way around Manchester's ever increasing variety of music venues was something Lol had long since become perfectly comfortable with. Allowed at last to grow his hair and beard he had easily assumed the look and persona of a typical early seventies student and in the days preceding his departure for College Lol had been to see both David Bowie, at Manchester's new *'Hardrock'* venue in Stretford, and Lou Reed, at the City's Polytechnic.

With this in mind he was subsequently a little disappointed, on his first night at College, to find some some particularly fresh faced looking first years dancing around, in the disco above the Students Union bar, to what, in Lol's opinion, was the frankly appalling and infantile sound of *Lieutenant Pigeon's 'Mouldy Old Dough'*.

He'd also been placed, seemingly at the last minute, in a large, College approved, semi detached Victorian Villa with five other male first years who each had the dubious delight of sharing one of the house's three bedrooms and its only bathroom.

Lol had no problem with any of his house mates, but equally he appeared to have little in common with them either. One late developing twenty something year old RE student apart...the others included two PE students, an Art student who supported Scunthorpe United and had the smelliest feet imaginable, and Lol's roommate, Sean, who was coincidentally following the same course...appeared not only very young but completely removed from any image Lol had previously entertained of what being a student was all about.

Arriving at College a little apprehensive about being able to cope, Lol suddenly found himself to be positively 'wordly' in comparison. None of his housemates, not even Robert, the twenty something year old, had lived away from home before, something that, after his four years at Boarding School, Lol now took easily in his stride. Few of them had encountered beer before, again something that Lol had been well acquainted with since long before his seventeenth birthday and as for any political or musical awareness...let's just say, there seemed little likelihood of any great scope for conversation in either of those two areas.

Despite the apparent belief amongst many of his contemporaries, that attendance at lectures was essential and scribbling down every word that the lecturers uttered equally so, it hadn't taken Lawrie long to realise that this wasn't actually the case.

Before long he had worked out that, as long as any course work was completed satisfactorily he could get away with just attending lectures that were *a)* of interest to him or *b)* run by those few lecturers who clung on to the antiquated practice of actually bothering to record attendance.

Even then, attendance in the second category was far from complete in Lawrie's case, but even he could not over-look the fact that there was one aspect of his College course that required his most serious and full attention.

Lawrie's course was structured in such a way that most students began on a three year course, successful completion of which would lead to a Teaching Certificate qualification. At the end of those three years, there was the option, for those who had achieved a sufficiently high standard, to do a final fourth Degree year which had the dual benefit of ultimately leading to better pay and, far more importantly in Lawrie's admittedly shorter term view, of postponing entry into the real world of full time employment and extending access to the relative 'fun palace' of College life.

Above all else though, an extended period of Teaching Practice had to be satisfactorily completed each year. What few exams there were could be retaken. A poor essay or assignment mark could be more than made up for with greater effort in the next, but Teaching Practice was the one thing no one could ever afford to 'flunk'.

FIRST YEAR TEACHING PRACTICE

First year Teaching Practice took a different and altogether less demanding form to that of the second and third years in as much as it was what was called a 'Group Practice' and only took place on two days a week over a period of five weeks.

Lawrie found himself placed in one of the City's biggest Primary Schools along with five other students all of whom he knew to varying degrees and including one of the PE students he shared a house with.

Like so many students, Lawrie and the others had existed largely in the artificial 'bubble' of College life. They'd venture out to local corner shops, to the cinema or the football ground perhaps, but Colleges and Universities alike tended, at the time at least and certainly as far as 'entertainment' was concerned, to be largely self sufficient, vaguely elitist even, organisations. The 'town and gown' partition may not have been quite as striking as that in Oxford but the 'real life' more hard edged parts of the City represented somewhere that most students remained blissfully ignorant of.

The Headmaster of Lawrie's host school apparently

wished to have as little as possible to do with any of his school's necessary but inconvenient student guests. The younger and infinitely more approachable Deputy Head however appeared to take a far greater interest and went out of his way to provide background information on the school and its catchment area in an attempt to entice his protégés from their 'ivory towered' existence.

The term 'ivory towered' is perhaps an exaggeration. Certainly Lawrie had never thought of himself as living a particularly 'privileged' existence and had no reason to suspect the same of any of his associates. Indeed the description has, perhaps, to be regarded as relative. In this particular part of the City however the little recurring terraced streets of red brick houses, built like some sort of subservient dependents around a huge, equally red brick, and regularly extended factory, bore more resemblance to Dickens' *'Coketown'* than anything Lawrie had previously experienced.

Unlike his own home environment where the abandoned cotton mills retained a certain grimy grandeur that dwarfed all around, here everything, with the exception of the protruding smoking and regularly hissing chimneys, was comparatively low rise and spread out, but there could still be little doubting the extent to which factory and housing had assumed a master-servant relationship.

The Deputy Head, Mr. Tressell, confirmed as much, going on to suggest that the school's environment had always been a hard one but that, with unemployment currently running at its highest level since the 1930's, the social problems that came 'with the territory' had recently been exacerbated. None of Mr. Tressell's thoughtful words though would illustrate the impact that both material poverty and it's not uncommon bedfellow, an absence of compassion, could have on the child more than two particular stories relating to children from the school.

The first concerns a ten year old pupil, Joanne, who

arrived at the school one morning, her hands quite literally dripping with blood. Up, as ever, before her demoralised and inadequate parents she had made herself and her younger brother a drink before looking for something that would suffice for breakfast.

All that a search of the bare kitchen cupboards revealed as being even remotely appropriate, was a long forgotten tin of sardines with one of the old fashioned key type openers. Tin openers in general of the sixties and seventies had a tendency towards being absurdly dangerous, but this type in particular, especially the hands of a young child, was nothing less than a recipe for serious injury.

Having used the ineffective opener to curl back the now razor sharp exposed edges of the lid as far as her limited strength and dexterity would allow, Joanne had set about trying to prise back the remainder of the lid with her fingers. Of course the results were predictably, to all but a hungry and determined ten year old, disastrous and Joanne arrived at school, her parents still blissfully asleep and hopelessly unaware, with blood pumping from three fingers of her right hand and the thumb of her left. As one of the teachers cleaned, treated and dressed the child's wounds, it became clear that at least two, and quite probably three of the fingers were almost certainly in need of stitches. Lawrie was amazed to note that the child remained cheerful and tearless throughout and astonished to find that a social worker, not the child's parents, provided the school's first port of call as far as a trip to A&E was concerned.

If that first example was the result of an act of determined kindness and an untimely attempt to accept responsibility on the part of one so young, the second involves a level of malice which Lawrie found hard to believe could be present in a Primary School in 1973.

In the days before such sophisticated devices as soap dispensers, let alone hand dryers, a largely to be avoided trip to any school toilet would involve acquaintance with either paper towels or the chronically unhygienic 'roll towel' along with single basic bars of soap that became ever smaller, filthier and more engrained with hair and germs the more they were used.

Into the centre of one of these bars of soap some, never to be identified and horribly mean spirited pupil had carefully inserted a needle, with the obvious and unavoidable consequence that eventually, someone washing their hands, in this case an innocent and totally unsuspecting nine year old, would as the soap neared the end of its 'life', effectively 'spear' the palm of their hand with the very sharp end of the doubtless germ ridden needle.

No stranger to bullying himself, Lawrie was amazed at the callousness and cruelty that had been involved in such a thought process and was no less puzzled at the randomness of the attack. There could have been no question of revenge as there was no way of anticipating the ultimate identity of the victim. It was nothing more than a simple act of malice, a hideous piece of malevolence, possibly one learned from an older, more cynical sibling, and certainly one that Lawrie found shockingly out of place amongst the otherwise overwhelmingly likeable children who were all, let us not forget, still only of 'primary' age.

These two eye opening incidents apart, Lawrie had actually enjoyed his first taste of teaching practice. Admittedly his experience hadn't yet included taking a full class, not even once let alone several times a day, like a real teacher. He had however taken a whole school assembly, creating a more topical version of the parable of the Good Samaritan by relocating the story to the Falls and Shankhill Roads area of Belfast. Of course the presence of every other teacher in the hall, while doing nothing for Lawrie's 'nerves', had done away with any real need for discipline on his part but his 'debut performance' had been well and enthusiastically received.

He had also produced a number of teaching resources aimed at providing pupils with improved coin recognition and money handling skills. Again the materials he had produced had been applauded and Lawrie had thoroughly enjoyed testing them out, albeit on a group of just half a dozen of the less able pupils.

Most of all though, Lawrie had simply enjoyed listening and talking to the children, whether it had been in the classroom, the school's endlessly long corridors or the play ground. They appeared to respond well to the young long haired 'Sir' who had only been out of school himself for a matter of months. They all had stories to tell, some if only by implication, and while Lawrie had been surprised at some of their matter of fact accounts of hardship, poverty and, in some cases, sheer neglect, this experience also represented a time when the first seeds were sown with regard to both Lawrie's future teaching career and his own first hand awareness of a *Billy Casper's* world of the *'haves and the have nots'*.

With his first experience of teaching practice satisfactorily completed Lawrie saw out the rest of the year well enough. The academic demands were, in Lawrie's opinion some way below 'A' level standard and he had little problem in managing to maintain a sufficiently high, if far from outstanding, standard in his course work while still picking and choosing which lectures to attend.

The pleasures of the Union Bar, representing the College at both football and rugby, albeit on very much a 'jack of all trades, master of none' basis and some memorable gigs, most notably those delivered by *King Crimson, Hawkwind* and the *Bonzo Dog Doo-Dah Band*, had dominated Lawrie's first year at College, as too had a first real 'adult' relationship with a girl called Bev, although as the year moved towards a close so too that relationship also drew towards its own inevitable and perfectly amicable conclusion.

SECOND YEAR

Just a few weeks before the conclusion of his first year, Lawrie had been approached by a girl from his course to see whether he fancied the idea of a flat share the following year.

Lawrie had never found the living arrangements particularly to his liking during that first year. It had served a purpose, but there were obvious drawbacks to sharing a room, not least in terms of his relationship with Bev.

The College accommodation contract also meant that the cost of three meals per day five days per week, regardless of whether or not they were eaten, which breakfast seldom was, along with accommodation and cleaning costs were deducted at source from his grant. So when the prospect of being both better off financially and swapping the practice of sharing a flat with five young men for this pre-Raphaelite like beauty arose, Lawrie was confronted with one of the easier decisions of his nineteen year old life.

Ali was almost three years older than Lawrie, infinitely more worldly, and with a head of dark curls and a partiality for dressing in what would, some years later, become identified as 'hippy chic', a combination of long Afghan coat, short skirt and knee length platform boots, Lawrie was hopelessly lost in what might euphemistically be described as 'admiration'.

Unfortunately for Lawrie, Ali was also a child of her time. She was no stranger to the 'free love' philosophy of the sixties and early seventies and came down very firmly on the side of sexual freedom as opposed to any concept of 'monogamy' which, despite the image and all pretence to the contrary, was exactly what Lawrie craved, at least as far as Ali was concerned.

Ali was to become a source of pleasure and pain in roughly equal measure. Being three years older and possessing a great deal more in terms of sophistication than her young 'flat mate', Lawrie's relationship with Ali was far from straightforward.

Having become familiar with the practice of self sufficient living even before her arrival in the Midlands, Ali was able to introduce Lawrie to a new way of life that covered everything from the most mundane to the positively esoteric. From not always entirely legal methods of making the most of trips to the discount supermarket, to the hitherto little known mysteries of eroticism and an introduction to soft drugs, Lawrie's life was definitely about to change.

Track 15. Angie. The Rolling Stones.

At much the same time as he had moved into his new flat Lawrie had also taken the decision to move the direction of his career away from Primary to Secondary Education.

There was to be no further period of actual teaching practice until the Spring Term of his second year however students were expected to make school visits in preparation during the autumn of Lawrie's second year.

Lawrie had enjoyed these occasions well enough although his increasingly hippyish appearance and the vague accompanying scent of cannabis smoke, barely masked by that of patchouli, hadn't gone unremarked upon.

His work too seemed to be in decline. In his first year Lawrie had found it easy to simply stay up late, in the company of copious amounts of tobacco and caffeine, and reel off a three thousand word essay the night before it was due in. Rarely had his grade fallen below a 'B', the average needed to gain entry to a fourth 'degree' year, but suddenly, like a cricketer whose runs have dried up, the 'B's' were no longer forthcoming.

Whether this was down to Ali's distractions, the increasing influence of cannabis, the academic expectations of a certain Mrs. Margaret Mantell, or even a combination of all three was debatable.

When deciding to change direction from a Primary to a Secondary course, Lawrie knew that he would also be leaving behind the kind, supportive and encouraging tuition of the affable Alan Davidson. What he hadn't fully recognised was that tutors could be tough task masters and that in Margaret Mantell he'd come across one of the most ruthless and least sympathetic.

One of the 'old school' lecturers and author of such riveting titles as *'The History of Primary Education in Leicestershire'* there was little about Lawrie that Margaret Mantell liked. She suspected him, rather exaggeratedly in actual fact, to be guilty of all sorts of depravity and, having in her head a sort of short back and sided, gown wearing, leather elbow patched image of a teacher she had confronted Lawrie with her damning appraisal of...'and what's more...you don't even look like a teacher!'

Stopping mercifully short of asking, '...And what the hell does a teacher look like then?' Lawrie did point out, only marginally more politely, that elbow patches, short hair, brogues, a mortar board and gown and a pipe were not actually the pre-requisites of what made a good teacher and that actually being able to *communicate* with young people might be marginally more important.

The lady however was, as a similarly intransigent female once said, *'not for turning'*. The damage was done and when Lawrie's next essay, one that he'd spent *'half the fucking night'* on, was returned marked as a 'D-' he did the only honourable, or at least sensible, thing and promptly sought out the genial Mr. Davidson to suggest that, after giving the matter *'much thought'*, he felt that he was *'perhaps better suited'* to the demands of Primary Education after all.

Over such inconsequential events are major decisions sometimes arrived at. If Lawrie was to make it to a fourth degree year it would be without any assistance from Mrs. Mantell, who appeared to have adopted an attitude of *'over my dead body'* towards the concept of Lawrie and any future career in teaching. Fortunately the significantly more benevolent 'Mr. D' was happy to welcome Lawrie back into the fold and his last essay before the Christmas holiday, which admittedly had witnessed a whole night of greater effort, saw a welcome return to a 'B' grade.

SECOND YEAR TEACHING PRACTICE; 'MALTLOW'

Track 16. 'Brass Buttons' Gram Parsons.

The whole process of assigning students to schools for the important periods of teaching practice was regarded as something of a lottery.

Having completed his first, relatively unchallenging 'group' practice in what was considered a tough 'inner city' type school, Lawrie now found himself 'rewarded' with placement in the canal side village of Maltlow about eight miles outside the City.

'You lucky sod', appeared to be the general consensus, not least from those who now had their first taste of going 'solo' amongst the comparative 'rough house' of perceived inner city deprivation and delinquency.

Lawrie however wasn't so sure. He'd enjoyed his contact with the kids on that much shorter and less demanding first practice. More to the point, it had been easy to get from the old shared student house to his placement in the industrial heart of the city. Given the new distractions in his life an eight mile journey each morning, for six whole weeks, really didn't seem that appealing.

'It'll be alright...you can take Bertha,' reassured Ali, inhaling deeply on an early evening 'joint' and making reference to her grey-green battered twelve year old Morris Minor, which spent most of each term abandoned in a nearby side street, while also simultaneously overlooking the fact that both vehicle and potential driver were completely lacking in the requirements of either road tax or insurance.

So it was, at a little after 8.00 o'clock on a dank and drizzly late January morning, that Lawrie found himself driving the unfamiliar, untaxed, uninsured and, almost certainly, un-roadworthy vehicle out of the city towards his preliminary visit at some unknown rural destination.

Of course, living in his student bubble, Lawrie had taken no account of 'rush hour' and the fact that the first three miles of his journey involved crossing the entire city. He was however distinctly aware that being late on his first morning was not the best of ideas and it was with this in mind that his ill advised and probably illegal lane change resulted in the distinctive thud of a motor cycle in collision with his passenger door.

'Fuck!' voiced Lawrie to himself, as all the possible implications began to miserably materialize in his head and he reached across to slowly unwind *Bertha's* misted up passenger side window and investigate the full extent of what damage had been done.

Being charged with driving without tax, insurance or, for that matter, *'due care and attention'* could so easily have been one of those occasions that signalled an early end to Lawrie's embryonic teaching career, but this was also one of those times when fortune was about to smile.

Accompanied by a background soundtrack of blaring horns and drivers now attempting evasive manoeuvres equally as outrageous as Lawrie's, the helmeted and entirely waterproof clad motorcyclist clambered back to his feet, raised two fingers of a leather gauntleted fist in an angry and entirely justified gesture, clambered back on board his bike and simply went on his way.

Quite why the motorcyclist had sought neither recompense nor retribution Lawrie didn't know. Nor, in all honesty, did he care, but as he left the outskirts of the city the largely motorway bound traffic began to gradually thin and, despite the events of the journey, he made it to the school with minutes to spare.

The headmistress, a lady of late middle years called Miss. Griffith, was welcoming from the start, providing Lawrie with a warming cup of tea, before guiding him in the direction of her tiny office, which she appeared, somewhat bizarrely in Lawrie's opinion, to share with her equally diminutive Chihuahua dog.

Miss. Griffith explained how she had returned to teaching in England via a spell in an armed forces school in Germany and, although Lawrie's idealistic anti-military leanings didn't exactly welcome such connections, he had to admit that the grey haired and tweed suited headmistress seemed very pleasant and appeared to be a huge improvement on the 'formidable' Mrs. Mantell. She also seemed to have taken something of a surprising shine to her young student and listened approvingly as Lawrie described, with genuine enthusiasm, some of the tales from his previous teaching practice and how he now genuinely believed that he wanted to work with more 'deprived' children.

Miss. Griffith's ears also appeared to prick up when Lawrie mentioned his interest in sport and willingness to take games lessons and even if this was actually, as he later suspected, only because Lawrie was the only male in the school and thus someone who could relieve the headmistress of her Wednesday afternoon trials with whistle, wellies and a muddy school field, it was certainly something else in his favour.

The best was yet to come however. Listening attentively to the details of Lawrie's 'rush hour' journey and showing appropriate levels of shock and sympathy at his slightly exaggerated and particularly graphic description of the unfortunate morning collision, Miss Griffith had an idea.

'How would it be if I were to suggest that you started at 10.00?' asked Miss. Griffith.

'Well...,' began a discreetly delighted but somewhat surprised Lawrie,'...it would certainly suit me, but I suppose I'll have to have a word with my tutor'.

'No need for that,' said Miss Griffith, waving her hand dismissively, 'My school, not theirs! You've got a long journey each morning and we want you at your best...if I say you can start at 10.00 o'clock each morning then that is what you'll do...suits us anyway,' she concluded with a twinkle in her eye.

It quickly emerged that, Miss Griffith and the part time secretary apart, there were only two other members of staff, one of whom was part time, and indeed only two classrooms in the school. One of these classrooms was assigned to the youngest pupils, the infants, while the other, where Lawrie would be based, was home to around twenty five eight to eleven year old 'Juniors'.

Miss Griffith herself had to teach for around forty per cent of the time and by doing Lawrie the enormous 'favour' of not requiring him to do any teaching before 10.00 o'clock each morning she had shrewdly managed to relinquish a large part of her own teaching duties while at the same time solving an emerging personal crisis for her part time Junior teacher. For the next six weeks, it seemed, everyone would be happy, not least the much relieved Lawrie who wholeheartedly approved of this first lesson in personnel and time management.

'You lucky, lucky boy!', announced Ali, after Lawrie had

confessed about the extra dent in Bertha's passenger door. 'You know...only you could do that...start off with the journey to hell...fall in the shit...and still come up smelling of roses!'

Mr. Kitchen, Lawrie's teaching practice supervisor, hadn't seemed too put out either when Lawrie had informed him of Miss. Griffith's 'insistence' that he shouldn't start teaching before 10.00 o'clock.

'Oh well, her school I suppose', was his only comment...accompanied by just the faintest of wry smiles.

In the two week hiatus between his initial visit and the start of his teaching practice Lawrie began, in between a variety of other distractions, to prepare for the six week stretch that lay ahead. In addition to delivering the standard curriculum of Reading, Writing and Arithmetic as well as Boys Games, students also had to deliver a 'topic based activity', something that would now be described as cross-curricular and that was to run through the whole of the practice.

Local knowledge, that is to say the advice of the better informed third years at the College, left Lawrie with little option as far as his choice of topic was to be concerned.

'You've got Kitchen at Maltlow? Only one way to go'... appeared to be the common consensus, and based on the entirely fresh information that Maltlow's very existence had depended on the importance of nineteenth century waterways, together with the fact that Mr. Kitchen was famed for his almost obsessive interest in canals and narrow boats, Lawrie's choice of topic was made.

As far as successful completion of any teaching practice was concerned, only full and uninterrupted attendance and the ability not to 'lose' any children were of more importance than a properly maintained 'Teaching Practice' file.

Each lesson, which at a rate of between four and five per day over a six week period, amounted to over one hundred and twenty over the whole practice, had to show appropriate and detailed evidence of planning and self assessment. Details of each and every lesson's *Aim, Introduction, Time available, Method, Development* and *Materials Required* had to be written up, as well as a *'Comments'* section, of around at least one hundred and fifty words, describing how well, or otherwise, each session had gone. All had to be properly recorded in the *'TP File'* the loss of which, or its absence when a 'supervisor' called, would, in all probability, be terminal.

Given the benefit of hindsight, if he was being totally honest, only Ofsted inspections would ever go on to generate as great a need for detailed preparation as Teaching Practice, at least as far as Lawrie was concerned. That though would come later, much later, and in the meantime Lawrie set off in the increasingly battered Bertha through the now free flowing and traffic free streets, armed with his all important file and a newly acquired familiarity with the history of narrow boats and the British inland waterway network.

After the social depravation in evidence during his first practice, together with the relative anonymity of the enormous, by primary school standards, corridors and the relative abundance of classrooms, Lawrie's experience at Maltlow represented a diametric opposite.

There were no needles wickedly hidden in bars of soap here. The children didn't have to get themselves to school or slash their fingers in a vain attempt to find some breakfast. The vast majority were either walked to school or delivered and collected in one of the family cars.

Differentiation remained an essentially futuristic notion that had yet to be invented, or at least implemented, so for the main part the children worked together in age groups as far as the basic curriculum was concerned and came together as a whole class for topic work and boys games only.

All well motivated, probably more by 1970's middle class aspiration than anything Lawrie had to offer, there were few problems, the pupils were largely well behaved and appeared happy enough with what Lawrie provided in the classroom. The most difficult aspect of games was crossing fifteen boys across the busy main road to a supportive farmer's field, but Miss. Griffith was sufficiently wise and worldly to ensure that she was always 'conveniently' available at the beginning and end of each 'games' session.

During one slightly boisterous maths lesson, in the unfortunate presence of Mr. Kitchen, Lawrie's TP Supervisor had been moved to observe, in red ink at the bottom of his lesson notes, *'Children should be treated like little puppies. They must understand who is in charge and show appropriate obedience.'*

'Well, thanks for that professional insight,' thought Lawrie, though they were words that would have a peculiar and entirely unforeseen resonance during Mr. Kitchen's next visit.

Unlocking the classroom to allow the children in for the lesson immediately after lunch, Lawrie was startled as a small missile shot straight between his legs and out through the newly opened door. His slow motion like recognition of Miss. Griffith's apparently distressed Chihuahua dawned only moments before his other senses were alerted to a vile smell emanating from within the classroom.

Unfortunately a number of children had entered the room with rather more speed and enthusiasm than Lawrie and although the now overwhelmingly stomach churning smell had made those towards the rear more reticent, the front runners had, with quite bewildering efficiency, managed to cover a collection of white knee socks and jeans in an all too generous coating of anxiety stricken Chihuahua excrement.

As if all this wasn't enough of a challenge, a glance through the window allowed Lawrie just enough time to register the never particularly welcome site of Mr. Kitchen struggling to park his shiny brand new sky blue Vauxhall Viva outside.

'Shit'...thought Lawrie, very appositely, if perhaps a little more vocally than he intended.

'Mr. Utting!'...he heard the concerned and slightly raised voice of Miss Griffith say through the chaos and fog of sensory confusion. 'What ever is going on here?', followed moments later by, as the headmistress' olfactory system eventually caught up with her altogether better trained senses of hearing and vision...'and whatever is that ghastly smell?'

'It's Maxi, Miss'...came an excited, near hysterical, girl's voice amongst the bedlam of shrieking and retching. 'He's been locked in the classroom all over dinner Miss,' continued the child.

'Aye...and now e's crapped his dinner all o'er the classroom, Miss', added one of the more outspoken and agricultural older boys, delighting in this unexpected opportunity to provide such an uninhibited and illustrative account in front of his head teacher.

'Come at a bad time have I?' came the temporarily forgotten Mr. Kitchen's voice moments before he too was hit by the pungency of the situation.

'Ah, Mr. Kitchen...little bit of a crisis I'm afraid,' replied Miss Griffith.

'Nothing to do with Mr. Utting...not his fault at all...erm, maybe it would be best if you were to call back later...on another day even...perhaps'...continued the headmistress, now equally as anxious as Lawrie to see the back of the lecturer.

'Circumstances beyond our control and all that...'

In truth, it didn't take much effort to convince Mr. Kitchen to leave. A combination of the, by now abominable, smell and the sight of apparently excrement stained children failing to hold any attraction whatsoever in comparison with a previously unlikely afternoon of relaxed narrow boat spotting.

Mr. Kitchen departed as discreetly, and a great deal more appreciatively, than he had actually arrived. Much to Lawrie's relief, Miss. Griffith took immediate and complete control of the situation, splitting the children into two groups, the clean and the unclean, sending out an urgent request for the school cleaner, who only lived a couple of minutes away, and instructing Lawrie to take the unaffected pupils on an impromptu 'nature walk' over footpaths at the back of the school while she dealt with the unfortunate results of her panic stricken, and apparently claustrophobic, Chihuahua.

Nothing was ever recorded by Mr. Kitchen about that afternoon at Maltlow Primary, but it is doubtful he ever offered his allegorical 'little puppies' advice again.

As for the remainder of the placement, Lawrie completed it well enough. Mr. Kitchen was delighted by some of the art and history work that had been produced on the subject of narrow boats and the history of canals. Although he wasn't quite so impressed, when a class trip that Lawrie had ambitiously arranged to the Stoke Bruerne Canal Museum, coincided with one of the coldest March days for years. Not only were all the canal locks frozen solid and totally inoperable, but the TP Supervisor, who had been looking forward to a free coach trip to one of his favourite destinations, took a tumble on the ice, much to the amusement of the children, bruising both his dignity and his rather ample backside in the process.

At the end of his final day, Miss. Griffith surprised Lawrie by shaking him warmly by the hand and telling him that he was exactly the sort of person that the teaching profession needed and that if he ever needed a reference, or a job, she would do all she could to 'oblige'.

Mr. Kitchen, it has to be said, wasn't quite so enthusiastic. Indeed Lawrie had begun to believe that enthusiasm was a concept that Mr. Kitchen was entirely unfamiliar with, unless in specific relation to narrow boats. He graded Lawrie's efforts and performance well enough however and that was all that mattered. Lawrie was unlikely to encounter his TP supervisor in any professional sense again and had already manipulated his career prospects so that future contact with the dreaded Mrs. Mantell appeared even less likely.

All that remained for the remaining term was for Lawrie to make sure his assignment grades recovered from, what he at least believed to be, Mrs. Mantell's malicious down marking and otherwise to do what students in the seventies seemed to do best...get drunk, get stoned, listen to loud music and enjoy their fair share of casual sex.

THIRD YEAR

By the start of their third year the two floors below the top floor flat that Lawrie shared with Ali had been taken over by a collection of apparently kindred spirits giving the whole block the feeling of a three storey commune.

The infinitely more 'gregarious' Ali was delighted with the new arrangements, although Lawrie had his reservations. Casual sex was all very well but the truth of the matter was that, however strong their friendship Lawrie really longed for greater commitment, something that, sadly for him, simply wasn't on the agenda as far as Ali was concerned.

Flowers, together with some hippy script about 'Peace and Love' and 'On The Eighth Day' were painted on the wall around the side entrance to the second and third floor flats.

The 'residents', no longer all students, were conspicuously unconventional and the selection of sounds, from Pink Floyd and the Stones to the Velvet Underground, Captain Beefheart and the New Riders of the Purple Sage, together with the scent of cannabis and patchouli that emanated both noisily and pungently from the building left little to the imagination as to what was going on inside.

As far as the local police were concerned there may as well have been a neon sign above the door announcing...*Cheech & Chong* live here...and it wasn't long before the inevitable 'bust' took place.

Alerted by the sound of raised voices from two floors below Ali and Lawrie looked down from their top floor window to see two police cars parked on the pavement and a group of burly police officers outside the front door.

'Quick', said Ali, dashing to flush the contents of an ash tray down the toilet. 'Grab that dope and let's get the fuck out of here'.

Lawrie picked up the stock cube sized polythene wrapped lump of resin and secreted it quickly in his underpants, before grabbing his cigarettes and a packet of red Rizla papers, stuffing them in his jeans pocket and making for the door.

'Not that way idiot', said Ali, grabbing his arm. 'We'll run straight into them...have to use the fire escape,' she went on, sliding the kitchen window open as quickly and quietly as possible and climbing out onto the black and largely rust coloured platform which formed the top of their rickety escape route. 'Just follow me...' said Ali, reassuringly and suddenly exhibiting an all too easy familiarity with such methods of escape, '...climb down as quietly as you can', whispered Ali, her eyes shining brightly with a mixture of excitement and fear. 'We'll have to jump the last bit...then run like hell across the back garden, use the tree to get over the wall and we'll bugger off in Bertha until things have calmed down...if they don't actually find us here there's not much they can do'.

Fortunately, Ali and Lawrie only weighed about eighteen stones between them and did not place too great a demand on the decaying and occasionally unreliable fittings of the fire escape. They were both sufficiently athletic to easily manage the final jump with the necessary degree of stealth, before sprinting the thirty yard length of long neglected dried earth that passed for a 'garden', hastily scrambling up the lower branches of a conveniently sited cherry tree and exiting over the six foot high back wall to safety.

By the time Lawrie caught up with her, Ali was already starting up *Bertha*, who thankfully coughed into life at only the third attempt.

'Christ!' exclaimed Ali, driving away down the network of side streets as rapidly as a combination of discretion and *Bertha's* limitations would allow. 'That was way too fucking close for comfort. You do realise that if we get busted...even just for dope, then that's the end of any hope of a teaching career don't you?'

It hadn't, Lawrie had to admit, been the first thing on his mind during their completely unanticipated *Bonny and Clyde* type escape. Now Ali mentioned it though!

'So what do we do now?' asked Lawrie, suddenly feeling a whole lot younger and more vulnerable than the three year age gap would normally suggest.

'Keep our heads down,' announced Ali authoritatively. 'We'll drive out to that big country park where no one knows us for the afternoon, spend the evening in the Union Bar as if nothing has happened and then go back later when everything has settled down...right now though, I think it's time you rolled us a 'J'!'

So, Lawrie and Ali spent a pleasant enough afternoon in the autumn sunshine getting cautiously and soothingly stoned. Any predictable attacks of the 'munchies' had been gently assuaged by two packets of Mackintosh's knowingly named confectionary and a bag of chips which they shared together while giggling inanely, much to the elderly stall holders baffled amusement.

Later on that evening the two of them made their way to the familiar sanctuary of the Student Union Bar. There were one or two curious questions about why the police had been spotted around their flat but the two young 'fugitives' answered with a carefully rehearsed display of blissful ignorance.

'Really? No idea, didn't know they had...we've been out all day'.

Only when they got back to the flat, venturing in by a rather more conventional route than the one they had so hurriedly left by, did the full seriousness of the situation become apparent.

The door to their top floor flat was ajar, the lock keep lying on the scuffed linoleum floor still attached to a piece of green painted splintered wood which, a few hours ago, had been part of the door frame. Both their rooms had been completely ransacked, their mattresses turned upside down, bedding scattered all over the place, drawers pulled out and emptied and the backs of speakers carelessly prised off.

The bathroom had escaped largely unscathed, but all the cupboards and drawers in the kitchen had been emptied, the crockery and cutlery having been scattered wantonly in piles on the floor and partly written essays swept off the table leaving just Lawrie's passport, positioned in the centre of the otherwise now largely bare kitchen table, and lying wide open, accusingly exposing his photograph and personal details.

'Fuckin' hell Ali, they know who I am', exclaimed Lawrie.

'They've got all my fucking details,..they even know where my Mum and Dad live!'

'Calm down', answered Ali. 'They'd know that from a simple follow up visit here. We flushed the roaches and we took the dope. There was nothing else to find'.

'The place was clean', she added, not entirely accurately. 'They've got nothing and they're just trying to frighten you'.

Lawrie was just about to confirm that they'd 'fucking well succeeded then' when both he and Ali froze at the slightly unnecessary sound of a knock on the broken front door.

Before either had time to head in the direction of the kitchen window for a second time a girls voice called out causing them to stop in their tracks.

'Hello...er hi, Ali...Lawrie...are you two in there?'

'Linda?' said the two voices in unison, as they rushed away from a second potential 'escape', back across the debris covered kitchen floor towards the front door, where they found an ashen faced girl, an occasional visitor to the flats below, standing forlornly in the doorway.

'What the hell's been happening Linda?' asked Lawrie. 'Where is everyone?'

'Busted!' replied the girl, a little unnecessarily. 'God, it was horrible man', she continued. 'The *pigs* came in and they were really heavy man.' 'One of them punched Graham...knocked a tooth out...'cos he made a dash for the bog.'

'Then they found Liz's GLF stuff...stickers and that...sent 'em bloody spare it did. Started calling us dirty lesbians...said what she needed was a *real man* instead of some student ponce'.

'What about drugs?' interrupted Ali anxiously, 'Did they find any drugs?'

'Course they bloody did,' answered an increasingly excitable Linda.

'Got all Graham's stash and some acid tabs too...got loads

of stuff off of that Baz in the bottom flat. Told him he'll be going down they got so much...'H', acid, speed and a load of dope too'.

Lawrie had to admit to having mixed feelings about this information. He'd never liked Baz, who had never made any secret of his licentious intentions regarding Ali. At an altogether far too urbane thirty, Lawrie felt him much too old to be living amongst the rest of them but sadly also far too 'handy' for him to do anything about.

'Got nothing up here though', added Linda.

'What...you sure?' asked Lawrie anxiously.

'Sure, I'm sure. Positive', replied Linda. 'Kicked the door in and made a right old mess but they never took owt...just kept going on about dirty hippies and fuckin' junkie students and left.'

'They're you go Lawrie. What did I tell you?' said a suddenly smiling Ali, linking her arm through his. 'We're just going to have to be a whole lot more careful in future.'

The implications of the 'bust' were not inconsiderable for some. Both Lawrie and Ali were called before one of the College's pastoral tutors but, as the police had found no evidence in their flat of anything more incriminating than *'weird posters'* and nothing more sinister than a squalid lack of any housekeeping prowess, there was no case to answer.

Baz was, much to Lawrie's delight, never seen again. Graham and another student, an artist called Kate, were sadly both forced to leave college as any, now unavoidable prosecution for possession, would inevitably lead to dismissal and a ban from working with children.

Despite the police's obvious objections there was nothing illegal about Liz's GLF materials. She and her partner Emma remained at both college and the middle floor flat where they were joined by the lovely but not terribly bright Linda, who led a sort of student-hippy type life style but actually worked in a newsagents during the day and did occasional evening bar work to make ends meet.

Two other student couples moved into the now vacant ground floor flat. All four were like minded as far as the use of 'soft drugs' was concerned but with the music turned lower and the giveaway flowers and slogans painted out from around the door there was a new atmosphere of discretion and a complete absence of any of the harder drugs, both of which would serve them all very well in the future.

Track 17. 'Landslide'. Fleetwood Mac.

As far as Lawrie was concerned he had just two 'academic' aims to meet during this, the third and possibly final year of his course. He needed to pass his third year teaching practice and maintain a sufficiently good average, as far as his assignment grades were concerned, to qualify for a fourth 'Degree' year.

Ali didn't really share Lawrie's enthusiasm for a fourth year. She wanted to get out into the 'real world' and start earning a proper living but before any of that was possible there were some choices to be made.

Part of the third year course involved choosing from an afternoon of 'Options' and both Lawrie and Ali decided to follow, as things would transpire for Lawrie, a 'career defining' option of learning about 'Special Educational' provision.

In the mid seventies there was a great deal less in the way of integration for pupils experiencing what would later be described as learning or behavioural difficulties.

Any notion of the mixed blessing of 'inclusion' was as yet unheard of and children who experienced such difficulties were insensitively referred to as being 'educationally sub normal'.

As a consequence, amongst the relative plethora of often inexpertly staffed schools seeking to provide for pupils labelled as anything from 'delicate' or 'school phobic' through to those who had broken the law and were now considered 'beyond parental control', there were schools for the majority of children with learning difficulties who were, at the time, non too respectfully and somewhat heartlessly defined as either ESN(M) -'moderately sub-normal' - or ESN(S) - 'severely sub-normal'.

The aim of Lawrie and Ali's course was, through the process of visiting a variety of such establishments and attending lectures by visiting Heads, to gain an overview of Special Educational provision within the area and indeed the country as a whole.

Their initial two visits were to establishments at either end of the spectrum. The first was to an old country pile situated in at least ten acres of fields and woodland on the edge of the city known as Sycamore Grange. It's brief was to cater for children of at least 'average' intelligence who happened also to have health or psychological 'issues' which prevented them from achieving their full potential within the normal (the term 'mainstream' had still to be invented) secondary school environment.

In reality, Sycamore Grange catered for children aged eleven to sixteen with a wide variety of ailments, hence the term *'delicate'*, ranging from asthma to epilepsy. The pupils were all taught in small class groups alongside those who, for whatever reason, couldn't deal with the sometimes harsh daily reality encountered in secondary school and fell into the category of having become 'school phobic', or as it would later be termed, 'school refusers'.

Some of the pupils attended on a residential basis from Monday to Friday and all came under the 'care' of the head-master, Dr. Silk and his wife who, despite possessing little in the way of qualifications, performed the doubtless pleasantly remunerative role of 'Matron'.

Lawrie had not encountered anything like it since his own days at the Boarding House. Having been shown around the once spectacular, but now increasingly dilapidated, building he was eventually led into Dr. Silk's office which he found quite breathtaking in terms of its pretentious opulence and extravagance.

The dining hall and gym apart, this was the largest room that Lawrie had been shown in the whole school. A huge and immaculately tidy solid oak antique pedestal desk, topped by a green and gold leather skiver, was found in front of a matching dark oak and green leather upholstered swivel chair. Both were positioned in such a way as to take full advantage of the view, through expensively curtained French Doors, overlooking two tiers of perfectly manicured lawns and the far reaching views beyond.

A chandelier hung from the ceiling and in the centre of the room was a green velvet chaise lounge upon which reclined the figure of Dr. Silk, a report of some description held carelessly in one hand and a glass of what appeared to be sherry, sourced from the nearby and apparently essential drinks cabinet, in the other.

'Ah, Mr. Utting I believe', began the headmaster, adjusting his gold rimmed half moon spectacles. 'Had a good look round have you? We deal with all sorts here as you'll have seen. Some of them are lost causes of course...quite, quite lost...no hope at all once they leave *The Grange* and go back to the outside world...but we do our best.'

Pausing briefly to take another sip of sherry, and appearing quite oblivious to the possibility that Lawrie might have any questions or observations of his own, the headmaster continued, 'Stopping for lunch I hope...just give my secretary your twenty five pence...we all eat at 12.30 on the dot...not a minute later...in the dining hall of course...and then we'll arrange some more observation time this afternoon'.

For once Lawrie didn't know what to say and his suspicion that the man was a complete fantasist was confirmed when, at lunch time the whole school had to rise as one, as Dr and Mrs Silk made their grand daily stage managed entrance, and were only allowed to reseat themselves after the 'good doctor' had gone through the ritual of an unusually protracted delivery of 'grace'.

Frankly Lawrie couldn't wait to leave. The two afternoon lessons had been little better and Lawrie had been shocked at the teacher's insensitive readiness to speak, gossip even, quite openly, in front of both himself and the whole group of ten pupils, about specific pupils' personal, private and individual social, family and health problems.

'A school totally lacking in sensitivity, catering for some of the poorest children in the area and run by a pretentious fantasist who apparently believes himself to be running some sort of minor public school', was Lawrie's forthright and damning indictment of his visit during the following week's feedback. His lecturer chose not to disagree.

Lawrie's next visit, which he made this time in the company of Ali, was to a nearby 'Community Home' with the not entirely inappropriate name of Bloodington Hall. Situated again in something once akin to one of the less grand stately homes, Bloodington catered, if that is the correct term, for an entirely different *clientele* to that found at Sycamore Grange.

The Hall, which stood in rambling grounds surrounded by a high wall or, in places where decline had turned into collapse, a perimeter fence, would have been unashamedly referred to as an 'Approved School' less than a decade earlier.

The staff were much less forthcoming and rather more intimidating than had been the case at Sycamore Grange, indeed one or two seemed as preoccupied as the majority of the 'pupils', *inmates* may have been a more appropriate description, with Ali, who had selected an ill judged length of skirt for visiting quite such a testosterone filled environment.

The pupils, all male and aged between 14-17, had all been found guilty of some offence or other but it was the diversity of offences which Lawrie and Ali found so shocking.

In between enquiries from some of the older boys as to the nature of Lawrie and Ali's relationship...'you shaggin' that Sir'... accounting for the commonest and most bizarrely respectful and synonymously disrespectful line of investigation, came the realisation that these 'children' had found their way to Bloodington via a variety of crimes ranging from shop lifting to murder.

Both Lawrie and Ali were astonished and distressed to find themselves talking to two young fourteen year old boys who were guilty of nothing more than repeated shoplifting, invariably as a direct result of parental inadequacy, poverty and subsequent hunger, but who now found themselves trapped in the same 'institution' as hardened young men who had committed far more heinous crimes including manslaughter, rape, aggravated burglary and even murder.

That the two students were both thankful to 'escape' from the atmosphere of fear and mistrust, which seemed to permeate virtually every corner of Bloodington, would be an understatement. Indeed, Robin Dale, the course tutor, offered only the knowing insightful suggestion of...'Sycamore Grange not as bad as you thought then?', following Lawrie and Ali's moving feedback.

Lawrie's third visit, this time to the 'Dovecote School' which was situated nearer the centre of the city and described at the time as a school for the 'Severely Educationally Sub Normal', was just as distressing but for wholly different reasons.

Here were to be found the pupils that Lawrie simply had no prior knowledge of. The school took children of all ages, from infant to sixteen, who exhibited such a variety of heart-breaking conditions and syndromes that Lawrie felt, both emotionally and practically, totally out of his depth.

There were children whose epilepsy was so severe that they had to spend their whole time in a cot like structure wearing some sort of protective 'crash helmet'. Others suffered enormous cognitive and sensory disorders often accompanied by huge mobility issues, and virtually all demanded and required a level of care, often in order to be able to complete even the most basic of human physical functions, that Lawrie knew he would never be able to provide.

Not for one moment did Lawrie ever doubt the commitment of staff at the 'Dovecote'. For the most part they were nothing less than 'angels' in his opinion, but to work within such an establishment was, so far as Lawrie could see, a 'calling'. More to the point, it was one he knew he would never be capable of.

Following the three visits Lawrie was beginning to doubt the wisdom of his choice of course. He had found it fascinating but equally had been shocked and appalled by various aspects of the three 'schools' he had spent time in.

Lawrie had missed a fourth visit because of '*illness*'. Actually that wasn't entirely true. He'd spectacularly 'overdosed' the night before, on a combination of alcohol and particularly potent Nepalese Temple Ball which had frightened even Ali so much that she'd thrown everyone out of the flat and held him in her bed throughout the night like the 'sister of mercy', lover and golden hearted soul mate she had become. As far as Robin was concerned though, Lawrie had 'a touch of flu'.

While Lawrie lay in bed recuperating from the excesses of the previous evening Ali herself had actually managed the afternoon visit to St. Anthony's Special School for those fitting the description of being merely 'moderately' ESN.

She returned full of enthusiasm for what she had seen going on there and for the headmaster in particular, a big, bearded, bear of a man who apparently led his own folk group and, with guitar in hand, had taken a particularly impressive assembly.

'You'd have loved him,' Ali eulogised, 'Really cool guy and a lovely vibe in the school too'.

'Yeah?' replied Lawrie, feeling regretful that the visit he'd missed appeared to be the one that was most worthwhile.

'Yeah...really', Ali continued, 'Anyway you'll get to meet him soon enough. He's coming in to give a talk next week and you really need to be there.'

Sure enough, just one week later, Lawrie had his first encounter with Bob Armstrong, the Head of St. Anthonys, and Ali had not been exaggerating.

Here for the first time was a Head whose ethos Lawrie felt entirely comfortable with. A surprisingly young and charismatic man, Mr. Armstrong spoke with passion and enthusiasm about his charges.

He talked about the difficult backgrounds and home circumstances that some of the pupils experienced. He spoke of the need for occasional 'tough love' and the difficulty of overcoming the perceived 'stigma', as many parents regarded it, of their child having to attend a 'special school'. Above all though, Bob Armstrong voiced the vital need for teachers to recognise the crucial importance of the 'triangle of support' whereby school and home alike had to act together to provide a firm foundation in order for the child to develop and grow.

Thinking back to the example of poor little Joanna on his first teaching practice, the unfortunate residential pupils at Sycamore Grange, the two shoplifting fourteen year olds now 'incarcerated' at Bloodington and, on a more positive note, the critical level of support he had received from his own parents, things all suddenly made sense to Lawrie.

The 'penny' had suddenly dropped with a reverberating clang. Mr. Armstrong was the real life personification of Mr. Farthing and Jeff Stone, only in 'Headteacher' form. If there was one person who Lawrie wanted to work for, it was Bob Armstrong. In the mean time, any lingering doubts had been dispensed with, as Lawrie experienced his 'eureka moment'. Any teaching career he was to have now needed to follow the path of working with disadvantaged children experiencing learning difficulties.

❧

THIRD YEAR TP

Track 18. Ramblin' Man. The Allman Brothers.

Unfortunately, in the mid seventies, completing any teaching practice within a Special School was simply not allowed, which led to Lawrie making an unusual request.

Driven by his recently discovered idealism and completely ignoring the accepted protocol of always hoping for the easiest and most comfortable of placements, Lawrie called to see his tutor and likely TP supervisor, 'Big Jim' Roberts, to ask if there was any chance of his final teaching practice being spent amongst the least able and most disadvantaged pupils in the area.

'Bloody 'ell Lawrie,' was the big man's initial reaction, 'I've never heard that one before I must say'.

Despite his bluff Yorkshire facade, Jim was a sensitive man and he was intrigued by Lawrie's request.

'What's brought this on then? You got Maltlow last time didn't you? So you weren't due another cushy one...but let me get this right...you want less able kids from a poor background? I mean...really?'

Lawrie nodded his assent.

'What the bloody hell for? I mean no one actually asks for that. Students have been known to offer bribes or fake bloody breakdowns to avoid that combination!'

Lawrie couldn't help but laugh at his tutor's bemusement, but went on to explain about his experiences on the 'Special Education' options course, his introduction to Bob Armstrong and, seeing as a practice within a Special School was apparently not viable, his desire to experience the 'next best thing'.

'Next best thing!' repeated an increasingly incredulous Jim. 'I have to say I've certainly never heard it called that before...still I'll see what I can do. You've got some balls Lawrie, I'll give you that!

Big Jim was as good as his word and arranged for Lawrie's final practice to take place at the notorious St. Marks Primary which was situated on the city's equally infamous and impoverished Wolvesden estate.

Lawrie was to be joined on the practice by another student who he barely recognised, a Maths specialist by the name of Cath Peake who had put in a similarly specific request to teach the more able but socially disadvantaged pupils.

Fortunately for Lawrie, Cath owned her own car and happened to have to drive past Lawrie's flat every day, so the first problem of actual daily arrival appeared, yet again, to have been fortuitously taken care of.

Unfortunately, for both Lawrie and Cath, one thing that Jim Roberts hadn't taken full account of was the oddity that passed as the Head of St. Marks.

Cliff Sullivan was a prissy little man who would have looked very much at home on Dr. Silk's chaise lounge back at Sycamore Grange. Sadly for him there was a spectacular lack of any such furniture anywhere in Wolvesden, but this didn't stop Mr. Sullivan from attempting to stamp his eccentric and pretentious view of the world on what he tended to regard as his own little empire.

Introduced to Lawrie and Cath for the first time, the Headmaster could barely conceal his contempt for Lawrie's long hair and the fact that he smoked, while at the same time displaying a level of obsequious largesse towards the attractive Cath which both students found positively unnerving.

'I will have absolutely no smoking in my school', announced Mr. Sullivan. 'If you must do it you will have to leave the premises and make sure you conduct your horrible habit away from the playground.'

To be fair this wasn't entirely unreasonable and was probably the only evidence ever shown by Cliff Sullivan of thinking which was ahead of its time. What followed next however was bizarre even by the standards of this despotic little man.

On being told of the two students' ambitions, Lawrie's to experience working with the less able in preparation for a career in Special Education and Cath's to work with socially disadvantaged but able pupils, the Headmaster looking completely aghast, held up his hand before pronouncing...

'No, no, no...that would never do.'

Lawrie and Cath looked at each other in wordless astonishment.

'Wh..what do you mean?' began Cath.

'Oh, I can't have that', continued the Head. 'Wouldn't do at all. Can't risk it...Mr. Renshaw takes the more able pupils

127

in that year group you see, while Mrs.Wrigley takes the er...the erm...*slower* ones shall we say.'

'Okay', said Lawrie cautiously, 'So what's that got to do with it?'

'What's it got to do with it?' repeated the apparently troubled Headmaster. 'What's it got to do with it? I'll tell you exactly what it's got to do with it young man! I can't have a female student with a male teacher...and I certainly can't have a male student with a young female teacher. It would never do...oh no, not in my school...just a recipe for impropriety you see.'

Lawrie couldn't believe his ears. This was one thing he had certainly never expected and only a subtle shake of the head from the obviously faster learning Cath prevented an incredulous Lawrie from telling the Headmaster exactly where he could stick his school.

'So what do you suggest', asked Cath, as politely as she could manage.

'Oh, I never suggest, young lady', replied the Headmaster with a slightly sinister and seemingly reluctant smile.

'No, it's quite obvious really...you Miss Peake will be placed with Mrs. Wrigley while you Mr...Mr...'

'Utting?' offered Lawrie.

'Yes, quite...you Mr. Utting will be overseen by Mr. Renshaw.'

'But...', Lawrie began.

'But me no buts, Mr Utting. You'll find Mr. Renshaw to be a fine example to you... Mrs Wrigley likewise. Now off you go the two of you, I have a great many other pressing engagements to deal with...Class 6 for you Mr. Utting and Classroom number 8 for you dear lady. You know where I'll be if you should need me.'

'God forbid we should ever need him,' spluttered Lawrie once they were both out of earshot. 'I can't believe it. What a twat!'

FINAL YEAR

Track 19. 'One World'. John Martyn.

With no more teaching practice demands to concern him Lawrie thoroughly enjoyed every aspect of his degree year. Ever since an eye opening confrontation with the loathsome National Front in Red Lion Square a year earlier, Lawrie had become increasingly involved in student politics.

He'd ended up giving evidence at Bow Street Magistrates Court on behalf of a friend from Sunderland Polytechnic who he'd witnessed being entirely wrongfully arrested.

News of his court appearance never reached 'MeMum' or 'MeDad' but even Lawrie had been shocked at the lengths the police had gone to in an effort to conceal the truth. They'd lied in Court and then again quite blatantly and aggressively when Lawrie had, unwisely and naively, challenged one particular officer in the corridor outside. Such incidents, along with the brutality shown at the demonstration which had led to the death of Kevin Gately, hardened Lawrie's political resolve and he enjoyed meetings with the likes of such soon to become media and political luminaries as Alastair Stewart, Sue Slipman, Trevor Phillips and Charles Clarke, all as a result of his involvement with the 'Broad Left'.

The academic challenges of the fourth year were far more demanding than anything that had gone before. Qualifying for a 'Teaching Certificate' had, in truth, barely lived up to the standard of 'A' levels but in this degree year the academic expectations were far more on a par with genuine University level.

Lawrie chose courses in Philosophy and Sociology, not least because they were run by Alan Davidson and Jim Roberts respectively, and he also had to follow a main course option in American Twentieth Century Literature and Drama as well as producing a twenty thousand word dissertation on 'Charles Dickens and Victorian Education'.

In all to qualify for his degree, Lawrie had to complete something approaching one hundred thousand words of essays and dissertations and twelve hours of final exams.

He'd loved every single minute of his final year, the Sociology exam apart, which probably cost him the difference between a 2.1 and the 2.2 he eventually emerged with. The best though was yet to come when, about a month before his final exams, Lawrie spotted an advert for a job as a classroom teacher at St Anthonys and the possibility of working for Bob Armstrong.

Lawrie painstakingly completed his application form, probably taking more time over the accompanying letter than anything he had ever done before in his life. He was called for interview, along with four others, but, with the help of excellent references from Messrs. Davidson and Roberts, together with the purchase of an improbable brown suit, proceeded to impress Bob Armstrong sufficiently to secure the position of 'Full Time Class Teacher at St.Anthonys ESN(M) School' from the following September and with it...entry into the real world of full time teaching.

LESSONS 4

1. Qualifying to become a teacher in the early 1970's was not the most academically demanding of tasks and, judging from many of those nearing the end of their careers at that time, it must have been alarmingly easy in the post war years of the 40's and 50's.

2. The difference between three year qualification for a Teaching Certificate and the final fourth degree year was as marked, and rewarding, as the

difference between 'O' and 'A' levels. Lawrie's final year had been by far his most satisfying and stimulating academically and it would now lead to him being paid more!

3. The majority of Head teachers at the time appeared a particularly self centred breed in what seemed to be a decidedly and unnecessarily male dominated environment. A decade or two earlier both Mr. Failsworth and Mr. Beaumont had stood out like beacons of fairness and excellence in comparison. Of those he had encountered during his training only Miss Griffiths could escape the label of 'delusional despot' although Lawrie had high expectations of Bob Armstrong.

4. Choose your battles carefully. Lawrie had learned to 'bite his lip' and hold his fire on more than one occasion. Confrontation with Margaret Mantell or Cliff Sullivan could easily have proved terminal to Lawrie's career before it had even begun. They held all the power and Lawrie did well to 'sidestep' both their prejudices.

5. Living both beyond the restrictions of College accommodation and in the company of young women was to prove a definite plus.

6. Policemen of the seventies were not known for their sensitivity, had little time for students and could, to say the least, be dishonest and brutal.

7. If you're going to smoke cannabis don't 'advertise' the fact, especially if you're pursuing a career in teaching!

8. Make the most of student days, they're some of the best of your life...and make the most of those lecturers and tutors who support you...for the most part they've 'been there, seen it and done it'!

FIVE

THE REAL WORLD

Situated within the relatively affluent western suburbs of the city, St. Anthony's was located well away from the more deprived and 'culturally diverse' areas which made up what would later become known as the school's 'catchment area'.

The school had been 'purpose built' in the early seventies, and although whether that purpose was one defined by architects or teachers remained questionable, St. Anthony's was nevertheless, a decent modern facility surrounded by plenty of much needed space including a good sized playing field.

The pupils were as diverse a bunch as it was possible to imagine.

Aged between six and sixteen, many fitted the old 'ESN (M)' or 'MLD' criteria of being typical slow learners - unhelpfully referred to at the time as 'backward' - who stood little chance of keeping up in the mainstream environment, whilst others demonstrated more complex learning needs.

In addition there was a not inconsiderable population of pupils whose problems were much more behaviourally based. Euphemistically referred to as 'maladjusted', these pupils probably made up about a quarter of St. Anthony's intake and had almost certainly been placed at the school by a local authority ruthlessly seeking to take full advantage of Bob Armstrong's enthusiastic and well intentioned, though perhaps slightly vain, claim that 'no child would be refused entry to *his* school'.

Most of the pupils were transported to and from school via two double decker buses or a veritable fleet of taxis, while many of the older pupils eventually made their own way and a minority were brought in by parents, alert to the possible dangers posed by a bus full of special needs children who were never placed in a class of more than fifteen, being temporarily supervised by one of two elderly and entirely unqualified ladies who 'enjoyed' the hopelessly understated and optimistic title of 'bus escorts'.

Lawrie, or Lawrence (Mr. Utting even)...as the minority of older members of staff chose to address him...was delighted to have been given responsibility for a 'middle school' group of pupils aged ten to twelve along with extra responsibility for 'senior boys games'.

He was equally happy to discover that the 'improbable' brown suit which had been worn successfully to interview was to rapidly prove entirely surplus to requirement.

'Smart/casual' would probably best typify the school's dress code and, however much the likes of Cliff Sullivan and Margaret Mantell may have disapproved of such *'unprofessionalism'*, it was the infinitely more relevant qualities of patience, commitment, empathy and communication that held rather greater status within Bob Armstrong's regime.

A dress code that was appropriate for purposes that often included a myriad mixture of paint, glue, snot, mud, tears, school dinner and occasional blood did not include any expectation of being 'suited and booted', or adopting the appearance of an early 1960's fashion victim.

Indeed while the two aforementioned representatives of a soon to be bygone era had displayed every indication of exhibiting some very real symptoms of actual pogonophobia, the wearing of a beard seemed, in comparison, almost compulsory, amongst the male staff at least, at St. Anthony's.

Any such tendencies towards casualness and the hirsute which would, just five or six years earlier, have had 'Bendover 'Bennett ranting about the school being a 'bally hippy colony', should in no way be allowed to disguise the fact that St. Anthony's was actually the epitome of care and professionalism. Indeed it may also come as some surprise, not least to those who think that educational testing was the invention of Education Secretary Kenneth Baker in the mid to late eighties, that tests and record keeping were very much in evidence long before the intervention of the soon to be Baron Baker.

More than a decade prior to the brave new world of 'Baker Days' and SATS, Bob Armstrong had been insistent on the need for records and testing and it was he, along with Terry Bird, the amiable and knowledgeable young Deputy Head, who would not only oversee Lawrie's probationary year, but also ensure that he was fully conversant with the twice yearly implementation and line graph recording of testing via the *Daniels and Diack, Neale Analysis* and *Young* tests in Reading, Spelling and Number.

Another insistence, on Bob Armstrong's part, and one that truly resonated with Lawrie, was that all children mattered and that the keys to educational and personal advancement and success, at whatever level, lay in the building of self esteem and an expectation of his staff to enable all pupils to achieve to their fullest potential.

Maybe it had something to do with his background as a mathematician, but Bob Armstrong was keen to reiterate his firmly held belief that the ability of a child to thrive and succeed was, in diagrammatic terms, dependent on a triangular structure where the child was at the apex with family and school providing the firm foundations from the base.

If the foundations were strong enough then the child

would develop and grow and if part of the base was to crumble and fail then the head teacher would be making, 'damned sure it wasn't the part that he or his staff were responsible for.'

Neither did Bob believe that parents and teachers should be working in isolation. St. Anthony's was quite physically detached from its catchment area and many parents lacked either the confidence, or sometimes even the ability, to make their way easily into school. Parents' evenings were often poorly attended and usually attracted those more committed and competent parents whose attendance was often the least necessary.

With this in mind Bob believed passionately in the value of home visits. Not only was it a case of 'if the mountain won't come to Muhammad' but it was also an opportunity for staff to familiarise themselves with the backgrounds of their pupils and gain a crucial understanding of the often far from easy environments that produced them.

'We see them in school from 9.30 till 3.30 each day', said Bob. 'What makes us think that the other eighteen hours are somehow less formative?'

'When things go wrong in the classroom there needs to be a dialogue between school and home and I don't just mean a hurried telephone conversation...should such a thing even be possible,' continued the head teacher.

Lawrie genuinely couldn't have been happier during that first year at St. Anthonys. Teaching his cosmopolitan class of mixed ability pupils brought with it few of the pressures that today's teachers often have to contend with. The job was to provide for the needs of children who, prior to their arrival at St. Anthonys, had known nothing but failure. Developing their literacy and numeracy skills was of course essential but so too were the development of social skills and personal esteem.

Working with his class was fun. He took huge pride in the work produced and displayed around his classroom together with the measured progress made by most.

Things sometimes went wrong of course and on occasions home visits were necessary, but Bob Armstrong was wise and professional enough to recognise the need for a little bit of 'hand holding'. He accompanied Lawrie on his first couple of visits, guiding him through the 'protocols' involved, always avoiding confrontation, never displaying shock at some of the living conditions that were all too regularly encountered and always gratefully accepting of any cups of tea offered, even that which, as seemed popular in many Asian households of the time, was made with condensed milk and, regardless of preference, copious amounts of sugar!

Lawrie learned so much about how to deal with parents who could be sometimes awkward, occasionally threatening but most frequently just inadequate, from Bob Armstrong. They were lessons that Lawrie would always value and sadly they were lessons given by the experienced to the uninitiated in a way which seems all too rare these days.

Not once had Lawrie felt patronised in the presence of his headmaster, although on the one occasion when he had decided to accompany Lawrie, along with the school football team to what, 'coincidentally', had been his head teacher's former school, Lawrie did have to admit to some degree of 'intimidation'.

Not only was this the first time that Lawrie had driven a mini bus full of pupils in the presence of another adult, it was also to a match that Bob Armstrong's vanity had made him increasingly keen to win, and while he had been willing to ignore the slightly erratic lane changes as Lawrie weaved his way through the unfamiliar rain swept streets of Burton upon Trent, there was no disguising Bob's increasing concern as half time approached with the score still locked at 0-0.

Thankfully Lawrie's half time team talk appeared to awake St. Anthony's answer to not so far away West Bromwich Albion's famous *'Three Degrees'*, and second half goals from each of Lawrie's triumvirate of Carlos, Winston and Benjamin, three strapping West Indian lads who took almost as much stopping as they did starting, restored a more reassuring, if slightly complacent, smile to the head teacher's face.

'I'll just pop in for a word with my old boss. Won't be a minute,' called a grinning Bob, leaving Lawrie to supervise his victorious and mud encrusted charges who he couldn't help but feel had combined that afternoon to save his own fledgling managerial career, and rather more besides.

Track 20. 'Roxanne'. The Police

So Lawrie, overseen by a combination of Bob Armstrong, Terry Bird and Harry Major, the local advisor who had significant experience of Headship in a similar school set amongst the 'mean streets' of early 1970's Salford, sailed blissfully through his probationary year.

Against a background of a rapidly collapsing, unwisely and hastily entered into, immature, marriage, Lawrie had few distractions. Work provided his great escape from the weekends and holidays which, far from providing oases of calm, had become more like some barren wilderness of hostility.

Lawrie spent the first three blissful years of his teaching career at St. Anthony's where he continued with the football team, developed something of a reputation for being able to handle the more 'challenging' pupils, organised sports days, wrote and directed school plays, cast the first black Jesus - which astonishingly still raised an eyebrow or two back in the late seventies - and familiarised himself with the requirements of residential trips...all of which stood him in good stead for...promotion.

BE CAREFUL WHAT YOU WISH FOR

Track 21. 'The Loneliest Man in the World'. The Tourists.

Promotion is something we probably all covet to some degree or other, for a combination of reasons relating to financial need, professional development and the sometimes misplaced ambition of sheer vanity.

Lawrie was no exception, however personal circumstances also played a part and the developing relationship between the recent probationer and Lisa, a more senior colleague and herself an escapee from an unhappy and rather more 'brutal' relationship, hadn't gone down entirely well with the more traditional aspects of Bob Armstrong's moral complexities.

This, alongside a blazing row that had taken place within earshot of some visiting local dignitaries and had clearly embarrassed Bob Armstrong, were the main reasons for Lawrie's move away from St. Anthonys.

Lawrie had unleashed an expletive ridden verbal assault on a colleague who he believed had been bullying one of his pupils after a drenched Colin Meek, as harmless and gentle a child as one could ever meet, had returned to class following an outdoor activities afternoon, claiming, in between sobs, *'He pushed me in the canal, Sir. He did, Sir...Mr. Harris, Sir...he pushed me in the canal!'*

The fact that Bob Armstrong appeared to perceive his own embarrassment as a greater 'crime' than that suffered by the hapless Colin, at the hands of someone who should have known better, had actually shocked and disappointed Lawrie.

He'd been called into the Head's office the following day and refused to back down.

'I apologise for the language and for the fact that you were embarrassed', said Lawrie, 'But if Colin Meek is right then perhaps you should feel much more concerned by what happened to him at the hands of Mr. Harris.'

That hadn't gone down well. Bob Armstrong, for all his undoubted strengths and virtues, loved receiving plaudits, but he was not one for being challenged. The fact that his onetime protégé had suddenly turned into a perceived 'young upstart', and one that was also now living with the 'senior mistress' to boot, meant that it was time to move on and, in the words of Alexander Graham Bell, as is so often the case… *'when one door closes another opens'*, although there were to be some unusual hcircumstances surrounding the speed of Lawrie's rapid from St. Antonys.

Lawrie's disagreement with his erstwhile mentor had come after the summer half term and so, in theory, too late for any immediate change.

The local authority however had belatedly agreed to sanction the retirement of Wilf Briggs the head teacher, for as long as anyone could remember at Meadow Lane Special School on the opposite and decidedly poorer, eastern edge, of the city. This had led to a seemingly spontaneous internal replacement by the existing Deputy Head, Bill Bagshaw, and had in turn created a Scale 2 vacancy.

Lawrie had visited the school once before when his newly kitted out St. Anthony's football team had accounted for the Meadow Lane outfit with almost embarrassing ease. He remembered a school in stark contrast to his own, where the buildings were made up of a mixture of typical Victorian Primary and 'temporary' wartime HORSA buildings, and in Bill Bagshaw he remembered a teacher in his early forties who's initial mask of geniality had slipped to something little short of embarrassed hostility as Carlos English had slotted in St. Anthony's fifth and final goal of the afternoon.

'What the hell?' Lawrie had thought, quite responsibly recognising that his relationship with Lisa might be unlikely to survive the prospect of spending every single hour together.

The job description, such as it was, appeared to be for the teaching of another group of Middle School aged pupils along with additional responsibility for the organising of swimming and outdoor activities throughout the school.

'But I'm rubbish at swimming!', Lawrie had announced when discussing his possible application with Bob Armstrong.

'Won't matter', replied his slightly disconcertingly enthused boss. 'It's just an organisational role. You'll arrange the booking, organise the transport, supervise the changing rooms and let those that can sort the swimming. Tell you what...I'll have a word with Mr. Briggs'.

And so it was, about a fortnight later and only a little under three weeks before the end of the summer term that, in the middle of a creative writing lesson, Lawrie's classroom door opened as Bob Armstrong, followed by an elderly looking gentleman with a thick head of carefully coiffeured white hair, came quietly into the classroom.

'Mr Utting...allow me to introduce Mr. Briggs from Meadow Lane,' announced the smiling headteacher to an astonished Lawrie. 'He's just popped in to see what he makes of you.'

Such was often the way of things in the late 70's. The new headteacher, who was due to take up his position just a month and a half later at the beginning of September, quite bizarrely took no part at all in the interview process which was conducted entirely by Wilf Briggs and Harry Major. Lawrie was shown round the school, asked a few unde-manding questions, asked again if he still wanted the job and that was that. He suddenly had exactly nine working days left at St. Anthony's and he would never set eyes on Wilf Briggs, who was destined for retirement on the Isle of Wight, ever again.

1. The greatest advantage children can be given in order to thrive is the support of parents and teachers alike. When the former fails it is the role of the school to compensate as best it can.
2. *Happiness is...*when work becomes fun. Always looking forward and never dreading going to work is a rare but enormous privilege in life and a major source of contentment.
3. We all learn best from those who have genuine experience of the knowledge they are attempting to pass on.
4. Don't ever lose football matches to your Headmaster's old school.
5. Try not to challenge your boss' self image, or his view of morality, without expecting repercussions.
6. No matter how strong and loving it may be, avoiding a 24/7 relationship is almost certainly for the best.
7. Bob Armstong had his faults, professional vanity being uppermost amongst them, but Lawrie couldn't have wished for a better initial head teacher to learn from, something he would never cease to be grateful for.

SIX

A STEP BACK IN TIME.

Track 22. 'Food for Thought'. UB40.

The second week of September 1980 was one of the most depressing in the whole of Lawrie's twenty six years.

Earlier in the year the perfect Spring weather had given way to an appalling Summer and now that the schools had returned the sun shone brightly again for the first time in months.

Having had no further contact whatsoever, beyond written confirmation of his new appointment, Lawrie drove his trusty old Fiat through the rusting metal gates of Meadow Lane at 8.15 that glorious early September morning in what he hoped would be ample time for the 9.30 start.

So bereft of vehicles was the car park that first impressions were that perhaps the school had succumbed to Margaret Thatcher's cuts without his knowledge during the summer.

The first door he encountered, one that betrayed the schools Victorian heritage by having 'GIRLS' engraved into the stone lintel above it, opened easily giving way to a small entrance area leading into the school hall where a stocky bearded man was putting the finishing touches to the gleaming parquet floor.

'Hold it!'...asserted the beard, which Lawrie assumed belonged to the caretaker...'And where do you think you're going?'

'Oh I'm sorry', replied a confused Lawrie. 'I'm Mr. Utting...Lawrie...the new teacher. I was just heading for the staffroom...looking for Mr. Bagshaw.'

'Not this way you're not', responded the caretaker. 'Staff room's through the main entrance...and I don't want any footmarks on this 'ere floor before the new Head's seen it.'

'But aren't you going to have hundreds on it in about an hour's time?' queried Lawrie.

'That's as maybe', continued the caretaker, showing no inclination to introduce himself further. 'By then Mr. Bagshaw will have seen it and realised that there's only so much as you can do before the little sods come in and ruin it.'

'Clearly a man who has his priorities sorted,' thought Lawrie, before conceding that entering into dispute with the school caretaker on his first morning was inadvisable and taking his polite leave with a cheery, 'Okay then, thanks...I'll try the other door, sorry to have troubled you.'

'No trouble to me', called the caretaker who's attitude had seemingly been somewhat defused by Lawrie's tactical display of deference. 'You'll not find him anyway.'

'Sorry?', replied Lawrie.'

'Mr. Bagshaw', answered the caretaker glancing at his watch, 'Never here before twenty past nine when he was Deputy Head so I don't see how that's about to change now he's the boss man', before adding with a knowing nod, equivalent to a finger tap to the side of his slightly bulbous nose, 'Busy man...Mr. Bagshaw.'

Lawrie was perplexed. His thoughts strayed longingly to St. Anthonys, just a few miles away on the other side of the

City. He pictured a hive of activity where just about every vertical internal surface in the building was covered with pupils' work or other monuments to their achievement.

Here there was nothing other than the caretaker's gleaming floor, which appeared to have been done entirely for his own gratification. There was no evidence of any art work, no photographs of any activities, no reference to pupil achievement and, most puzzling of all, with little time to go before the school term was due to start, no sign of any teachers.

The staff room couldn't have been more different from the entirely functional set up at St. Anthonys where modern, purpose built seating was fitted against all four walls around two long document covered and shin bruising coffee tables.

Here the 'inner sanctum' resembled some sort of cluttered living room from the early 1960's with a selection of haphazardly placed wingback chairs, a *Gas Miser* fire, identical to the one 'MeMum' and 'MeDad' had had installed almost twenty years earlier, and a tray of what looked like gilt-edged bone china cups and saucers which shared a rather kitsch green polka dot pattern and were probably of about the same vintage as Lawrie himself.

Unlike St. Anthony's there were no pigeon holes and no notice boards providing timetable details and the familiar NUT and NAS/UWT posters. Indeed the only item on the wall was a solitary white plastic clock which ticked monotonously towards 9.10 in a staff room still devoid of any sign of life.

Just then Lawrie's thoughts were interrupted by the noise of what he supposed to be the front door closing and the sound of footsteps coming briskly towards down the corridor towards him.

'Morning', said a young woman brightly, offering her hand in greeting having dumped an assortment of bags and files on one of the chairs...'I'm Jan...Mrs. Lucas...Class One'.

'Lawrie...Lawrie Utting, I'm meant to be starting here today.'

'Good to meet you at last Lawrie. We've heard a lot about you...you'll certainly bring the average age down anyway.'

'Ah...go with the furniture do they?'

'Lawrie...most of them **are** part of the furniture, you'll soon see...', laughed Jan, cutting herself short as an elderly looking balding gentleman, who might have been a role model for Margaret Mantell's favoured dress code, dragged himself through the staffroom door closely followed by Bill Bagshaw.

Lawrie's dismay had only intensified as the day progressed. Bill Bagshaw had seemed friendly enough, but he'd only shown Lawrie his classroom ten minutes before the arrival of the school buses and, whereas, at Moor Lane Bob Armstrong would have welcomed both pupils and new staff during an organised and well planned whole school assembly, here the rag taggle collection of pupils simply gathered in the pristine but otherwise soulless and barren school hall to have their names read out and be allotted to the appropriate class room and class teacher.

Neither did things improve as the day wore on. By morning break it became apparent that the school actually had more in common with Edgemoor of the fifties and sixties than anything he had experienced in those three largely blissful years at St.Anthonys. His first mistake had been to sit in the 'wrong' chair which apparently 'belonged' to the senior teacher and acting deputy headmistress, a formidable looking lady in her early sixties, who could easily have passed for being ten or even fifteen years older, by the name of Mrs. Pitchford.

There was none of the friendly free for all banter over

break time drinks which had existed at St. Anthonys. Here everyone was addressed by surname as *'Mr, Mrs or Miss'* and tea or coffee was provided, via termly order and in the gilt rimmed green spotted cups and saucers, by an elderly and earnest little spinster called Miss. Berry who appeared to be about the only member of staff that Mrs. Pitchford deferred to.

Indeed, as the week progressed, and Bill Bagshaw appeared to take more and more opportunities to *'just slip out for a while'*, it occurred to Lawrie that Miss. Berry - who appeared to incorporate responsibility for staff refreshment, with being a bus escort, having complete control of the school dining hall and being the only member of staff, school secretary apart, allowed to operate the antiquated Gestetner duplicating machine - might actually be covertly in charge of the whole school!

'So', began Lawrie, finding Jan Lucas to yet again be the only remaining member of staff, cleaners and caretaker apart, to be left on the premises just minutes after the departure of the pupils.

'What's actually going on here then?'

'How do you mean?' responded a slightly cautious Jan.

'Well I really don't know what I've come to. It's not like any school I've ever been in before...not since about 1961 anyway,' added Lawrie ruefully.

'No they can be a bit old fashioned,' replied Jan. 'I suppose I've just got used to it, and it is my first school'

'Hmmm, it's not just to do with being old fashioned though', replied Lawrie. 'I mean, yeah...they do seem to have a monopoly of the nation's supply of cavalry twill trousers, sports jackets, leather elbow patches, brogues and twin sets...but it goes much deeper than that. They just don't really seem to give a damn, take now for instance'.

'What about it?' asked Jan.

'Well it's only a quarter past three and we're the only ones still here! It's been like that every single day. They arrive two minutes before the kids...you'll be lucky if there's anyone left by the time the school bus has reached the top of the street...there's nothing at all in the way of staff meetings...there's no evidence of any display work on the walls...I've yet to see any sort of assembly...and, as the Head appears to spend most of his time elsewhere, the school actually appears to be being run by two elderly ladies one of whom isn't even a teacher!'

'Is that it?' grinned Jan.

'Well no, actually...I could go on, but honestly'...continued an increasingly frustrated Lawrie, 'I mean...where the hell is he? He's meant to be a new Head and half the time he's just never here!'

'Probably distracted by his other responsibilities I suppose'...answered Jan.

'Other responsibilities...'queried a slightly startled Lawrie. 'What *other* responsibilities?

'Oh, didn't you know? He's got bit of a building business. Runs it with his brother, or so I'm told.'

'You're kidding me!'answered an astonished Lawrie.

'No honestly. Must admit, I was surprised at first. He was often out when he was Deputy and I suppose that's only going to get worse now', explained Jan.

'But why do people put up with it?', asked Lawrie, remembering Bob Armstrong's sideline as a folk musician, but how that never impacted on the school other than positively, as a result of his twice yearly sell out fund raising gigs.

'Just how it is', shrugged Jan. 'What can you do? He's not all bad, besides things will improve once the new Deputy is in place after Christmas. Dorothy Pitchford's really not up to it, just seeing out her time. Mind you, from what I've heard, don't you be at all surprised if her replacement is someone very well known to Bill!'

Things hardly improved for Lawrie as the term wore on. He could barely remember not enjoying a day of teaching during his first three years at St. Anthonys such was the enthusiasm and commitment of the staff, but at Meadow Lane things were decidedly different.

There had been just one, seemingly very much resented, staff meeting before half term at which Lawrie had raised the possibility of introducing an after school football club and some occasional weekend outdoor activities similar to those he had been involved in at St. Anthonys. He'd wondered aloud whether anyone might be interested in offering some support, but the silence was deafening, as if nothing could have been more preposterous than the idea of actually choosing to spend more time than was absolutely necessary with the pupils.

There'd been an embarrassing standoff with the woodwork and cookery teachers when Lawrie had dared to suggest that perhaps there might be an opportunity for girls to visit the 'Workshop' and boys to learn some kitchen skills.

'Boys! In my cookery room...over my dead body!' uttered Mrs. Radcliffe, the dour looking Scottish cookery teacher, whose curriculum appeared to be devised entirely around variations on the theme of iced fairy cakes and jam roly poly.

While the woodwork teacher, a rapidly balding and overweight man who, although only apparently in his early fifties already seemed to be seeing out time, appeared equally aghast at the idea.

'Teach girls woodwork?' he'd said in dismay. 'But you'd

have to get close to them...have to stand next to them...work *over* them!'

'And how do you suppose the rest of us manage?' asked Lawrie.

'Well I wouldn't know Mr. Utting...that's none of my business, but I do know one thing...there'll be no girls in my workshop... and I suggest you keep such new fangled notions to yourself in future!'

Finally Lawrie had, deciding discretion to be the better part of valour, walked out of the staffroom when, one lunchtime in early December, Mrs. Pitchford had haughtily decreed, much to the agreement of the majority, 'Well that'll damn well teach him to claim that the Beatles were bigger than Jesus won't it?' following the murder of John Lennon in New York the previous evening.

'How can it possibly have come to this?' thought Lawrie later in the day, as Mrs. Pitchford, her right foot pressed hard to the piano pedal, 'accompanied', some might even say 'bullied', a recalcitrant group of junior pupils through a reluctant and apparently tone deaf rendition of 'Silent Night'.

LESSONS 6

1. Schools and school teachers alike take many and varied forms. Despite being in the same city and catering for much the same *'clientele'* Meadow Lane bore no resemblance whatsoever to St. Anthonys.
2. The older people are the more resistant to change they can become.
3. Despite all their protestations about 'young people today' and how it 'wasn't like this in my day', older teachers could be both complacently and offensively rude. They also seldom worked as hard,

154

or showed the same commitment, as their younger counterparts.

4. There's a great deal of truth about 'the grass not always being greener'. Always know when you're well off.

5. Be careful what you wish for and take care to ensure that promotion doesn't involve jumping from the proverbial frying pan into the fire!

6. Done properly, the job of Head teacher is a difficult one. There is absolutely no place for them having other jobs *on the side*...a lesson certain current politicians might do well to be mindful of.

7. Even as recently as the early 1980's the 'philosophy' that woodwork was for boys and cookery only suitable for girls was being accepted as a serious proposition by allegedly educated people who worked within the UK education system.

PART II
WHISTLEBLOWER

SEVEN

CHANGES

Debbie Mason was to be the new Deputy Headteacher, taking up her post immediately after the Christmas holidays.

True to Jan Lucas' prediction, Debbie - *'call me Debs'* - was already well known to Bill Bagshaw having worked in the school where his wife was head teacher. Indeed there were rumours that Debbie had provided something of a 'shoulder to cry on' when Brenda Bagshaw had become both emotionally and physically entwined with a local Educational Psychologist, with whom she'd embarked on a brief affair.

Whatever the veracity of this claim it certainly soon seemed that Debbie was to assume a huge responsibility in the running of the school, allowing a happily relieved Bill to concentrate on his other *enterprises*.

So complacent did Bill become that the staff always knew whether he'd last the day or not from which vehicle they'd find in the car park. If his nearly new, sparkling white Audi Quattro was present then it would be a 'school day', either that or they could expect visitors, but if, as was more often the case, his battered blue Bedford van, full of bags of cement, overalls, tools and lengths of timber, was in evidence...then it would be rare for Bill to last beyond morning break.

Track 23. 'In the Air Tonight.' Phil Collins.

Despite the, mainly discreet, allegations of nepotism regarding her appointment, Lawrie found Debbie to be something of a breath of fresh air as far as the running of the school was concerned.

Bill Bagshaw had been seemingly content to allow things to continue as they had for years. The school remained like a throwback to the early sixties at best, where pupils were largely deferential to elderly ladies, there was no testing, no display work, no regular staff meetings, no morning assemblies and things seemed to exist solely for the convenience of the staff and the head teacher in particular.

This though wasn't what Debbie had signed up for and there were two incidents, both involving Lawrie, which inadvertently helped bring matters to a head.

The first came as a result of Lawrie's regular Monday afternoon excursions to nearby Nottingham University where, as a condition of his acceptance of the post the previous summer, he had been granted a special dispensation to follow a two year part time post graduate course in *'Special Educational Provision'*.

In his absence the agreement was that Mrs. Pitchford would, somewhat begrudgingly, take his class and Lawrie was amazed, upon entering his classroom one Tuesday morning, to find four of his six rotating blackboard surfaces covered in beautifully hand written details of *'The Origins of the English Parliament'*.

As his dishevelled group of fifteen pupils entered the classroom Lawrie took Terry Moore, one of his brighter pupils, to one side to ask about the work on the boards.

'Oh that, Sir...that's all we did when you weren't 'ere

yesterday afternoon. Right flippin'boring it were, Sir...I mean, I'm one of the best readers in 'ere, and even I don't have a clue what any of that's about. Patrick, threw a right wobbler...but you know what *Pitchfork's* like Sir...we just had to copy it all down.'

Lawrie did indeed know what Mrs. Pitchford was like. She was an aged primary school teacher, another whose main educational philosophy appeared to be that *'children should be seen and not heard'*...except of course when singing Carols. She arrived five minutes before the pupils and left five minutes after them. She had moved into a Special School because she thought it would be easy. There would, after all, be far fewer expectations, and now, entirely as a result of her seniority, she had been placed in charge of the school leavers, a group of fifteen and sixteen year old pupils with whom she had absolutely no credibility and for whose well being she was equally devoid of enthusiasm.

Lawrie knew from his own experience at St. Anthonys, and the fact that he was now living with the member of staff responsible for school leavers back there, that such pupils should be having access to work experience placements and college courses along with all sorts of activities aimed at fostering independent living skills. At Meadow Lane there was none of that. Here there was just more of the same, and their only escape was, for the boys, to Lawrie's games lessons and the workshop or, for the girls, the mixed blessing of Mrs. Radcliffe's fairy cakes.

'Mrs Pitchford...have you got a minute,' began Lawrie, entering the leaver's classroom after deciding he couldn't let this particular matter pass and opting to follow his mother's frequent advice to *'take the bull by the horns'*.

'Well as long as it is just a minute, Mr. Utting...I need to get off quickly tonight.'

'That'll make a change then', thought Lawrie to himself.

'It was just that I couldn't help noticing the work that you did with my class yesterday afternoon...the Origins of the English Parliament, I believe it was.'

'Yes...what of it?' replied the older teacher, slightly indignantly.

'Well...to be blunt...what was the point Mrs. Pitchford?'

'I beg your pardon?'

'Mrs. Pitchford, the kids in my class have an average reading age of about seven. They're already resentful of being unable to read and write as well as they should...what on earth was the point of giving them something more suited to 'A' level to copy from?'

'Hand writing practice', replied Mrs. Pitchford, stubbornly.

'But they can't read it and they barely understand a word of it', answered Lawrie. 'Can't you see that all yesterday afternoon achieved was to leave them frustrated and, to be completely frank, totally pissed off!'

'Mr. Utting! I'll thank you not to use such language in front of me and remind you that, while you may have been teaching for all of three years I have approaching four decades of experience under my belt! The last thing I need is advice from the likes of you and now, if you'll excuse me, I must get home,'continued an increasingly stentorian and thoroughly exasperated Mrs. Pitchford as she swept past Lawrie slamming the classroom door on the way out.

'Whatever was all that about?' asked a concerned looking Debbie Mason who had heard the door slam and witnessed an indignant looking Mrs. Pitchford exiting the school hall in the direction of the car park like a galleon in full sail.

'Professional disagreement', answered Lawrie sullenly.

'Care to explain?' queried the Deputy Head.

'How long have you got?' sighed Lawrie.

'Well, if there's something I need to know about...' began Debbie.

'Just look around you Debs', interrupted Lawrie. 'Does

this look like a classroom suited to the needs of sixteen year olds who'll be leaving to set out in the big bad world of work in just a few months? She doesn't have a clue. It's a Victorian Primary School classroom and she might as well be a Victorian Primary School teacher. There's nothing on the walls, nothing in the way of careers advice or work experience and when you look at what she did with my class yesterday afternoon...'

'What do you mean?' asked Debbie.

'Come and have a look,' answered Lawrie leaving Mrs. Pitchford's classroom and striding through the school hall in the direction of his own.

'This!' gestured Lawrie in the direction of the two, still unwiped, rollerboards covered in meticulous cursive chalk written sentences.

'This is what she did with my class for the whole of yesterday afternoon while I was at the University. They were just expected to copy words and sentences they can neither read nor understand off the blackboard for an entire afternoon!' continued Lawrie, *'The Origins of the English Parliament'*...I mean...honestly...what is the bloody point?

If that first incident might best be regarded as a *'generational clash'*, the second was much more a reflection upon the Headmaster himself.

Lawrie had been having some difficulty with a thirteen year old girl in his class called Mary Muldoon. Never the most forthcoming or enthusiastic of children, Lawrie had noticed Mary, nicknamed *'Mardy Mary'* throughout the school, becoming increasingly withdrawn, to the point where just about the only interaction with her classmates appeared to stem from a foundation of anger and frustration.

Things had come to a head when Mary had launched a

sudden attack, not to mention a classroom chair, at an admittedly intensely irritating classmate called Wayne Humphries. The previously taciturn Mary had, without any apparent warning, suddenly turned into the ultimate harridan and it is unlikely that Wayne would have escaped the need for medical treatment had Lawrie not rapidly intervened.

'Fucking get off me! Get your fucking hands off me!' screamed Mary as desks and chairs went flying and Lawrie wrapped his arms around the suddenly inexplicably crazed pupil in an effort to protect the astonished, if probably quite deserving, Wayne.

Alerted by the untypical cacophony, a passing Debbie had done a rapid about turn and rushed into Lawrie's classroom to be greeted by the unedifying sight and sounds of a cowering Wayne Humphries, and Lawrie clinging onto the enraged Mary while she continued to hurl expletives at both her teacher and her apparent tormentor.

'Mr. Utting!' uttered the somewhat shocked Deputy Head, 'Whatever is going on here?'

'You tell me'...answered Lawrie, a little breathlessly. 'But if you could give me a hand to remove Mary and ensure Mr. Humphries' survival in the process it'd be greatly appreciated!'

Between them Lawrie and Debbie managed to negotiate the collection of startled pupils and upturned furniture to manoeuvre the by now pale, shaking and tear stained Mary across the Hall and into the sanctuary of the medical room...so called because it contained a small lockable cupboard with the obligatory red cross on it (circa 1950) which housed a rudimentary collection of antiseptic cream, bandages, plasters and painkillers.

'I'll go and keep an eye on your class while you see if you can get to the bottom of all this', suggested Debbie.

'Fair enough', said Lawrie, before returning in the direction of the now sobbing Mary, 'but there'd better be a damned good explanation'.

'Go easy, Lawrie', advised a departing Debbie, 'it's only about fifteen minutes till break time...I'll come back and see what you've discovered then.'

'So'...began a still rather startled Lawrie, taking a seat opposite Mary, 'what on earth was all that about?'

Mary shrugged her shoulders and looked away, fixing her gaze on the blank medical room wall.

'Not good enough, Mary', said Lawrie sternly. 'I know exactly how irritating Wayne can be, but....'

'You don't know nothing...' interrupted Mary, as the tears began to fall again.

'What does that mean?' asked the bemused teacher.

'You...,' spluttered Mary in between shoulder shaking sobs. 'You and all them other teachers...you know nothing about what goes on outside here...but HE knows!'

'Who? Who knows what, Mary?' asked Lawrie, beginning to sense and dread what might be about to be revealed.

For the next thirty minutes, latterly in the company of Debbie for which Lawrie was inordinately grateful, Mary poured out the shocking details of her life.

A long term resident of Marlborough Street, one of the more notorious areas of the city which bore absolutely no resemblance to its illustrious Wiltshire namesake, it turned out that Mary lived with her relatively elderly parents and her eighteen year old brother, Malcolm.

Her parents' better days, if indeed they'd ever had any, had long since gone and the brother, whose physical strength far outweighed any intellectual or emotional capacities, appeared to rule the roost to the extent that Mary's parents had long since abdicated any responsibility for what went on behind closed doors.

As a consequence, Mary knew nothing of the safety and security that children should be entitled to and went home each night wondering what 'demands' would be made of her thirteen year old mind and body by her bullying and emotionally retarded, but unfortunately all too sexually charged older brother.

If it was possible for things to be worse, Malcolm (as is often the way of such individuals) craved the 'respect' and acknowledgement of those such as the much younger Wayne Humphries. The two spent time together, sharing a small shop lifting racket, and Malcolm had actually boasted of his iniquitous activities with his sister to her classmate, leading to the younger boy making the all too recognisable gesture for sexual intercourse towards Mary and in the process, tipping her completely over the edge.

Lawrie could hardly believe his ears and was doubly grateful for Debbie's presence on the basis of both her gender and her greater experience. Had he still been at St. Anthonys, Lawrie would have known exactly what to do. Even before the days of an official Child Protection system a procedure would have been in place where an identified senior female member of staff would have been informed before the matter was taken on to Bob Armstrong and referred to Social Services.

Referring the matter to Mrs. Pitchford would have possibly only led to her suffering immediate and life threatening palpitations, and he was immensely grateful for Debbie's involvement together with her comparative calmness.

Taking the matter to Bill Bagshaw was however, to prove another eye opener.

'Mary who?' asked the Head Teacher looking impatiently at the clock on his office wall.

'Muldoon', replied Lawrie, irritated to think that, in a school of only about one hundred and twenty pupils, such verification was necessary.

After Lawrie and Debbie had provided their account of all

that had been reported the Head Teacher reclined thought-fully in his chair.

'So Mary Muldoon', he mused. 'Mardy Mary...dumpy little thing...lives in Marlborough Street'.

'She does' agreed Lawrie.

'Well there you have it', continued Bagshaw, glancing again at the clock on the wall.

'Sorry?' queried Lawrie.

'Marlborough Street', continued the Head as if this provided some instant and ultimate form of explanation. 'Just about the worst council housing in the whole city. Nothing would surprise me about what goes on there and there's nothing, from a car stereo to a blow job, that can't be bought in the Marlborough Arms. No...I'm very sorry, but that's just how it is Mr. Utting...that's how people live in that den of iniquity. That's life!'

'But she's bloody thirteen...' exploded Lawrie, '...with Special Needs!'

'And I'm sorry too, but we can't just allow this to happen, Bill,' interjected Debbie, shooting Lawrie a warning look.

'Times have changed. Lawrie's right. We have both a moral and a legal responsibility. The days of turning a blind eye to some of the things that go on, even at this little educational back water, have gone, Bill.'

'No good'll come of it, you mark my words', replied Bill Bagshaw. 'She'll only end up in care and you know as well as I do what that means!'

'Got to be a damn site better than what she's going home to at the moment!' said Lawrie angrily.

'Oh has it? Has it indeed young man...and you know that how exactly?' responded the Head bitterly. 'Well if the two of you want to take this further then so be it. You'll have my backing...but it'll be you two who'll have to accept responsi-bility for the consequences...'and with that he grabbed his van keys from the desk and stormed angrily out of his office, simultaneously, had he only but known it, dragging Meadow Lane kicking and screaming into the so far largely unrecognised world of 'Child Protection'.

Although both appreciative and supportive of the changes that Debbie was attempting to introduce, Lawrie was grateful that it was her, rather than he, who had been tasked with winning over the staff.

First came the introduction of regular fortnightly staff meetings which, although a weekly version had been routine for years at St. Anthonys, proved particularly unwelcome amongst those older staff who seemed to believe that their working day included some divine entitlement to a 3.00 o'clock finish.

As if that wasn't enough, once Debbie started a debate on the need for staff to show greater awareness of the pupils' social and emotional needs and the possibility of introducing some procedure for recording relevant events then, despite her seniority and position as Bill Bagshaw's *'chosen one'*, the voices of dissent were not slow to emerge.

'Hang on a minute...we're not flaming social workers you know...' opined Mr. Crossley, the woodwork teacher, predictably.

'Well I know it's all terribly important, but I've got quite enough to do clearing up after them...' added Mrs. Radcliffe, 'Sometimes I don't think people quite appreciate how much mess can be made by eight of our children all trying to produce half a dozen fairy cakes'

'And I simply have to be home by 3.30' said Mrs. Pitchford sternly. 'My Ernest is my first responsibility... he's really not a well man...', before adding, much to Lawrie and Jill Lucas' disbelieving ears and barely concealed hysteria, '...and pussy won't feed herself you know.'

'Well that went well', laughed Lawrie later, knowing that Bill Bagshaw had left almost as speedily as everyone else, and that only he, Debbie and Jill were around to hear.

'Yes..well'...muttered the Deputy Head. 'Like it or not they're going to have to change...social workers, fairy cakes and Dorothy bloody Pitchford's pussy included!'

LESSONS 7

1. Comfort and complacency are the enemies of change.
2. Relevance is essential for education to succeed.
3. What goes on behind closed doors can be shocking and deeply unpleasant to deal with. Turning a 'blind eye' is not an option. What we all need to remember is that it doesn't even begin to compare with what the actual victims of such abuse have to deal with on a regular, and possibly daily, basis.
4. Proper Child Protection systems run by experienced professionals are essential in all schools.
5. Introducing change is unlikely to make you popular.
6. Just like their schools, Bill Bagshaw and Bob Armstrong had nothing in common and exemplified the extraordinary differences to be found amongst head teachers.

EIGHT

A NEW DAWN

Track 24. 'Avalon'. Roxy Music.

As things transpired Debbie Mason had rarely spoken a truer word.

Realisation was beginning to sink in that, in Bob Dylan's immortal words, *'The Times they are a-Changin',* and, for the likes of Mr. Crossley, Mrs. Radcliffe and Dorothy Pitchford, that their *'old road'* was indeed *'rapidly ageing'* .

Confronted by the recognition that a five and a half hour day was no longer likely to be the norm, that reports might have to be written, staff meetings and parents' evenings attended and that some degree of *'in loco parentis'* responsibility might have to actually be accepted, they collectively opted for retirement at the end of the year.

'Not a moment before time,' had been Lawrie's discreetly spoken opinion.

The *'leaving do'* had been a tedious affair, its only redeeming feature being that it had ended as abruptly as the three 'dignitaries' typical school day, and Lawrie had been able to make it back home by half past nine.

He'd also benefitted from a further promotion, it having

been agreed that Lawrie would take over Mrs. Pitchford's responsibilities straight after the summer holidays, although Lawrie always believed this to be much more through the combined efforts of Debbie Mason and Harry Major, rather than anything approaching respect and approval on the part of Bill Bagshaw.

The reasons for quite why Lawrie and Bill Bagshaw struggled to get along better were many fold. Bill was perhaps best described as a working class Conservative who idolised Margaret Thatcher to much the same extent as Lawrie loathed her.

Bill shared the *'Iron Lady's'* mistrust of foreigners and preached about the need for a better national work ethic, ironically totally failing to recognise that it was precisely such work of the same name -*'foreigners'* - indulged in at the expense of the school, that had enabled him to purchase the shiny white Audi and the second home in Lanzarote which he holidayed in each Christmas and Easter and happily rented out for the remainder of the year.

He had perhaps been irritated at being curiously left out of the process of Lawrie's appointment and, having just a Teaching Certificate to his name which had led to him qualifying as a PE teacher in 1965, he possibly felt threatened by Lawrie's more advanced and still ongoing post graduate qualifications.

He even came close to throwing his proverbial *toys out of the pram* at the end of year school sports day when Lawrie had inadvertently ensured that, for the first time ever, Bill didn't win the staff race.

In previous years the only competition to the then Deputy had come from a collection of middle aged ladies, the increasingly rotund Woodwork teacher and, if he could be located,

Stan the bearded caretaker, who always looked about ready to expire after the first ten faltering steps had been completed.

This year though was to be different. Had the two of them gone 'head to head' at the peak of their respective powers it seems likely that the former PE specialist may well have won...but Lawrie, twelve years younger and nothing if not determined, got off to a flying start before comfortably beating his disgruntled Head into second place.

're run!..re run!' demanded an agitated Bill. 'False start...Mr.Utting got off to a flyer'.

'Oh for God's sake', muttered Debs, who had finished a perfectly creditable third. 'Get a grip Bill...it's just a bit of fun. It's not the Olympics you know! You lost...get over it!'

It was noticeable though that Bill never ever entered the staff race again.

Bill was all for maintaining the status quo. He was more than satisfied with the way in which the school was able to tick along largely without him. He didn't want to attract attention and if the appointment of Debbie Mason allowed that to happen while also enabling him to spend more time off site, then that was absolutely fine by Bill.

The unlikely and un-envisaged alliance between Deb's professionalism and Lawrie's idealism however did not go down well.

In truth the arrival of Debbie Mason at Meadow Lane had signalled a sea change for both the school and for Lawrie.

He had taken over the school football team from Mr. Crossley's occasional half hearted efforts, and although crossing twenty odd pupils over the busy Loughborough Road, to the turd (mostly canine) and condom (emphatically not) infested park pitches that lay beyond would have tested even Miss Griffiths' traffic management skills, the Friday afternoon 'coaching' sessions and resultant fixtures against other schools soon became a source of pleasure.

Indeed Lawrie couldn't help but smile when, after an 18-0 thrashing at the hands of a tough local residential school, little Mark Braithwaite, a flying winger who seemed quite unable to tell his left foot from his right, ambled alongside Lawrie to happily and innocently enquire, 'Who won Sir?'

PTERODACTYLS AND VULTURES

Towards the end of his first year Lawrie had also led his first ever residential trip from Meadow Lane to spend two nights Youth Hostelling at Pen-Y-Pass in the heart of Snowdonia and at Llanbedr near Harlech, where Lawrie had spent so many happy childhood days.

The trip had actually been the source of another minor confrontation between the head teacher and Lawrie when the former had refused to allow Lawrie to take any support.

'But you're only taking half a dozen boys!' had been Bill Bagshaw response.

'Yes I am', replied Lawrie, 'but I'm taking half a dozen boys from 9.00 o'clock on Monday morning until sometime on Wednesday evening. What happens if something goes wrong? What happens if for some reason I'm unable to drive?'

'You'll be fine, Mr. Utting...I have every confidence in you...and besides, we just can't spare the staff.'

'You mean you might actually have to bloody do something yourself,' thought a frustrated, but ultimately untypically silent, Lawrie.

So it was, that on the first day of the penultimate week of Lawrie's first year at Meadow Lane, six pupils and Lawrie had clambered into the converted ten year old VW camper van for the trip to Wales.

By today's health and safety standards the vehicle should never have left the school car park. It had two long bench seats, running the length of each side of the van which had been bolted to the floor by Miss Berry's garage owning brother, along with seating for an additional two people in the front alongside the driver. Only those in the front seats benefitted from the security of seat belts and all the pupils' luggage was just dumped in the foot space between the two sets of bench seats.

By the time they'd reached a few miles west of Uttoxeter, a horribly ominous knocking noise, coupled with a disconcerting inability to steer accurately, had alerted Lawrie to the fact that they'd got a flat tyre, and he'd had to spend twenty minutes at the side of the road changing the rear near side tyre while numerous HGV's sped past, each one making the clapped out old camper van rock alarmingly.

Without any sort of support, and not daring to get the pupils out onto the dubious and unsupervised 'safety' of the thin weed ridden pavement that ran along the side of the road, it was amongst the longest twenty minutes of Lawrie's life, and each time a vehicle sped past he inwardly cursed Bill Bagshaw and imagined the potential newspaper headlines, 'TEACHER (27) AND HIS SIX PUPILS KILLED IN ROAD-SIDE CARNAGE.'

The rest of the journey passed by uneventfully enough and once the drabness of Stoke and west Cheshire was passed through it wasn't long until the route gave way to the infinitely more spectacular scenery on the approach towards Llangollen and Corwen.

Lawrie was pleased to notice that the further they travelled into North Wales and towards Snowdonia the more seduced into silence by the increasingly dramatic scenery the pupils became. 'Nothing like where we live is it Sir?'

'The rivers are different here...all clear and winding like the roads. They're all straight and dirty at home',

'That's because you live next to the canal...ya div!'

'Wouldn't want to have to do my paper round here...these hills are massive...you'd be fu....soz Sir...I mean right knackered!'

'Sir...sir...I've just seen a Ter...a Terra...a Terrywotsit...a Terrydadkil, Sir', shouted little Elvis Williams.

He wasn't being daft, but had actually just caught sight of an enormous grey heron landing in the shallows at the side of the River Llugwy, and which Lawrie was very well aware, for a fourteen year old who had only just experienced his first ever sighting of a sheep, did indeed bear more than a passing resemblance to the prehistoric Pterodactyl.

The kids were mesmerised by the landscape, and an evening walk in the foothills of Snowdon, which might just as well have been in the Himalayas for all they knew, provided more stimulation than any classroom.

There were soaring buzzards, or *'vultures'* as Elvis preferred to identify them, and along with lonely mysterious lakes and the alien dusk time cries of foxes and owls, there was more *awe and wonder* to be found in that Snowdonia evening than the pioneering designers of the National Curriculum could ever have believed possible.

The following morning which, much to Lawrie's relief, had dawned bright and sunny, began with the second of three minibus related problems which would plague the expedition.

Having loaded everything and everyone into the bus and started the engine, Lawrie went to put the minibus into reverse. A number of unwanted and discouraging crunching noises apart, nothing happened. Reverse gear would simply not locate.

'Shit', muttered Lawrie under his breath.

'What's up Sir. What are we waiting for?'

'Seem to have a problem with the gearbox,' answered Lawrie, whose knowledge of mechanics pretty much matched Elvis' ornithological expertise. 'Doesn't seem to want to go into reverse.'

'Be alright Sir', piped up Terry Moore. 'We're on a slope. We can just roll back.'

'And then what?' queried an exasperated Lawrie.

'Well you never know Sir...the other gears might work. We can still go forwards. Me dad's van ain't 'ad no reverse gear for years, but he still gets round in it okay.'

'Really? But what about his MOT?'

'His what Sir?' asked a confused Terry.

'Never mind,' replied Lawrie, who had to admit to there being some degree of unlikely logic in the teenager's suggestion.

From Tuesday morning until Wednesday evening then, Lawrie and his six young adventurers continued their intrepid journey through Snowdonia, onwards to the Welsh coast and eventually back to the Midlands without the benefit of a reverse gear.

Just as Terry had suggested, the four forward gears worked perfectly well and although Lawrie had to spend the rest of the trip parking in a position which gravity would allow him to 'reverse' from, when that hadn't proved possible he moved to 'plan B' which involved three of the lads pushing the van out of its parking place enabling first gear to be located and the journey to continue.

A drive across the causeway to Shell Island and the magnificence, by any standards, of Harlech beach, with its background of the iconic thirteenth century coastal fortress and the view across Tremadog Bay to Criccieth and the Llyn Peninsula, were to prove the highlights of the trip.

Lawrie though would never forget the words of Elvis Williams as they walked to the top of the untypically sun drenched dunes which separated the fortunate and expansive flatness of the car park from the vast expanse of beach and seemingly never ending sea.

'Sir...Sir...can we go in, Sir? Sir...which is the deep end, Sir?

They say that bad things come in threes, and following Monday's puncture and the mishap with the gearbox it was perhaps inevitable that, having got to within fifteen miles of their home destination, a large stone chipping should have been flung up by the car transporter in front, crashing into the windscreen with an enormous 'crack' and shattering it into thousands of pieces.

'Fuck me!' reacted Terry Moore, who had been sitting alongside Lawrie in the front and rather echoed Lawrie's own thoughts, as he braked heavily and quickly punched a hole through the now disconcertingly opaque windscreen.

'Erm...sorry, Sir', apologised an ashen faced Terry, as Lawrie pulled up to the side of the road and prepared to sweep away the little cubes of broken glass and ensure that the hole was big enough for him to be able to continue the last few miles of the journey safely.

'Don't worry Terry, we all sometimes say things we don't mean when we've had a shock.'

'Never said I never meant it, Sir,' said Terry with endearing honesty. 'Just shouldn't have said it...but it were a right shock. It were like bein' flamin'' shot, Sir.'

'Could have been a lot worse and at least it's warm and not raining...no harm done,' said Lawrie, attempting to calm everyone's nerves.

'Not sure Baggy...erm...Mr. Bagshaw will see it like that, Sir'.

'I'm sure he'll be fine, Terry', replied Lawrie, with rather more certainty than he actually felt.

Lawrie was later than usual into school the following day. After driving the one hundred and twenty odd miles back from Harlech and then having taken all six pupils to homes which seemed to involve traversing the whole City, and where only Elvis' mother had bothered to thank him, he was tired and the 6.40 radio alarm had proved unusually ineffective.

Without any reverse gear Lawrie had been unable to park the minibus in the inconveniently sited school garage the night before, and had opted instead to park the flat fronted VW as close to the school wall as possible in an effort to minimise the admittedly unlikely risk of any theft.

He'd then climbed into his trusty old Fiat, engaged the luxurious novelty of reverse gear, and sped off home in what, for the first (and only) time, suddenly felt like some sort of high performance sports car.

STANDING HIS GROUND

Returning now, just ten hours later, the first thing Lawrie saw, as he drove through the rusting school gates, was his disconsolate looking head teacher closely examining the gaping hole in the VW's shattered windscreen.

'What's been going on here?' demanded the Headmaster, no sooner had Lawrie retrieved his brief case and locked his car door. 'Looks like some little vandal has smashed the windscreen...why ever didn't you park the bus in the garage properly when you got back, Mr. Utting?

Lawrie really wasn't in the mood and answered tetchily... 'Erm...it was just a bit difficult with no reverse gear.'

'No reverse gear? What on earth are you talking about, Mr. Utting?

'Well let's see', continued an increasingly unamused

Lawrie, 'Do you want me to start with the puncture, the clapped out gear box or the shattered windscreen?'

Just at that moment the two adversaries were interrupted as Terry Moore skidded through the school gates and came to an abrupt halt on his still much coveted, if no longer quite gleaming, red Raleigh Chopper.

'Told you, Sir', said Terry with a disarmingly discreet wink in Lawrie's direction.

'Classroom, Moore,' ordered the Headmaster.

'But it weren't Mr. Utting's fault, Sir...he couldn't have done nothing. We're lucky to be alive, Sir!' continued the boy.

'I said...classroom!' repeated the Headteacher menacingly, '...and I think you and I had better go to my office, Mr. Utting.'

To what extent his pupil's well intentioned and impromptu description of their good fortune in remaining alive had helped or hindered his cause, Lawrie wasn't sure. He was however certain that, after all the events of the previous three days, the circumstances had yet to be discovered whereby he would simply roll over and accept any sort of wholly unjustified rebuke from his pompous, overbearing and ungrateful boss.

'Mr. Utting', began the headteacher from across his desk. It would seem that over the last three days your little jaunt to Wales has cost this school the small matter of one new tyre, one new windscreen and, in all probability, a new gear box too!'

'I've always believed in telling it like it is...'continued the bombastic Headmaster, 'I won't pussy foot around...and it has to be said that this just isn't acceptable...you were meant to be providing an outdoor activities excursion...not bankrupting the damned school! Now what have you got to say for yourself?'

Lawrie couldn't believe it. Even by Bagshaw's standards

this was an entirely undeserved tirade, but Lawrie somehow managed to maintain his self control.

'I'll tell you what I have to say for myself,' began Lawrie in an ominously calm voice. 'I'd just like to say thank you...'

'You what?' snapped Bill, '...What the hell do you mean...thank you?'

'I'd just like to thank you, Bill', added Lawrie in a tone of growing sarcasm,'For taking such trouble to find out this morning how the trip went...how the kids behaved...what they got out of it...for checking that we all got back safely despite the various mishaps...'

'Well I...' blustered the Head teacher in a vain attempt to interrupt Lawrie's flow.

'...and I'd just like to thank you also...' continued Lawrie, his anger only partially betrayed by the slightly raised tone of his voice,'...for sending us all off in a clapped out and barely roadworthy vehicle with absolutely nothing in terms of adult support for when things went horribly wrong, just as I'd warned you they might!'

'Now just a minute Mr. Utting...you listen to me...'

'No, Mr. Bagshaw...you listen to me!' continued Lawrie, now in full flow, and beginning to enjoy getting the stresses of the last three days off his chest.

'I'm not at all sure how it's meant to be my fault that we picked up a three inch nail in a tyre, that the gearbox is shot, or that a large stone was flung into the windscreen by the vehicle in front...but if you want to continue to bask in the reflected glory of children at this school being offered such outdoor activity trips then you might need to get things sorted. We need a decent and reliable vehicle and staff will need a reasonable level of support...'

Lawrie paused briefly for breath, as the stunned head teacher stood open mouthed, before continuing.

'The last three days could easily have ended in complete

disaster and without those conditions being met you can count me, and in all probability anyone else, out!'

'In the meantime...' concluded Lawrie, before opening the door and brushing past a rather startled looking school secretary, 'If you do want to know how the trip went, then I suggest you ask Elvis Williams what he thought of the vultures, the Pterodactyl and his first ever view of the sea!'

'Everything alright, Sir?' asked Terry Moore as a rather red faced Lawrie sat down at his desk to take the register.

'It is now Terry', answered Lawrie with a knowing wink.

LEAVERS...

With the beginning of a new school year Lawrie had moved out of his original classroom and into the one vacated by Mrs. Pitchford, where he immediately set about trying to create an environment more suited to his soon to be sixteen year old, final year pupils.

Encouraging the pupils to bring in the sort of images they would like to be surrounded by, Lawrie had firmly rejected one or two *'page three'* pictures, resulting in a chorus of disgruntled *'Oh why Sir?'* from the miscreants.

Otherwise though, the collection of contemporary 'cultural icons' - ranging from Adam and the Ants and Madness through to Abba, Kim Wilde, Duran Duran and The Specials on the music front, characters from Star Wars, Superman and the Blues Brothers in the world of film, and sports related additions made up largely of Liverpool, Manchester United and some lesser local 'stars', along with Daley Thompson and an incongruously youthful looking Nigel Havers from 'Chariots of Fire' - had soon spread rapidly into a lovingly created collage across the front wall of the classroom.

The fact that Mrs. Pitchford would have probably viewed the creation as nothing more than a collection of 'trouble makers and anarchists' bothered Lawrie not one jot. In any case, he very much doubted that such disparate and 'dissolute' individuals as 'King' Kenny Dalglish, Harrison Ford and Agnetha Faltskog would have been anything other than highly amused to find themselves described in such a way.

He was also happy to make a point of welcoming the Careers Officer, a bubbly young Irish woman called Bernie, who Mrs. Pitchford had viewed as an entirely superfluous distraction and, for the purpose of interviewing pupils, had incarcerated in a dimly lit and windowless stock room.

In place of the hopelessly unventilated store room, Lawrie commandeered the medical room for Bernie's fortnightly visits and ensured that she was admitted to and acknowledged in the staffroom as a vital cog in the progress and development of his group of school leavers.

In return for such consideration (otherwise known as simply treating another professional with the respect they deserved) Bernie helped Lawrie enormously in the setting up of College courses and work experience placements until something akin to the 'Leavers' Programme' he'd seen Lisa establish at St. Anthonys was similarly in place at Meadow Lane.

NEW ADDITIONS

The welcome addition of several new replacement staff members, much closer to Lawrie in terms of age and outlook, had also helped drag Meadow Lane into at least a more appropriate decade. The curiously outdated convention of addressing each other as *Mr, Mrs* or *Miss* was quickly and naturally replaced with the less formal use of Christian names and some much needed stress relieving banter became the order of the day at break and lunchtimes, making Meadow Lane a much happier place to be in Lawrie's eyes.

Whether it was the replacement of the 'old guard' and the emergence of a more youthful staff, the desire not to uproot his own children from their settled home and school environments, or just sheer lack of genuine ambition that led to Lawrie spending so much of his career at Meadow Lane is difficult to say. Maybe a combination of all three, either way, despite his continued misgivings over Bill Bagshaw, Lawrie was to be there for a great deal longer than had ever seemed likely during his far from fondly remembered first term.

Track 25. '99 Red Balloons'. Nena.

Mindful of Lawrie's words of warning following the trip to Snowdonia, and suddenly aware of how there was no longer any hiding from his ultimate responsibility, Bill Bagshaw had uncharacteristically climbed down over a number of issues.

He still sought to spend round a fifty per cent of most working weeks off site, looking after his other business interests, and could rarely be found in school after a quarter past three, except when there was one of the by now weekly staff meetings which even Bagshaw didn't have the audacity to avoid. He had however belatedly recognised some of the dangers that Lawrie had spoken of and, just as a hired and properly maintained minibus would now always be made available for lengthier expeditions, so Lawrie gained the additional staffing he needed for crossing the increasingly dangerous main road and running an afternoon of 'Upper School' games in the park opposite.

Such support came in the form of Tom Clay, the newly employed woodwork teacher, who had not only taken over responsibility for woodwork, or CDT as it was soon to be dynamically rebranded, but also, quite spectacularly by Meadow Lane standards, Cookery too.

Just a few months younger than Lawrie, the two would become both close friends and allies at Meadow Lane, and the Friday afternoon football matches, which would include no little degree of rivalry between the two young teachers, would go on to become a thoroughly pleasant end to the working week.

'What's the boss all about then?' asked Tom one afternoon as they enjoyed an after school coffee in the workshop.

'Honestly?' answered Lawrie, aware of the need for balancing professionalism with truthfulness. 'Can't say I'm a great fan...very skilled at looking after number one, but beyond that...well, he's a bit of a prick in my opinion', answered Lawrie.

'Doesn't seem to interfere much', commented Tom.

'No, hardly at all, he's just an over promoted Phys.Ed teacher really...doesn't generally care until things go wrong. Debs pretty much runs the place...the more he can get away with the better it suits him...not a man to be on the wrong side of though', advised Lawrie, before adding ruefully, 'and certainly not one to *kowtow* to either.'

'Do your job...put your hand up if you're in the wrong...stand your ground if you're not and you'll be fine', added Lawrie, 'Besides you don't seem like someone who's likely to allow themselves to be bullied.'

'Message received and understood...and thanks for the heads up,' said Tom, emptying his coffee dregs down the sink, with a knowing look.

Track 26. 'The Power of Love'. Frankie Goes to Hollywood.

Following the changes brought about largely by Debbie Mason, and the introduction of some newly recruited replacement staff, Meadow Lane embarked on possibly the most settled, productive and professional period in its history.

As the LEA had decided that the school was now to cater exclusively for secondary aged pupils, largely those presenting behavioural difficulties within the mainstream sector, there was to be a much needed shift away from class based to more subject based teaching.

Lawrie retained his responsibilities for School Leavers, senior boys' games, and outdoor activities but his first responsibility was for 'Upper School' English, a situation he wholeheartedly welcomed.

Meanwhile, Tom Clay had transformed the CDT room, where girls now worked happily alongside their male classmates, but it was in the adjacent Domestic Science (Cookery) block where the greatest changes had taken place.

With a lifestyle still joyously not greatly removed from the student one he had left behind some years earlier, Tom was very much aware of the requirements of being able to live on a budget. As far as he was concerned being able to feed yourself well on a limited budget was a hugely important real life living skill and one that seemed particularly appropriate to the Meadow Lane pupils. Fairy cakes were no longer central to a Domestic Science curriculum aimed exclusively at girls as, with the twenty first century getting ever closer, the realisation that boys too might need to cook had suddenly dawned.

Two other welcome additions to the staff were Esther Jacobs a young West Indian teaching assistant who was only about four years older than the pupils in Lawrie's Leavers' group, and Megan Owen, an experienced and enthusiastic Art teacher.

Esther, as Lawrie would relay in the years ahead, was to become, his wife and family apart, the person who he 'holidayed' with more than any other, as she became his 'go to' as far as residential school trips were concerned. While Megan rapidly set about reorganising the previously drab old class-room into a veritable gallery of replica images from the likes of Van Gogh and Monet through to Picasso, Lowry, Warhol and the rather more daring, as far as pupils' paint contain-ment was concerned, Jackson Pollock. The room had become as diverse as 'MeDad's' chimney breast all those years ago.

Even more spectacular was Megan's enthusiasm for school drama productions. Nothing so adventurous had ever been attempted before at Meadow Lane, but with the support of Esther in drama classes and both Lawrie and Tom, in terms of the provision of sound and lighting systems, some genuinely impressive 'productions' were launched. Indeed, so impressed was Bill Bagshaw that, after one particular Christmas event, he arranged for bouquets of flowers, albeit ones bought hastily from the local garage, for Megan and Esther, and promised to look into the purchase of some stag-ing, enabling the rather disgruntled late arrivals amongst the parents to see the performances of their offspring more clearly.

JOB SATISFACTION

Track 27. 'Brothers in Arms'. Dire Straits.

Over the next few years Meadow Lane grew beyond all recog-nition from the school that Lawrie, had joined from the other side of the city. Where once there had been bare walls, an abundance of art work, photographs of school trips and drama performances now blossomed.

Those in their final year now attended courses at the nearby College in such subjects as Catering, Bricklaying and Painting and Decorating. Previously nonexistent Work Expe-rience placements were found in a range of environments from the local Sainsburys and Kwik Save to tyre fitters, hairdressers, nurseries and old peoples' homes and there were trips across the Channel to France and more locally, after an annual succession of disappointingly damp weeks under canvas in Wales, to Edale at the foot of Kinder Scout in the far north of Derbyshire.

Here Lawrie had established contact with the local vicar, a warm and committed man by the name of Jeremy Lloyd Bowen, who ran an outdoor activities centre in an imaginatively converted and extended old barn. The vicar was also an expert rock climber and over the years, scores of pupils were to be provided with the opportunity to live together for a week in the comparative wilds of the 'High Peak', and take part in such activities as hill walking, riding the numerous bike trails, rock climbing and abseiling.

Of these, abseiling, usually from the viaduct in Millers Dale down to the River Wye, provided the single most spectacularly memorable activity, and one which virtually all the pupils showed rather more proficiency in than Esther. Even after years of annual practice, and much to the amusement of all, Esther had never really mastered anything more graceful than a peculiarly unique horizontal abseil. She always seemed to end up returning to terra firma backside first. Indeed it became almost an annual Edale tradition for at least one puzzled pupil to ask fondly of Tom or Lawrie, 'Sir, why does Miss. Jacobs always have to come down on 'er arse?'

For Lawrie attending and managing such trips was the most satisfying part of his job. This, along with the arranging of numerous theatre trips was where he believed he was really doing what he had entered the teaching profession to do...to make a difference.

Track 28. 'Dignity'. Deacon Blue.

The trips to Wales, France and the Derbyshire Peak District, along with theatres across the Midlands, were providing these largely disadvantaged pupils with opportunities such children would otherwise not have had access to. Indeed this was a view perhaps best encapsulated by the words of a troubled fifteen year old called Marvyn whose brief life was to end, as the victim of a gang fight, and whose funeral Lawrie would attend just a couple of years later.

Most doubted the wisdom of Lawrie and Esther taking Marvyn to Buxton Opera House for a stage performance of the 'Hobbit', but he'd promised to be on his best behaviour and Lawrie's one condition was that the generally unruly teenager occupied the seat next to him throughout the performance.

True to his word and recognising that for once he was actually being trusted, Marvyn had been mesmerised by the performance and had behaved perfectly, even remaining next to Lawrie throughout the interval and staring wide eyed at the century old ornate ceiling, cherubic images, white alabaster scrolls and columns of African onyx, before making his most telling of comments, 'Amazin' innit, Sir! Ain't for the likes of us though, is it?'

Lawrie didn't know whether to laugh...or cry.

TROUBLE AHEAD

It's hard to identify the exact cause of the difficulties that would come to unfold at Meadow Lane over the coming months and years, but they perhaps began from an indirect and unlikely source, with the retirement of the school secretary, Joyce Jackson, who had been in place at the school for longer than anyone could remember.

Now in her mid sixties and sporting a purple rinse to, not entirely convincingly camouflage her rapidly greying helmet of hair, Joyce was a more than capable 'old school' secretary with excellent shorthand and typing skills. She had been a keen admirer of Mr. Briggs and had chosen to turn a blind eye to his successor's shortcomings but, with rumours of inspections along with something called 'Ofsted' on the horizon, and with her 66th birthday fast approaching, Joyce had decided it was time to call it a day.

In itself Joyce's departure should have been easily manageable. She was competent and loyal, desirable but had hardly irreplaceable virtues in a secretary, but it was the nature of her replacement, a gym fit thirty something year old called Nicola Fullard, who would prove the catalyst for an unwanted and unanticipated degree of change.

Track 29. 'Into the Great Wide Open'. Tom Petty.

It wasn't Marvyn's fault that he was the first to discover the new school secretary's 'secret'. Having arrived late he just happened to have been sent to the office to book himself a school dinner at precisely the time Mrs. Fullard had been bending over while facing away from the glass office hatch window, to reveal an unknowing glimpse of the heart and angel wings tattoo that occupied the small of her back.

'Nice *tramp stamp*', Miss' observed Marvyn, will all the conflicting innocence of one who was sufficiently street wise to be familiar with such terminology, but who correspondingly possessed none of the wisdom or sophistication to recognise the risk of such usage towards a recently appointed and highly ambitious school secretary.

'I beg your pardon!' replied a rapidly reddening and somewhat flustered Mrs Fullard.

'Your *slag tag*, Miss', continued Marvyn, hardly helping his cause, 'Me Mum's got one just like it...only 'ers is like a red rose where you've got an 'eart.'

'Yes, well...I don't think that's any of your business do you?'

'Just saying, Miss, didn't mean nothing,' answered a chastened and slightly aggrieved Marvyn.

'Well don't just say! Just mind your own business and make sure you're not late again tomorrow...why wasn't you here for registration anyway?' continued the new school secretary, by way of reproach, and slipping into language that somehow betrayed the image of power dressed office efficiency that had materialised for interview a month earlier.

'Stroppy cow'...muttered an indignant Marvyn on his return to class.

'I'm sorry Marvyn...good morning to you too,' said a confused Lawrie, 'What, or perhaps I should ask, who, are you talking about now?'

'That new woman in the office, Sir...she's right up 'erself. Nowt like Mrs. Jackson, Sir...she might have been old but she were kind. She'd have asked me how I was, 'ow my little brother was getting on...stuff like that. Not this one, Sir...she just gave me a right bollocking...and all I did was say I liked her *tramp stamp*.'

The arrival in recent times of the newly appointed and altogether more enthusiastic staff to Meadow Lane had allowed Lawrie, in his capacity of 'Head of Upper School', to introduce a system of accreditation known as the *Youth Award Scheme*.

This was another first for the school and allowed the year pupils in Years Ten and Eleven at Meadow Lane to benefit from a programme of cross curricular activities based around real life skills, enabling them to leave school for the first time with an externally recognised level of accreditation to their name.

Tom and Lawrie had put their heads together to devise additional CDT and Domestic Science modules and the *YAS* now formed the basis of the 14-16 curriculum in such areas as Literacy, Numeracy, Games, Art and Drama, R.E, Domestic Science, CDT and Information Technology.

Things had gone well, and from an introductory two years when just a handful of students had managed a Bronze Level Award, the school had now reached the stage where, of Lawrie's sixteen school leavers, only one, who seldom attended, would fail to leave with any accreditation while, of the rest, there would be a dozen Bronze Level successes and three who had gone on to achieve Silver Level passes.

Now, with the first ever Ofsted Inspection imminent, the school's success had been recognised. Lawrie had been asked to introduce other schools to the benefits of the scheme which was to become a further topic of debate when one of the LEA's Senior Advisors called a pre-Ofsted planning meeting at Meadow Lane with the SMT triumvirate of Bill Bagshaw, Debs and Lawrie.

Track 30. 'Rotterdam'. Beautiful South.

It should be acknowledged at this point that Lawrie had little time for advisors. He recognised they had a job to do, but believed that, all too often, they were unsuccessful escapees from the classroom who now sought to teach others to perform tasks they themselves had often never adequately mastered. *'He who can, does. He who cannot, teaches'*, had been George Bernard Shaw's original damning indictment of the teaching profession, and while Lawrie clearly disagreed with such a sentiment, he found himself infinitely more comfortable with the notion that, *'He who can, teaches...he who cannot, advises.'*

Lawrie's admittedly somewhat jaundiced view had only been strengthened earlier in the year when, again as part of the Ofsted preparations, a Maths advisor had singled out one of the Meadow Lane teachers for what was generally considered to be ill informed and unfair criticism. 'Okay, fair enough...so how about demonstrating how you'd have handled this particular group,' had been Lawrie's response...a stance which Bill Bagshaw had surprisingly supported.

Perhaps unwisely the advisor had taken up the challenge and prepared a demonstration lesson with the same disenchanted group for the following week. The fact that he lasted just under twenty minutes before walking out of the classroom declaring the group, *'unteachable'*, had only reinforced Lawrie's theory and it was, within this context, that a cautious Bill Bagshaw introduced Nancy Palmer, one of the LEA's Senior Advisors, to the school's SMT.

Lawrie knew only a little about Nancy Palmer who was known widely by the abbreviated nickname of *'NaPalm'*, not least because of her inflammatory and somewhat incendiary reputation. She'd struggled to progress far within the teaching profession and had never held a senior position in any school, yet here she now was, a senior representative of the LEA and, apparently, a leading exponent of what was to be considered 'best practice'. 'The world works in a mysterious way', thought Lawrie to himself, although the meeting was civil enough and entirely uncontentious, until Nancy brought up the schools YAS figures.

'These accreditation figures, Mr. Utting...they're very impressive.'

'Thanks', acknowledged Lawrie. 'The scheme seems to have been accepted very well.'

'Yes indeed', replied Nancy, '...and Ofsted are going to be most impressed, but what are your projections?'

'I'm sorry?' queried a puzzled Lawrie. 'Not sure I understand.'

'Your projections, Mr. Utting', continued the Advisor. 'These results are good...very good...but they must now be seen as just a benchmark. How do they help you predict the performance of pupils in future years and where are those projections.'

'Yes Mr. Utting,' interjected Bill Bagshaw, not least because a part of him was secretly relishing Lawrie's apparent discomfiture and partly to diffuse any ensuing argument, 'How do they help...and where are the projections?'

'Well they don't,' answered a slightly bewildered Lawrie. 'We don't have any projections.'

'Oh but you must, Mr. Utting...data is everything. Percentages and pass rates are there to be built on.'

'With respect, Mrs. Palmer' answered Lawrie, in grave danger of meaning the exact opposite, 'Schools don't quite work like that. We are not conveyor belts, or machines, churning out endless facsimiles of what has gone before. The achievement of this year's cohort bears absolutely no relevance to what may be achieved next year or the year after.'

'So you're saying you aren't going to learn anything from the achievements of the present?' continued the advisor raising her eyebrows questioningly.

'I'm saying nothing of the sort,' replied an increasingly irritated Lawrie. 'We're learning all the time...and seeking to improve too. But until we know the nature of the pupils we're dealing with, and the sort of issues that impact upon all schools throughout the year, we're not in any position to make worthless projections.'

'Ah...I see. The age old *can't make a silk purse out of a sow's ear argument*', countered Nancy.

'Not exactly...no, although I suppose there is some element of that,' answered Lawrie. 'Seeing however as you've introduced a vaguely agricultural perspective, I'll take the farming analogy a little further.'

'Meaning?' interrupted the advisor sharply.

'Meaning, if you'll allow me to finish...' continued Lawrie. 'If a farmer produces a magnificent crop yield in a year when the growing conditions are perfect, do you consider the following year, which may be ravaged by disease, drought or floods, to be a failure if the yield is not as good?'

'Well I...I...' began the advisor.

'We are like farmers, Mrs. Palmer,' continued Lawrie calmly, 'We learn from experience and we always aim to get the best results we can, but the *growing conditions* vary and one year will, in all likelihood, bear little resemblance to the next. To think otherwise,' continued Lawrie, warming now to his agricultural analogy, 'Is, frankly, just bullshit.'

'Well er...I think we all take Mr. Utting's point on board,' interjected a rather startled Bill Bagshaw, anxious to avert any further disagreement between his Senior Teacher and the influential LEA representative. 'Perhaps these year on year projections might not be all they seem after all,' he concluded.

'Apparently not,' added Nancy Palmer a little tersely, unable to provide any counter argument in support of her beloved 'data','I can only hope Mr. Utting will be as willing to explain their absence so forthrightly to the Inspectors when they ask...as they most assuredly will.'

'Happily', replied Lawrie.

OFSTED WEEK

Track 31. 'Nothing Lasts Forever'. Echo and the Bunnymen.

Ofsted, in its current form, as with virtually any form of inspection, can be an understandable source of stress. Back in the early days however, when Meadow Lane had been given ten months notice of the inspection dates, Lawrie displayed little sympathy for those who were winding themselves up into states of high anxiety.

'They're coming in to see how we operate for four days and feeding back on the fifth. If, having been given ten months notice, people can't make sure their marking is up to date, their classrooms look decent and their lessons are well prepared then, to be honest, they deserve to be found out!' was Lawrie's take on the matter.

'But we don't know which lessons they'll be coming into,' remarked one of the almost tearful and less efficient Lower School teachers.

'Then you'd better make sure they're all well prepared,' answered Debs, a little frostily, while tactfully missing out the words *'for once'* as an unspoken codicil to her response.

Lawrie's greatest concern had been that the inspectors might take the form of 'pen pushers' like Nancy Palmer. He had always been of the opinion that only those who had actually proved themselves in the job should be in a position to judge others, and he was delighted to find that all four of the inspection team, the decidedly odd couple of 'Lay Inspectors' apart, had previous experience of working in schools like Meadow Lane. Indeed the team leader, who was now a University lecturer, had, it transpired, co-authored a book called 'Real Life Reading Skills' which, entirely coincidentally, was Lawrie's literacy skills 'bible'.

Far from presenting themselves as the 'jobsworths' that Lawrie had feared, the main inspection team, who seemed happy to distance themselves from the obligatory 'lay inspectors', proved to be polite, constructive and knowledgeable.

The only surprise, as far as Lawrie was concerned, was that, because he was teaching four 'subject' areas (English, YAS, Games and a double period of preparation for a forthcoming Outdoor Activities Trip) he had an unprecedented ten lessons inspected during the week, a fact which didn't go unnoticed by Marvyn who, as yet another inspector arrived to take up their customary seat at the back of the room, was heard to mutter under his breath, 'God, not a-bloody-gain!'

All of Lawrie's lessons went well. The lead inspector was delighted to see his text book being put to good use and impressed by Lawrie's own more 'bespoke' supplementary materials which had been designed to provide increased local relevance to such real life literacy skills as understanding bus and train timetables, cinema showing times, local street maps and the like.

Fortune also smiled on the weekly ordeal of crossing the busy main road to the park for the weekly games lesson. This weekly nightmare had been made much easier since Tom Clay had been timetabled to share the responsibility of 'Senior Boys Games', however on this week of all weeks, upon reaching the park pitch Lawrie had been astonished to find a machete lying behind the goal.

Not lacking in imagination as to the dangers of where such an item falling into the hands of one of his less 'predictable' pupils might lead, Lawrie rapidly abandoned his sweat shirt and tracksuit bottoms, quickly covering the machete from view. Fortunately no one noticed and the rest of the afternoon's proceedings went as planned. What was more noticeable however, was how, on the way back to school, the sight of two, bearded and mud stained men, one apparently carrying a machete, seemed to make the business of stopping the traffic to direct a large group of teenagers across the busy road a whole lot easier than usual!

'Interesting method of traffic control,' commented the bemused Inspector afterwards.

Offensive weapons apart, the only other slight mishap related to the female lay inspector, who had already gained something of a reputation as an attention seeker, having turned up late on the third day claiming to have had her sleep disturbed when a strange, and never to be identified, man had mysteriously materialised in her hotel bedroom.

Later that same day she was due to visit the local College, only ten minutes walk from the school, to witness a Brickwork lesson in action. Unfortunately, rather than asking Lawrie for directions, she'd naively sought advice from a mischievous lad called Gurdip, who'd already had more than enough of *'weirdos following us about all week, writing stuff down.'*

Rather than providing the perfectly straightforward instructions of crossing the main road and turning right at the roundabout, Gurdip had failed to mention crossing the road at all and advised his unknowing victim to turn left at the roundabout. The poor woman never did locate the college and spent most of the afternoon hopelessly lost and walking miserably up and down the canal tow path, where she was probably in considerably more danger than had ever been the case overnight in her hotel room.

'Oops...soz, Sir', exclaimed a seemingly contrite Gurdip the following morning, 'You know me...never could tell me right from me left!'

By Friday it had become obvious that Ofsted week had been a success. The inspectors had made some slightly questioning comments about Bill Bagshaw's 'eccentric leadership style' but otherwise the 'feedback' had been overwhelmingly favourable and Lawrie hadn't once been asked about any 'projections'.

Moreover, in an age when Ofsted still provided 'C1' forms as written evidence of 'Particularly Good or Bad Teaching', it was unusual to have four staff - Lawrie, Tom and Megan, together with Gloria Carney, a more recently appointed Science teacher who Lawrie hadn't really taken to - all officially recognised as displaying clear examples of the former.

'Does it mean we get paid more?' enquired Tom enthusiastically.

'Sadly not...no,' replied the lead inspector, '...but at least you get the recognition.'

'Hmmm...' responded Tom glumly, 'Can't ever remember paying any bills with recognition.'

Only much later that same evening, during the drunken post Ofsted celebrations at the local 'Midland Hotel', when Lawrie had caught a fleeting glimpse of Bill Bagshaw's podgy fingers sliding furtively over a heart and angel tattoo and beneath the waistband of Nicola Fullard's skirt, had he begun to realise there may be problems of an altogether different nature ahead.

LESSONS 8

1. School vehicles always need to be safe and well maintained.
2. Don't ever appear to be faster, brighter or more knowledgeable than your Head teacher. They really don't like it!
3. Always stand your ground when you're absolutely sure that you're right.
4. No amount of Sociology lectures will ever teach you as much about the 'Social Construction of Reality' as taking deprived kids on trips to theatres and the nation's National Parks.
5. To the innocently untrained eye, Herons really can resemble Pterodactyls, and there are few better examples of 'awe and wonder' than seeing one land for the first time.
6. Pupils invariably value being shown trust and provided with opportunities.
7. Acknowledging pupil achievement and creating a positive environment really does matter.
8. George Bernard Shaw had never heard of 'advisors'.
9. There is limited value in attempting to measure the achievements of pupil cohorts in relation to one another. Like crops and financial products, how well they perform in one year may well, for a vast variety of reasons, bear no resemblance to the next.
10. The best Ofsted Inspectors are those who've been there, seen it, done it...aren't on a mission to catch you out and then say nice things about you! Even adults benefit from praise.

11. There is much more to understanding than the production of 'data' alone. For instance, showing a teenager the sea for the very first time is both an enormously humbling privilege and something the value of which advisors and inspectors would find very difficult to measure.

NINE

CRIME...AND LIMITED RETRIBUTION

Albert Higgins, the elderly Chair of Governors at Meadow Lane, who'd been as likely to fall asleep in meetings as he ever had been to question any of Bill Bagshaw's suggestions, had decided that with a successful Ofsted to his name, this was the time to step down.

Now, buoyed by the successful outcome of Ofsted, and, even more encouraged by the realisation that he was most unlikely to be troubled by further inspection for at least another four years, Bill Bagshaw had not been slow to spot an opportunity.

As ever, with such thankless and voluntary posts, there was hardly a queue of willing candidates and the Head teacher saw the opportunity to strengthen his own position via the appointment of his best friend or, as some would go on to describe...partner in crime, a man called Michael Donovan.

Donovan certainly looked the part. He was a dapper man in his late fifties, all steel grey hair, perma-tan and sharp suit in the Michael Heseltine tradition of well to do successful businessman. Never introduced as having any previous connection with Bagshaw, Donovan claimed to have all manner of contacts with those in high office and, as the owner of an allegedly successful I.T. company, was very forth-coming with suggestions of how useful his contacts could be to the school. Michael Donovan however was not to be quite all he seemed.

With Nicola Fullard having already taken over from Joyce Jackson as Clerk to the Governors, Donovan as Chair and one of a couple of 'tame' parents, who Bill Bagshaw had charmed and flattered into joining the Governing Body, now forming the Finance Committee, it was obvious where the power now lay and how unlikely it would be for any of Bill's initiatives to be challenged.

Esther Jacobs, as ancillary staff representative, and Gloria Carney, as teacher rep. (because no one else wanted to do it) made up the remainder of the Governing body, and while no one would ever question Esther's loyalty or integrity, she was hardly the most outspoken, while Lawrie had privately identi-fied Gloria as just another 'glory hunter' looking out for herself.

Track 32. 'Race for the Prize' Flaming Lips.

It was against such a background that Debbie Mason had discreetly taken Lawrie to one side during lunch time and suggested that she could do with 'a word' in her office at the end of the day.

Bill Bagshaw had long since changed into his work boots and disappeared in his van by the time the school buses left and Lawrie had joined Debbie in her office with a couple of mugs of tea.

'So what's up then?' asked Lawrie.

'Long story,' answered Debs, a little forlornly, 'I'm thinking of calling it a day, Lawrie.'

'What?' said Lawrie, who was genuinely shocked...'But why?'

Lawrie knew that Debbie had taken it personally not to have been deemed worthy of the 'C1' recognition that her four colleagues had received, and there could be no doubt that she'd deserved it, having done more than anyone to drag Meadow Lane into something at least resembling the nineteen nineties.

'Is this to do with Ofsted?'

'No...no...nothing to do with the Inspection', answered Debbie who was clearly becoming upset. 'I'll admit to feeling a little under appreciated, but that's just one of those things. This is much more serious.'

'Serious?' queried an increasingly alarmed Lawrie. 'You're alright aren't you?'

'I'm fine. It's nothing like that...but there are things going on here that you don't know about Lawrie.'

'What like Bill shagging Nicola, you mean' said Lawrie with a knowing smile.

'That's part of it...yes,' answered a slightly surprised Debbie. 'So you know?'

'I'd guessed,' corrected Lawrie, describing what he'd seen at the post Ofsted celebrations. 'Old boss screws young secretary...he gets to feel young and virile and she doubtless picks up a few other perks. It happens Debs...always has, always will...not worth getting upset about.'

'There's rather more to it than that' replied Debs, 'and what I'm about to tell you mustn't go any further...you have to promise me that'.

'Okay', agreed Lawrie, hesitantly, 'Go on then...'

'It's about Michael Donovan' began Debbie.

'What, Tory Boy...the creepy new Chair of Governors?' What's he got to do with it? Hey old Bill's not arranged a threesome has he?' laughed Lawrie.

'Oh for Christ's sake Lawrie!' snapped Debbie. 'I thought you of all people would listen! If you can't take this seriously then...'

'No, no...I'm sorry', said Lawrie holding up his hands, both to stem further reprimand and acknowledge his fault in appearing dismissive of his colleague's concerns.

'Michael Donovan is not all he appears', continued Debbie. 'He isn't someone who Bill has just discovered...he's Bill's oldest friend. More to the point...it's only just over ten months since he was released from prison!'

'You're joking!' gasped Lawrie. 'Prison? What the hell for?'

'It's all here,' answered Debs passing Lawrie a carefully folded if rather aged local newspaper.

Lawrie could scarcely believe his eyes. There, on the front page, in a report from Stafford Crown Court, was a photograph of a younger looking, but still quite unmistakeable, Michael Donovan, under the headline 'BANNED BUSINESSMAN JAILED FOR THREE YEARS'.

The newspaper was dated September 14th 1994 and went on to describe how a 'thoroughly dishonest businessman had breached a previous court order to fund his lavish lifestyle'.

With little head for business Lawrie couldn't pretend to understand all the ramifications of the newspaper article. It seemed however that Donovan had fallen foul of Government legislation and been the subject of two disqualification orders both of which he'd been in breach of while clearly continuing to manage his IT business and simultaneously using the company's money to fund what the newspaper described as his own 'profligate lifestyle'.

'Christ, Debs...how long have you known?' asked Lawrie.

'I met him once...at one of Bill's parties,' answered Debbie. 'Fifteen, maybe nearer twenty years ago...I thought I recognised him so I got a friend to do a bit of digging.'

'And this is what they came up with?'

'It gets worse Lawrie', said an increasingly distraught Debbie passing across a type written sheet of A4 paper.

The letter, which was as succinct as it was poorly written, was addressed to the Head of Staffing at the Local Authority Education Offices and read as follows:

Dear Gillian,

At the recent annual review meeting of the Head teacher's salary the Governors recommended that Mr. Bagshaw's salary should be increased to spine point 34 backdated to 1st September. The decision was made after consideration of the results of an OFSTED inspection held earlier in the year and in accordance with professional management guidelines in addition to the standard criteria.

Yours sincerely,

Michael A Donovan

Chairman of Finance Committee

Meadow Lane School.

'The bastard!' exploded Lawrie. 'So you bring about all the change, the staff work their bloody balls off and he picks up the reward?'

'That's about the size of it'.

'But what about Esther and Gloria? They must've known...they're Governors, how come they've kept quiet?' continued an angry Lawrie.

Debbie gave a small resigned chuckle, 'You really can be naive at times Lawrie...what goes on in the Finance Committee doesn't get back to the rest of the Governors, not beyond the initial splitting of the budget...Esther and Gloria would never be allowed on that.'

'So who is privy to the bloody Finance Committee then?'

'Haven't you worked it out yet?' replied Debbie to an ever

more incredulous Lawrie. 'Well, let's see...there's Bill himself, Michael Donovan of course, he's the Chair...Nicky Fullard keeps the records and Mrs. Lowe, who as you know doesn't know what day it is half the time, as the obligatory parent.'

'And what does this increase add up to then?' questioned Lawrie, hardly daring to ask.

'A huge amount for a school this size.' replied Debbie.

Lawrie was quite incredulous. He'd known for a while that Bill Bagshaw couldn't be trusted but he'd never suspected anything like this.

Lawrie's main source of comparison however was with one of his closest friends, Ron Sherwood, an experienced Head teacher who had only recently finished his career, opting for a stress relieving early retirement over the potentially perilous benefits of continued employment.

Ron had worked in a number of schools across the Midlands, eventually finding himself, in his second headship, at one of the biggest primary schools in the city where he had responsibility for over 400 pupils, about four times as many as would currently be found at Meadow Lane.

Unlike Bill Bagshaw, Ron was a charismatic man of integrity. His school had been in a notoriously poor area but he did what was expected of a good head teacher, taking responsibility for discipline within the school, providing informative and entertaining twice weekly assemblies, ensuring he was on first name terms with all his pupils, dealing with some enormously challenging parents and managing the staffing, running and administration of the school in a way which won the virtually universal praise and approval of his colleagues.

Unfortunately Ron's one shortcoming was his timing, and just as Tony Blair's election was within months of signalling an escape route from the permanently underfunded world of Thatcher's educational wasteland, so Ron...recognising that if things were, in the words of *D:Ream* and the shiny new 42 year old Prime Minister, to *'only get better'*...they'd have to do so without him.

So it was that, on the last day of August and technically the last day of Ron's employment, he and Lawrie were to be found in the late summer sunshine on a celebratory walk in the High Peak of Derbyshire.

It should have been a stiff ten miler, including a breezy and spectacular ramble across the top of Stanage Edge. Not for the first time however, Lawrie had misread his OS map and ten miles had become not far short of thirteen by the time they stumbled into the *Cheshire Cheese* at Hope, still some way ahead of their wives whose combined navigational skills made Lawrie look like Columbus.

During the walk Lawrie and Ron had talked about the latter's forthcoming holiday to the Loire Valley, a trip he planned to joyously begin on the day the new school term was due to start. They'd exchanged anecdotes about their rugby playing days, about politics and about teaching too of course, but it hadn't been until the first couple of pints had loosened their lips that the talk had shifted to how difficult Ron had found the last few years and how, in order, to keep his school functioning he'd never actually been able to sanction his own salary rising above £35,000.

Lawrie had never forgotten that, nor Ron's sage advice about tackling the issue of Ben Bagshaw's absenteeism and unethical second source of income.

'Don't be a hero, Lawrie...the world is full of them. The ones on the battlefield are largely dead and the whistle blowers are mainly redundant. There'll be plenty who happily step aside to let you, but just don't go it alone.'

Lawrie thought back to that conversation now. 'Such a

salary for a man who abdicated responsibility at every opportunity...a man who was happy to take such a salary while running another business...and a man who had now created a situation whereby he, along with his best friend and his lover ran the Finance Committee in exactly the way they wanted...it just couldn't go on,' thought Lawrie...but it did!

Debbie Mason lasted another year. Lawrie knew she'd been struggling, but other than offer subtle and prudent support there was little he could do. He couldn't confront his head teacher without betraying Debbie's confidence and she had sworn him to secrecy. Neither could he share his knowledge with anyone else as, again, the source of his information would have had to be revealed.

Debbie didn't return to Meadow Lane again after the end of the school year. There was vague official, and superficially sympathetic, talk of some sort of 'breakdown' and her entitlement to early retirement, but Lawrie knew the real reasons. She had never really recovered from Ofsted's failure to recognise her contribution to the school, she was consumed by a devastating combination of guilt and outrage at the things she knew but felt the need to keep secret, and she was sick and tired of hearing *'Nic thinks this and Nicki says that...'* from her erstwhile friend, Bill Bagshaw.

NEPOTISM

In Debbie's absence Bill Bagshaw was quick to act. In order to continue with his alternative and lucrative business interests he had to ensure that there was an official second in command and with that in mind he persuaded Lawrie to relinquish his afternoon teaching commitments and extend his role as Senior Teacher to taking on responsibility for discipline throughout the school.

The additional role came with a small salary enhancement and a promise that such experience would stand Lawrie in good stead should Debbie, as looked likely, be unable to return and the position of Deputy Head become permanently available.

He also, with all the necessary approval of the Finance Committee of course, upgraded Nicola Fullard from her position as secretary to that of 'Business Manager' which came with a far from small salary increase and the additional appointment of an office clerk...or the *secretary's bloody secretary'* as Tom Clay was quick to describe her.

Track 33. 'Two Seconds of Your Love'. Laura Cantrell

Unfortunately for the besotted head teacher, as is so often the case, arrogance and dishonesty began to lead to complacency on the part of Bill and Nicola, and when it became apparent that the new office clerk was in fact Nicola's sister in law and that one of three newly appointed teaching assistants was none other than the new Business Manager's sister...tongues quickly began to wag. The final straw however came when it was announced that Nicola Fullard would be taking over Debbie's responsibility for the vital role of Child Protection.

'But she has no experience...and absolutely no qualifications,' remonstrated Lawrie.

'I'll send her on a course', answered Bill Bagshaw, 'She's a bright girl...fast learner and besides she does have some personal experience'.

'Personal experience?' asked a puzzled Lawrie.

'Her father'...replied the head teacher before adding with a frown, 'Keep it to yourself...but a bit of a wrong 'un...if you know what I mean.'

'The apple seldom falls far from the tree', thought Lawrie.

News of Nicola's 'promotion' and the appointment to the staff of two of her family members hadn't gone down well. The usually laid back Tom Clay, who'd been particularly close to Debbie Mason, had done the sums as best he could and was untypically outraged.

'Do you realise there's probably over forty grand being spent on running that fucking office now Lawrie, but never any money for more teachers. Just a few years ago we had old Joyce doing exactly the same job for a fraction of the money...and she could bloody spell!'

Lawrie couldn't disagree.

Neither did such dissatisfaction stop with Tom. Gloria and her Departmental Head, Molly, were equally outraged at the planned change in the business manager's role to include Child Protection.

'It's just bloomin' ridiculous' announced Molly,...her broad northern accent becoming noticeably more pronounced the angrier she got. 'What does she know about children? That should be a career opportunity for a teacher here, someone who's trained for three or four years, one of us who's completed the course and actually understands the kids. She's welcome to screw Baggy...each to their own and all that...but she's not bloody screwing us too!'

TURNING POINTS

'I know you two don't exactly see eye to eye, but there's more to her than you might think', said Esther Jacobs to Lawrie as he gave the TA a lift to her flat just off the City's busy ring road.

'She's brave you know.'

'You what?' laughed Lawrie. 'We are talking about Gloria Carney? Brave...how do you work that out?'

'There are things you don't know,' continued Esther, blissfully ignorant of the irony of that particular comment. 'It's not easy speaking out in Governors' meetings you know...I mean that new Chair...I know at least this one stays awake, but he always just seems to support Mr. Bagshaw...and with Nicki Fullard there too...well it's hard standing up to them.'

'Standing up to them...how exactly?' asked Lawrie.

'Well, like all this stuff about Nicki taking over Child Protection, Mr. Bagshaw wants it to happen, Nicola too...obviously, but Gloria keeps standing up to them...goes on about how it needs to be done by a properly qualified teacher.'

'And what do you think?' asked Lawrie.

'Me? Oh I agree with Gloria. It needs to be done by someone who's properly qualified...someone who knows the kids...not some glorified typist. Not sure I'd have the courage to say so though...not like Gloria'.

The impromptu conversation with Esther, someone who he liked and trusted, had provided Lawrie with food for thought. Perhaps he had misjudged Gloria Carney, maybe there was more to her than he thought and she wasn't just out for number one after all.

Lawrie's thoughts were interrupted when, having just finished helping his youngest son with his English homework, the telephone rang.

'Hi Lawrie,' came the familiar voice of Jane Bryson, a social worker who had become something of a family friend. 'Just ringing up to say congratulations.'

'Well that's nice Jane,' responded Lawrie, 'but you must

know something I don't and we're a bit past the new additions stage.'

'Don't be daft you silly sod,' laughed Jane, 'I mean your new appointment.'

'Appointment? What appointment...I honestly have no idea what you're talking about Jane.'

'Oh c'mon', continued Jane, 'What's with all the false modesty? I was in a meeting this afternoon with your boss...that Bagshaw bloke.'

'Bit odd really'...continued Jane quizzically...'Scruffy old bugger...seemed anxious to get away and looked more like he was on his way to a building site than a Social Services meeting. Anyway, he made it perfectly clear that you are his new Deputy... any issues we have with the kids from Meadow Lane and you're our first port of call. What's happened to Debs anyway?'

It was nothing more than a simple case of serendipity that saw Lawrie crossing the car park after school the following afternoon at precisely the same moment as Gloria Carney.

'Gloria, have you got a moment?' said Lawrie seizing the opportunity to initiate some sort of dialogue. 'I know we don't usually have much to do with each other but I've been talking to Esther, and for what it's worth, I really do admire the stance she tells me you've been taking in Governors' meetings'.

The neat and natty little science teacher paused from loading stuff into the back of her people carrier and looked up at Lawrie, the makings of an unfamiliar smile breaking out across her face. 'Wow...well there's a turn up...I really didn't expect that.'

'What does that mean?' asked a questioning Lawrie.

'Well you know...Senior Management and all...I just thought you'd be on their side'.

'Is it about sides?' asked Lawrie.

'Lawrie, I think we need to talk!'

ACTIONS SPEAK LOUDER...

Emboldened by Lawrie's words of support, Gloria had wasted no time in organising an after school meeting of the ten teaching staff. A few eyebrows had been raised amongst the teaching assistants, but any doubts had been largely allayed by Gloria's explanation that this was nothing more than an opportunity for her, as teacher/governor, to feed back from the most recent meeting on matters that related specifically to those she represented .

Gloria spoke freely for the first time about how difficult she had found opposing the decision to place Nicola Fullard in charge of Child Protection.

Molly and Tom were particularly outspoken. 'It's just bloody ridiculous,' said the former...'insulting to us as professionals and unfair on the kids. They deserve someone who's familiar with what they're going through...someone with proper training, someone who knows them...not Baggy's bloody knock off.'

'I agree,' joined in Tom, 'But it's not just Child Protection. The whole business with Debbie was handled dreadfully and the money that goes into that office these days...it might as well be being chucked into a flaming black hole!'

'Why are we suddenly employing two of Nicki Fullard's family anyway?' added Megan...'and I don't remember there being any interviews either.'

'Actually there are more than two of Nicki's family benefitting,' said Gloria.

'What?' said Tom. 'Two's more than enough but they're the only ones that I've heard of.'

'Employed directly by the school...yes,' replied Gloria, but you know that new CCTV system we've just had installed?'

'Oh God!' said Tom...'don't even mention it...I tried to use it the other day to see who'd been messing about with the bikes in the bike shed. Complete waste of bloody time...just a bunch of shadowy figures...couldn't identify anyone at all. What about it anyway?'

'Installed by *SecurityNet*', said Gloria.

'You've lost me...?' said Tom.

'The owner of *SecurityNet* is...' replied Gloria pausing briefly, '...none other than Nicki Fullard's brother!'

'I don't fucking believe it!' said Molly.

'I'm afraid there's more,' said Lawrie who had so far remained silent throughout the meeting but had now heard more than enough to realise that his continued silence was no longer an option. What was it they said? *'All that is needed for wrongdoing to prevail is for good men to do nothing'*.

The room quietened again, partly out of deference to Lawrie's seniority and the fact that, since Debbie's departure, he had been regarded as the Deputy Head in all but name.

'I can't tell you how I've come to know the things I'm about to tell you, and you're going to have to trust me on that one, but there are things you need to know and need, at least for now, to keep secret', continued Lawrie.

Track 34. 'Cigarettes and Chocolate Milk'. Rufus Wainwright.

Steve 'Archie' Archibald, the school's NAS/UWT representative, was the first to break the silence after Lawrie and Gloria's bombshells.

'So...from what I'm hearing...we've got a boss with a sideline in a building business, an ex-con, who's also the boss's best mate, as Chair of Governors, and a Business Manager who's having it a way with the boss while she and three of her family reap the benefit', surmised the Union rep in his typically succinct and forthright manner. 'Does that just about sum things up?'

No one could disagree. 'I think it's time to involve the Union', continued Archie.

'Or the flamin' police!' added Molly, her neck reddening in anger and indignation at all she'd just heard.

'Archie's right...let's start with the Union,' argued Tom.

'And get the teaching assistants on board too,' suggested Megan Owen.

'Sorry, but no. We can't do that, Megs!' stated Lawrie emphatically.

'Why on earth not?' asked a disappointed Megan, 'They're our colleagues and our friends, we all need to stick together'

'Absolutely', replied Lawrie, 'But they include Nicola's family and friends. We can't be seen to be being selective. Once we start inviting some of the support staff and not others we start to raise suspicion. I'm sorry, I know it's horrible and I feel bad about it too, but as far as I can see, we need to let Archie get on to our Union and go from there...until then I'm afraid this has to be kept secret'.

Reluctantly, Megan and the other teachers had to accept Lawrie's point.

'So how long have you known about all this, mate', asked Tom, as he and Lawrie sat together in the sanctuary of the workshop.

'Some of it for a while...other bits, like the CCTV stuff, have been as much of a surprise to me as to you to be honest,' replied Lawrie.

'How did you find out about the Donovan creep?'

'I really can't say,' replied Lawrie, 'Not even to you.'

'Oh c'mon...you're not going down the, *it's tough at the top, with great power comes great responsibility* route with me! Won't wash mate.'

Lawrie laughed, 'You know me better than that, Tom...I just can't say.'

'Debs then?'...asserted Tom, looking his friend straight in the eye.

Lawrie shrugged, 'You said that, not me.'

The Jubilee Vaults, which smelled of smoke and stale beer and sounded infinitely grander than it actually appeared, was about to get a significant boost to its early evening trade, as an unlikely collection of ten teachers and one suited and booted Union official, joined the scattered half dozen or so customers who appeared to have spent their unexceptional afternoon benefitting from a diet of cheap lager, crisps and Sky TV.

Chosen only because of its proximity to the school, and the need to hold the meeting off site and away from prying eyes, the teaching staff had been joined by Jack Beckett, the local Union organiser.

He listened, with growing astonishment, to the account of what had been happening as relayed largely by Gloria, Lawrie and Steve Archibald, along with occasional and increasingly indignant interjections from Molly who was soon tucking into her second large glass of Pinot Grigio.

'These would appear to be very serious allegations', concluded Jack Beckett.

'No shit Sherlock!' said Tom to Megan in rather less of a whisper than he might have imagined.

'If you're sure of your evidence...'

'We are!' interrupted Molly...'Absolutely bloody sure!'

'Then, as I was saying', continued the Union official patiently, 'If you're sure of your allegations then this has to be brought to the attention of the LEA as quickly as possible.'

'And how are we to do that then, Jack?' asked Steve Archibald.

'I have to warn you all that this isn't going to be pleasant,' began Jack Beckett.

'The LEA don't take kindly to whistleblowers and if this all gets out things aren't going to reflect very well on them at all.'

'But we're not the ones in the wrong. It's not us fiddlin' the bloody finances...' interrupted Megan to general murmurs of approval.

'Exactly so', agreed Jack. 'You're absolutely right...but as I've just said, it isn't going to be an easy process. It's not something to go into lightly and you are going to have to stick together so if anyone has reservations it'd be better to raise them now.'

One or two of the younger, more recently appointed staff looked a little anxious, but there was no backtracking and the overwhelming mood remained one of defiant determination.

'In which case', began Jack again. 'I believe the best course of action is for you to compose a letter, which you must all agree with and all sign, calling for the resignation of the Head teacher on the grounds that you no longer have confidence in either his integrity or his ability to run Meadow Lane School. There's no need to be more specific at this point, that'll all come out later,' continued the official. 'The key point to get across is your collective loss of confidence in his integrity and ability as Head of the school.'

'Once you've done that,' I'll need a copy of the letter delivered to me, preferably by tomorrow lunchtime, and someone will then need to deliver a copy of the same letter to Mr. Bagshaw himself at the end of the school day tomorrow.'

'If he's still bloody around for once,' muttered a disconsolate Molly, wondering quite how her second glass had already become half empty.

'I'll then present your letter to the LEA on behalf of the Union and as for how your Mr. Bagshaw reacts...well, we'll just have to wait and see,' concluded Jack.

It was quickly decided that Gloria would compose and type out a suitably succinct letter that evening and discreetly have it photocopied and signed by all the teaching staff the following morning. Steve Archibald, who always welcomed any opportunity to visit a pub, would meet up with Jack in the *Vaults* at lunchtime to hand over one copy, leaving just the small matter of delivering the original to the Headmaster himself.

As the remaining staff got up to leave an eerie quiet suddenly seemed to have descended across the rest of the pub and all attention appeared riveted on the brand new flat screen TV in the corner, where what looked like some sort of disaster movie was showing, only curiously with a Sky 'banner' across the top of the screen and a reporter's name at the bottom.

It was Tuesday 11th September 2001.

Lawrie barely slept that night. His head was full of images of the atrocity. Of a plane being flown into the World Trade Centre towers...the second tower being engulfed in flames...the sheer desperation of those who had flung themselves from the burning buildings...smoke pouring from the Twin Towers polluting the clear blue New York skyline like two enormous cotton mill chimneys from his Lancashire childhood, and dust covered people frantically running from the dense clouds of ash that seemed to chase them through the monolithic glass lined 'corridors' which made up New York's grid system of streets.

As if that wasn't enough, he pondered what was going on at Meadow Lane. His mind just wouldn't switch off. Were they doing the right thing? Had he behaved correctly in relaying the details of Bagshaw's longstanding friendship with Michael Donovan and exposing the latter's criminal conviction and subsequent prison sentence? How would the Local Authority react? How would Bagshaw himself react?

All through the night those images and questions punctured his dreams and prevented his sleep, and yet each time the answer was a variation on the same theme, *'all it takes for wrongdoers to succeed is for enough good men to do nothing'*.

Throughout the drive into work a bleary eyed Lawrie listened to Radio 5's depressing reports from across the Atlantic.

The rest of the World's news no longer seemed of any relevance, as unfamiliar names like Rumsfeld and Giuliani superseded not only that of the U.S. President, but also the more parochially topical ones such as the slightly bizarre Hamiltons, who had just been cleared of sexual assault, and Iain Duncan Smith whose dismal term as Tory Party leader now needed to be briefly delayed as a result of the catastrophic events in New York.

The mood at Meadow Lane was flat. The attacks on New York and Washington had shocked everyone, and while the teaching assistants remained in blissful ignorance as far as events at the school were concerned, the teaching staff exchanged knowing looks and wary glances as they gathered in the staff room.

Only with the arrival of the school bus and the appearance of a tear stained little Indian boy named Shiv at the staff room door did the more immediate consequences of events in New York, even for life at faraway Meadow Lane, begin to emerge.

'They kept calling me bin Laden'...Sir, 'Told me I was a terrorist', stammered the tearful and clearly terrified young boy. 'They said they're gonna put me in the big bin and set fire to it at break time,' he added breaking down again in entirely understandable floods of tears.

'We can't have this. We need an assembly,' announced Molly. 'I think Baggy should come up with something straight after registration.'

'Not possible I'm afraid,' interrupted Nicola Fullard, 'Mr. Bagshaw...' she continued, placing great emphasis upon both the honorific title and unabbreviated completeness of the Head teacher's name, '...and I have a 9.30 meeting at Area Office to discuss splitting the budget.'

'I hope that's not a euphemism?' commented Tom, to stifled sniggers from those who'd heard.

'I have no idea what you're talking about Mr. Clay,' replied Nicola with unknowing and equally untypical candour. 'But I can assure you that the Headmaster will not be available this morning.'

'Lawrie?' said Molly, '...something really needs to be said.'

Lawrie agreed. Shiv was one of the loveliest pupils he'd ever had the pleasure to teach. He excelled at virtually nothing but tried his hardest at everything. He had a 100% attendance record and always had a smile, though never a bad word, for everyone. He was, not that it really mattered, from a Hindu background and thus had nothing whatsoever to do with the targets of the Islamophobia that would spread like a cancer from the wreckage of the Twin Towers. Bill Bagshaw may have had other priorities, but Lawrie was damned if he was going to allow racist bullying to take a hold at Meadow Lane on top of everything else that day.

The assembly went well. Given his audience, Lawrie had had to strike a balance between explaining to some pupils that what they had seen on TV had actually been real life and not just yet another disaster movie scene, while also getting the message across that terrorists were very much a tiny minority who were not at all reflective of any particular religious or ethnic group and that picking on people at Meadow Lane because of anything to do with their colour or religion would not be tolerated.

Shiv beamed beatifically throughout the assembly, miraculously arriving at Lawrie's side at the end as if seeking one final validation...'I'm not one of them flippin' terrorists am I sir?'.

'Absolutely not, Shiv...in fact I don't know anyone who is less like a terrorist than you,' was Lawrie's reassuring and completely honest response.

At least he'd made one person happy that day.

During Assembly, Gloria had been able to take advantage of Bill and Nicola's 'absence' and had photocopied the letter which made a point of including the typed names of all the teaching staff in strictly alphabetical order, removing the possibility of any individual teacher being singled out as a ring leader.

By lunchtime all the teaching staff had signed and Archie wandered up to the *Vaults* where Jack Beckett had a pint waiting for him.

Lawrie's afternoon was spent in a Case Conference on the other side of the City which had been called after Amanda Knowles, a fifteen year old girl in his class, had disclosed to him that she was being abused by her grandfather. There was the usual mixture of police, social workers, parents (or in this case just a single mother) LEA legal representatives and, of course, a solicitor to act on behalf of the alleged offender.

There was always one of those and although Lawrie understood why they were needed. He also invariably left such meetings struggling to understand how people could earn their living by defending the indefensible. That afternoon had proved no exception and Lawrie only got back to Meadow Lane just as the school buses were leaving.

'So what now?' seemed to be the general sentiment amongst the teaching staff.

'Well someone has to give Baggy the letter,' said Molly, joining the consensus in not exactly pushing herself forward.

'Oh, for Christ's sake,' said an already agitated Lawrie, give it to me...I'll do it.'

'Don't you want Archie to go in with you?' asked Megan anxiously.

'Not unless we want to add bloodletting to the procedure' replied Lawrie, remembering the Union rep's reputation as something of an outspoken pugilist.

'Just give me the letter, I'll give it to him and I'll see you in the *Vaults* in about fifteen minutes.'

Lawrie knocked on the head teacher's door barely waiting for an answer before entering to find Bill standing at his desk with Nicola Fullard sitting to the side of him.

'What is it, Lawrie?' asked the slightly surprised Headmaster.

'I just wondered if I could have a word with you...in private.'

'No time for that now Lawrie...things to get on with and all that. I'm sure anything you've got to say can be said in front of Mrs. Fullard.'

'Well...' began Lawrie.

'Spit it out man. I haven't got all day.'

'Okay then', sighed Lawrie. 'Well, I'm sorry that it's had to come to this Bill, but there's something I have to give you,' said Lawrie as he passed across the envelope.

'What's all this then?' asked the now somewhat mystified headmaster. 'Not your bloody resignation is it?'

'Not exactly, no,' answered Lawrie looking his boss in the eyes.'It is something I think you need to look at now though.'

Bill Bagshaw's hand was shaking and his skin had visibly paled to match the greyness of his hair, by the time he had read the short missive from his staff.

He passed the letter to his new Business Manager almost automatically, as his mind struggled to deal with the implications of what he had just read...'*no confidence*... *integrity*...and *ability*...' were the words that kept going round in his head.

'Good grief...what...why... is there still time to talk about this?' were about all the disjointed words he could utter in response.

'Not really, no...' answered Lawrie '...and I think you know why. A copy of this letter was delivered to our Union at lunchtime today and will have been presented to Area Office by them this afternoon.'

'You bastard, Lawrie,' snarled Nicola Fullard loudly and in a voice filled with loathing as she rapidly began to digest the likely consequences of the teachers' action for her own 'position'. 'You're behind all this aren't you? You never was in favour of me being made Business Manager was you?' she continued, her anger and fury as ever betraying her grammatical limitations.

'I agree completely with the contents of the letter Nicola. Obviously I do...but I think you'll find it to have been signed by each and everyone on the teaching staff', replied Lawrie calmly. 'As for being *behind all this*...I'd suggest you look a little closer to home for that.'

'And what the hell is that meant to mean?' demanded Nicola.

'Not now, Nic', interrupted the remarkably resigned voice of Bill Bagshaw. 'Not now...' he repeated, all traces of his earlier bumptious arrogance having disappeared.

As he departed the office, leaving his head teacher sitting on the edge of the desk with his head in his hands wondering what to do next, Lawrie was surprised to find Tom and Molly sitting and waiting for him in the school's reception area.

'Sounds like that went well, mate,' observed Tom cheerily, having doubtless overheard the raised tones of Nicola Fullard. 'Doubt you'll be on *her* Christmas card list .'

'Yeah...well', added Molly with typical bluntness, 'If the silly bitch could've managed to keep her legs in the same postcode then maybe none of this would have happened!'

One or two of the staff were just leaving as Lawrie, Tom and Molly arrived in the car park at the *Jubilee Vaults*.

The others had been joined by Jack Beckett and all were anxious to hear what had gone on when Lawrie had handed over the letter to Bill Bagshaw.

'Not much to tell, really...he hadn't got a clue why I needed to see him, obviously hadn't seen it coming...asked if we could talk about it. I said things had gone too far...he seemed shocked and Nicola started shouting the odds a bit before Bill told her to pipe down,' reported Lawrie. 'I think we've all had better days but it needed doing and now it's done.'

'Question is...what happens next?' asked Archie.

'Well one thing's for sure,' replied Lawrie, 'There's sure as hell no going back now!'

Gloria, Tom, Archie, Molly and Lawrie had all hung around in the *Vaults* discussing further courses of action with Jack Beckett, still against a background of disturbing images of the destruction in New York City played out endlessly on the pub TV and interrupted only by the sporadic click of pool balls from an unseen table around the corner.

'Turn up for work exactly as normal, do your jobs exactly as you usually would and wait and see,' had been Jack's advice.

'Doesn't actually sound, from what you've all said, as if Mr. Bagshaw being there makes much difference one way or the other, but if the shit hits the fan Archie knows how to get hold of me. My guess is...' continued the Union rep '...that the Local Authority will be putting in an appearance in one form or another tomorrow morning. Probably send in Nancy Palmer for starters.'

'Oh great!' sighed Lawrie, his heart rapidly sinking.

As Lawrie arrived at Meadow Lane the following morning the first thing he noticed was that Bagshaw's latest car, a metallic black BMW 5 Series, was parked next to Nicola's silver MX-5 Convertible, rather betraying the likelihood that they had, very unusually, arrived both early and at much the same time.

By the time Lawrie had crossed the concourse area, where Tom and Molly had loyally waited like a pair of anxious parents the previous evening, Nicola Fullard had moved from the office to stand in the narrow staff corridor where she blocked Lawrie's path and virtually ordered him into Bill Bagshaw's office, as if by edict, spitting out the words, 'The Headmaster would like to see you now.'

'Here we go,' thought Lawrie, entering the inner sanctum, now cast in his new and unaccustomed role of villain.

'Mr. Utting,' said the Head, obviously and thankfully dispensing with any need for pleasantries. 'After the events of yesterday I shall be leaving the premises shortly. I have no idea how long for but until I return you will be in charge'.

'Not much change there then,' thought Lawrie to himself.

'Until then let's remember that all that now matters is the well being of the children', added the Headmaster.

Lawrie couldn't believe his ears. 'Excuse me?' he said.

'I think the Headmaster made it quite clear...' began Nicola Fullard. 'The only thing that matters to all of us now is the safety and well being of the pupils,' she continued, as if recalling lines from some sort of pre-prepared script.

'Well it's a pity you couldn't have thought of that before!' responded Lawrie, utterly incensed by this entirely unexpected exhibition of hypocritical self righteousness.

'Meaning what exactly?' demanded the Business Manager.

'Meaning this exactly...' replied Lawrie angrily '...and you'll be sorry to know that I've got more sense than to go into all the details right now, but if this school had not been being run for the betterment of you and your family and for the personal convenience of the bloody head teacher then we wouldn't be in this mess. So don't either of you dare start getting on your fucking high horses now with some sort of sanctimonious lecture about the wellbeing of the kids.'

With that Lawrie left the astonished pair, slamming the office door behind him, before striding up the corridor and into a stunned staff room where he suddenly remembered that, sound travels and he may well have been speaking very loudly.

LESSONS 9

1. Never judge a book by its cover. The same goes for secretaries and Chairs of Governors.
2. Being a whistleblower is hard and uncomfortable. Try and avoid entering into it alone and be aware that once you've started there's no going back.
3. Greed and dishonesty go hand in hand and often lead to complacency.

4. Unions can be a source of great comfort and advice. You never know when you may need them.
5. Bravery comes in many forms. Gloria Carney may have been a little lady and an ordinary teacher but she stood up to be counted when it mattered.
6. Don't put your name to something unless you're sure you're prepared to go through with it.

TEN

UNEASY LIES THE HEAD...

Since Debbie Mason had introduced a greater level of professionalism into the school than had ever seemed previously likely, it had become customary at Meadow Lane for each morning to begin with a fifteen minute briefing which served as an opportunity to go through the diary, discuss any specific child based issues to take account of during the day, and mention the prospect of any visitors who might be coming round. When present Bill Bagshaw would run the meeting, but in his unremarkable absence it was often Lawrie or Molly who would take control.

'What's going on?' asked one of the later arrivals amongst the teaching assistants. 'Mr. Bagshaw has just stormed off across the car park and taken off in his car with a face like thunder? He wouldn't even look at me when I said *good morning*.'

'It's seems that we do have a problem this morning...' answered Lawrie, '...and that the Head is unlikely to be in school today. Beyond that I really can't say, but we will be a man light as they say.'

'Better make that two,' added an elderly bus escort who doubled as a TA and had just arrived on the school bus...

'Mrs. Fullard has just zoomed off through the school gates as if her tail's on fire'.

'Splitting the budget again?' observed Tom wryly. This time nobody laughed.

Lawrie was about fifteen minutes into his first lesson of the day when Julie Cooper, the Business Manager's sister in law, or *'secretary's secretary'* as Tom had memorably christened her, put her head around his classroom door to say 'Mrs. Palmer would like a word, Mr. Utting.'

'Tell her I'll ring her back as soon as I get a moment, will you please Julie,' replied Lawrie who was busily engaged in some work on Michelle Magorian's classic wartime novel, *'Goodnight Mr. Tom'*, with a lively group of Year 10 pupils.

'I would...' answered the secretary, '...only...she's not on the phone...she's in the staffroom.'

'Ah...okay', answered Lawrie, sounding far calmer than he felt. 'In which case, can you explain that I'm teaching, but that I'll be with her as soon as I can, five minutes hopefully, ten at the most.'

Fortunately for Lawrie his teaching assistant in that particular lesson was Esther Jacobs. Lawrie knew she was sufficiently experienced and competent to see out what remained of the lesson, and having established what needed to be done he reminded the class that if Miss. Jacobs came to him with any complaints, then the culprits could expect to be spending their dinner hour with him doing their work all over again.

'Morning Nancy', said Lawrie as he walked into the staffroom...'Cup of tea...coffee?'

'Maybe later', answered the senior advisor who, if rumour was to be believed, was actively chasing an appointment as Acting Deputy Director. 'I think we need to get to the bottom of all this first...don't you? Is there somewhere we can go where we won't be disturbed? Mr. Bagshaw's office perhaps?

'Lawrie I have to say...' began Nancy as the two sat opposite each other across Bill Bagshaw's large, contemporary executive desk, '...that there are many in the Authority who have taken an exceedingly dim view of what has been happening at Meadow Lane.'

'I'm very glad to hear it...' answered Lawrie. 'There's been too much wrongdoing going on here for far too long...it couldn't be allowed to go on and....'

'I think,' interrupted Nancy Palmer, her eyebrows rising in tandem with the stridency of her tone, 'You misunderstand me Lawrie. It is precisely the manner in which this matter has been dealt with by the staff...the quite unnecessary involvement of the Union...and the secrecy involved in taking steps to remove a respected Headmaster that is the source of concern at Area Office!'

'Whoa!' interjected Lawrie. 'Hang on a minute...that's hardly fair...and since when was Bill Bagshaw a *respected* Head? He's been playing fast and loose with public money and running this place for his own convenience for as long as anyone can remember.'

'Mr. Utting!' cut in the advisor, beginning to live up to her inflammatory nickname.

'You shouldn't have to be reminded that I cannot have you making completely unsubstantiated allegations like that...it simply will not do...it is quite improper!'

'But, that's the point...they're not!' responded Lawrie.

'Not what?'

'Not bloody unsubstantiated!' continued Lawrie. 'Do you honestly believe that the teaching staff at Meadow Lane have nothing better to do than fabricate stories about someone to get rid of them? There is absolutely nothing that we have alleged that we haven't got evidence to substantiate. The fact that the teaching staff have chosen to no longer ignore matters which this Authority turns a blind eye to is not our fault and I don't need a lecture from anyone upon what has been *improper!*'

'Mr. Utting!'

By the time Lawrie had spelled out all the details of Bill Bagshaw's *activities*...his business sideline, the appointment of his best friend and a man with a conviction for fraud as Chair of Governors, his manipulation of the Finance Committee, his promotion of his secretary and paramour to Business Manager and the subsequent way in which no less than three of her family had benefitted from the Meadow Lane coffers...the Senior Advisor's incendiary inclinations had been well and truly extinguished.

'I'm sorry Lawrie,' said a suddenly more contrite Nancy Palmer. 'I honestly didn't know. There've been rumours of course, always are, and I've always thought of Mr. Bagshaw as being a little erm...eccentric, shall we say?'

'That's one word for him', replied Lawrie.

'Either way...' continued Nancy, waving a hand dismissively, 'The question is where we go from here.'

'Indeed', agreed Lawrie. 'The TA's and ancillary staff are still in the dark. We all need a sense of direction.'

'They weren't involved then?' queried Nancy.

'Couldn't be', answered Lawrie. 'We couldn't afford for things to get back to Nicola and Bill. This action only involved the teaching staff, doubtless some will know something given the friendships that exist, but there needs to be some sort of explanation.'

'I understand', said Nancy, almost sympathetically. 'In the

meantime we need you to take over the running of the school and I think I'll have to bring Simon in to address the whole staff at the beginning of next week.'

'Simon?' asked Lawrie.

'Yes, you know, Simon...Simon Wolf...the Deputy Director.' Lawrie couldn't actually claim to know him...but he had, most certainly, heard of him.

DARK ARTS

Simon Wolf was a man whose reputation preceded him. It was one he had built by successfully heading up a Maths Department in one of the city's bigger comprehensives, before following the advisory route as a means of escaping the classroom and establishing a potentially less stressful and more lucrative career working out of Area Office.

Always smartly suited and with prematurely greying hair, he'd been regarded as something of a 'silver fox' and rapidly risen to the position of Deputy Director. Now though, with only ten months to go until retirement, he'd followed the delusional path of so many men who find themselves 'follically challenged' in late middle age, and adopted the goatee and neat short ponytail look, swapping the appearance of successful accountant for one of hippy chic. The accountant look would have been a far truer reflection, but then truth and Simon Wolf, who was, unbeknown to most, a close friend of Bill Bagshaw, were unfamiliar bedfellows.

Nancy Palmer had done her best to stage manage proceedings so that by the time of the Monday afternoon meeting in the school hall, when all was expected to be explained to the whole staff, there looked to be clear signs of unity.

'You, of course, must sit alongside Simon and myself,' Nancy had virtually ordered Lawrie.

'Why's that?' asked a rather reticent Lawrie.

'Lawrie...you are likely to be Acting Head at Meadow Lane for the foreseeable future! As such it is important that the staff recognise that you and the Authority, in the form of Simon and myself, are singing from the same hymn sheet,' explained Nancy moving, a little patronisingly, into political animal mode.

Lawrie knew better than to argue at this particular point. He was however quite certain where his loyalties lay and saw little point in publicly aligning himself with someone he had no knowledge of and who, in turn, could have only the most limited understanding of the impact recent events had had at Meadow Lane.

The 'audience', made up of all the teaching staff, the vast majority of the TA's and other ancillary staff, along with a couple of parent Governors, quickly grew silent as the Deputy Director, rose to speak.

'Well good afternoon everyone...I have to say it is with the greatest sadness that I find myself speaking to you all in such circumstances here at Meadow Lane this afternoon', he began, sounding for all the world as if he was addressing some sort of funeral gathering.

'Mr. Bagshaw has, in my opinion, achieved great things in his many years of commitment to this school, a conclusion that, as has been noted by the LEA, your recent Ofsted inspection was happy to support.'

Flanked by Nancy to his right and Lawrie, a little more distantly to his left, the Deputy Director continued as if he was delivering some sort of eulogy and Lawrie couldn't help but notice the questioning raised eyebrows amongst many of the teaching staff as the accolades continued to flow

'Unfortunately however', continued the Deputy Director, 'Certain allegations have recently been brought to our attention, meaning that it now seems very unlikely that Mr. Bagshaw will be able to continue as Head teacher at Meadow Lane...'

At this point the words of the Deputy Director, which until that moment had been heard in total silence, were interrupted by the sudden scraping of chairs on the parquet flooring as two figures rose together, in almost synchronised harmony, and began to walk out of the hall.

'You've not heard the end of this. This is a total disgrace...it's nothing more than a stitch up...a witch hunt... and you lot...' spat out Nicola Fullard, her outstretched finger sweeping aggressively to include the whole of the teaching staff, '...are all in on it!'

With that Nicola and her sister Natalie stormed out of the hall, almost slamming the door off its hinges behind them.

'Seems to have taken it well', muttered Tom to Steve Archibald, as an uncomfortable murmur replaced the previous hush.

'As I was saying', continued a visibly chastened Simon Wolf, pausing only briefly for some sort of order to return... 'Unfortunately, as a result of the actions of a few of the staff here today, you all need to understand that it now appears very unlikely that Mr. Bagshaw will be returning to Meadow Lane...'

If Nancy Palmer had been ill prepared for the impact of Nicola and Natalie's dramatic exit upon her contrived display of unity, she was to be even more taken aback as Lawrie intervened.

'I'm sorry Mr. Wolf, but you seem to have been misinformed,' interrupted Lawrie.

Simon Wolf paused for a second time as Nancy Palmer looked daggers in Lawrie's direction.

'I'm not sure I understand,' said the Deputy Director, quietly.

'Apparently not...' continued Lawrie. 'It's just that you

referred to *a few of the staff here today*...which is simply incorrect. A letter of no confidence in Mr. Bagshaw was delivered from the whole of the teaching staff. It was an uncomfortable thing to do, but an action unanimously agreed by us all and signed by each and every one of us.'

'Yet not, it would appear, by any of the teaching assistants or ancillary staff,' responded Simon Wolf, in a tone which suggested he had just won a point that he'd never actually expected to be competing over.

'For exactly the reasons you have just seen an example of...,' replied Lawrie.

'The teaching staff had to keep the details of this action to themselves given the personnel involved amongst the teaching assistants and administrative staff. It was an extremely difficult and, for some, distressing thing to have to do, but you've just witnessed the reason why. Of course, if you wish to open up this meeting now to discuss what motivated the teaching staff to take the actions we have I'm sure we'll be very willing to explain.'

'Forty fifteen', whispered Tom Clay, to anyone near enough to hear.

'I don't think that will be necessary now,' interrupted an agitated and anxious looking Nancy Palmer to murmurs of disappointment amongst the TA's. 'What matters right now is where we go from here.'

'Indeed', continued the Deputy Director, who did not take kindly to being disagreed with and was still recovering from finding himself in the unlikely position of receiving criticism from both sides of the dispute.

'What needs to be understood now is that, as I've been trying to say, Mr. Bagshaw will almost certainly not be returning to Meadow Lane. In the short term...' (prior to Lawrie's interruption he was going to say *for the foreseeable future* but could no longer bring himself to do so) '...Mr.

Utting will be Acting Head of the school and an entirely new Governing Body are shortly to be sworn in.'

'As I've already intimated, personally I very much regret that such actions have had to be taken but I believe these steps are in the best interests of all at the school. Now, if there are no further questions?'

Of course there were many further questions, but professionals like Simon Wolf knew enough about orchestration and intimidation to be able to avoid the potential pitfalls of allowing such inquisition during any sort of public forum.

'Was that absolutely necessary?' demanded a clearly irate Nancy Palmer following the Deputy Director's departure.

'Well yes, in my opinion it was.' replied Lawrie. 'I'm not sure which, but either he'd been genuinely misled or he was making a deliberate attempt to belittle the actions of the teaching staff in that meeting,' continued Lawrie forcefully. 'Either way there was no need for it, it was likely to cause further division amongst the staff and was totally disrespectful as regards the actions the teaching staff have been forced to take.'

'I'll tell you what, Lawrie...' said Nancy spitefully, '...sometimes I think you're more cut out to be some sort of Union Rep. than a potential Head!'

'And I'll tell you something too, Mrs. Palmer...I'd take being a Union Official over a crooked head teacher or some complicit LEA official any day of the week,' replied Lawrie venomously.

The next day passed off peacefully enough. The LEA hadn't seen fit to bring in any cover so Lawrie still had to manage the majority of his morning teaching timetable while using the afternoon to deal with more administrative matters the first of which had been introduced by a knock on the door and the arrival of Julie Cooper...the *secretary's secretary*...or as things had now transpired, just *'The Secretary'*.

'I know you're probably very busy Mr. Utting...but I wonder if I could have a word,' asked a seemingly chastened Julie.

'It's just that I need to know where I stand', she continued.

'I'm not entirely sure I'm going to be able to answer that...'answered Lawrie, feeling horribly out of his depth but appreciative of the fact that at least Julie hadn't been part of the faux exhibition of rage and unrighteous indignation from the previous evening. 'Grab a seat and I'll tell you as much as I'm able.'

'I know it all looks bad, Mr. Utting...' began Julie, clearly close to tears, '...but I don't think I've done anything wrong. Our Nicola told me about the job coming up and she said that Mr. Bagshaw had asked if she knew anyone who might be suitable. I don't know anything about what they've been getting up to, don't want anything to do with all that, but I do like this job, I am qualified and I don't want to be out of work again.'

While all too uncomfortably aware of the fact that he might well be encouraging some sort of 'spy in the camp' situation, Lawrie couldn't help but feel sorry for Julie who, despite being an undeniable beneficiary of nepotism, quite probably and just as she'd implied, might not have actually done anything wrong.

'To be honest Julie I'm not quite sure what to say,' answered Lawrie, deciding that common sense and honesty probably represented the best policy.

'Given these difficult circumstances I do appreciate you coming in to work today and coming to see me this afternoon, but it would be wrong of me to try and give you any reassurances at this point,' continued Lawrie, seriously hoping that his words were not going to lead to the young woman's tearful breakdown.

'At this precise moment we can't be sure what the situation is as regards the futures of Mr. Bagshaw or Nicola and Natalie. That will be a matter for Area Office and, I imagine, *'Personnel'*, but as far as you're concerned, I'd be grateful if, for the time being and as long as you're happy to do so, you could just carry on with your work and I'll do my best to try and get some clearer guidance from Mrs. Palmer, Mr. Wolf and the new Governors.'

Lawrie hoped his response hadn't transgressed any rules. He'd answered as honestly as he could and, for the time being at least, Julie seemed consoled and had remained, thankfully, tear free.

The Governors meeting wasn't due to commence until 6.00 p.m.and Lawrie was deep in conversation with Gloria and Esther, the two school based governors, when he spotted a power dressed Nancy Palmer walking purposefully across the car park.

'Oh God, here we go...*Napalm's* just landed', announced Lawrie. 'Wonder what fire and brimstone she's got in store for us this time.'

'Evening Lawrie', said Nancy Palmer as Lawrie opened the front door for her. 'How did your first day go?'

'Well, as you can see, we're still standing,' answered Lawrie, 'Although there are a couple of personnel issues that need addressing.'

'Personnel?' repeated Nancy...'Don't you mean Human Resources?'

'Yes I suppose I might,' responded Lawrie dismissively,

showing Nancy into the room he was still struggling to regard as *his* office. 'Either way, I've had Julie Cooper in to see me this afternoon. She's very anxious over what is to happen with her job'

'I sincerely hope you didn't contribute in any way to that anxiety, Lawrie', answered the Senior Advisor, clearly identifying the possibility of yet another potential staffing crisis at Meadow Lane and seeking to immediately apportion blame elsewhere.

'Of course not,' said Lawrie. 'I simply said that I appreciated the effort she'd made today but that, as yet, I didn't know what would be happening with either her, Nicola, Natalie or Bill Bagshaw and that I'd endeavour to find out more this evening.

'Well as far as Natalie is concerned, that's easy,' replied Nancy. She resigned this morning. Probably realised she hadn't been in post long enough to make anything out of prolonging matters so she's gone...not at all complimentary about you though.'

'I'll live with it,' laughed Lawrie ruefully. 'What about the others?'

'Mrs. Fullard went off sick this morning', answered Nancy, '...and Mr. Bagshaw is in consultation with his Association so we'll know more later. As for Mrs. Cooper, again we'll know more once HR have had more time...let's just say I doubt that a sacking is likely to be in order.'

Just at that moment there was a knock at the door as it opened almost simultaneously, allowing a grey bearded and pony tailed head to peer into the office.

'Ah, Nancy...er, Mr. Utting, there you are. Allow me to introduce Alan Haynes, our new Chair of Governors...' announced a smiling Simon Wolf.

Although Lawrie was only too aware that the new Chair of Governors was more than likely to be a local authority stooge, put there in all probability, to ensure both that things didn't get even further out of hand and that a lid was kept on the potentially extremely embarrassing events at Meadow Lane, he couldn't help but quickly warm to the man.

The other two governors, a slightly severe looking woman called Jenny and a teacher and local councillor, who Lawrie estimated to be in her early forties, named Sue also seemed decent enough.

Simon Wolf called the meeting, which was being hosted in Lawrie's classroom, to order and explained, after everyone had introduced themselves, that he would provide a brief introduction before handing things over into the capable hands of Alan Haynes.

'We have a very complex, sensitive and possibly quite unprecedented situation here this evening where the previous Chair, erm...Mr...Donovan, has relinquished his position along with Mrs. Lowe, one of the parent governors, and of course the Clerk to the Governors, Mrs. Nicola Fullard, is also unavailable,' began the Deputy Director. 'In addition we are also, of course, without the long established Headmaster of Meadow Lane, Mr. Bagshaw and, as part of our effort to address at least two of those issues, Mr. Lawrence Utting has stepped up to become Acting Head and Mr. Alan Haynes has been invited to replace Mr. Donovan as the new Chair.'

'Have steps been taken against Mr. Donovan and Mr. Bagshaw yet?' asked Gloria Carney with rather more urgency than was necessary.

'I'm afraid I'm not in a position to comment on that,' replied Simon Wolf, before adding brusquely, '...and I'd further advise that such matters are no longer the concern of this Governing body.'

'Seems strange,' said Lawrie, earning a reproachful look

from Nancy Palmer. 'I mean that's why half of us are here isn't it? I'm only here because Bill Bagshaw has been suspended and we only have a new Chair because the previous one was shown to have a criminal record and to be in cahoots with the Head and Business Manager.'

'Mr. Utting!' began Nancy Palmer, her imminent explosion curtailed by the intervention of her immediate senior.

'If I might be allowed to continue,' asserted Simon Wolf. 'Firstly Mr. Bagshaw has not been officially suspended, secondly this Mr. Donovan would currently appear to be out of the country and thirdly there is absolutely no evidence of anyone being in *cahoots*, as you put it, with anyone else.'

'Really?' replied Lawrie, vaguely aware of Gloria touching his arm in a subtle attempt to suggest that discretion might be called for. 'You have to be joking...have you not heard anything that has been said to you about what has been going on here?'

'*Allegedly*...been going on here...' said Simon Wolf by way of clinical correction, '...and I can assure you Mr. Utting,' he added, his words becoming ever more menacingly staccato, 'That I never, ever, joke about such matters.'

'Finally,' said the Deputy Director, 'I have to add that you, or any other member of staff must now understand that it would be extremely unwise to go about making further allegations without the necessary proof. Allegations, we should remember, are one thing...*proven* facts quite another, and on that note I'll take my leave with the hope that this group will be able to look to the future of the school rather than dwell on the events of the past. I'm sure Mrs. Palmer will be happy to report back to me in the morning,' he concluded as a parting shot aimed, it was assumed by all, primarily in the direction of Lawrie.

For all that Lawrie recognised that Alan Haynes had been put in post to protect the interests of the Local Authority he also saw a decent and capable man who, for absolutely nothing in terms of financial reward, was making a huge time commitment towards the well being of the school.

Alan exhibited none of the antagonism shown by Simon Wolf and moved smoothly through the rest of the meeting drawing attention to the necessity for a new Clerk to be found, the election of replacement parent governors and, somewhat surprisingly, his personal desire for the teaching staff to have their *'brave whistle blowing actions'* acknowledged by the local council.

At the end of the meeting he was happy to actively seek out Gloria, Esther and Lawrie with a tone that was, in direct contrast to that of those representing the LEA, conciliatory, sympathetic and optimistic about the future.

The same could not be said for Nancy Palmer who loitered with intent throughout and, knowing that Lawrie would have to wait for everyone to leave before he could eventually lock up, was clearly waiting for an opportunity to catch him alone.

'This really can't go on,' Lawrie, opened Nancy.

'What's that?' answered Lawrie wearily.

'You've got to let things go. What's done is done. You can't keep dredging things up.

Bill Bagshaw's not likely to return, Donovan appears to be somewhere in the South of France and there's little chance of Mrs. Fullard returning to post either. You've won Lawrie.'

'Right,' said Lawrie. 'So *not likely to return* and *little chance of returning* are meant to be reassuring in your book are they...because they sure as hell aren't in mine!'

'Oh, for Christ's sake grow up, Lawrie!' exploded the Senior Advisor, acutely aware of the personal need for her to furnish Simon Wolf with positive news the following morning. 'Shit happens...and it's time to move on. More to the point...if you want your application for the Headship at Meadow Lane to be taken seriously you need to recognise that...and pretty damned quick!'

Track 35. 'There Goes the Fear'. Doves.

Lawrie was shocked at the brazenness of this attempt to silence him and have him toe the line.

'But I don't, Nancy,' he replied.

'What do you mean...you don't?' replied the Senior Advisor sneeringly. 'You don't what?'

'I don't want my application for the Headship to be taken seriously because I have absolutely no intention of making one...never have had.'

A stunned Nancy Palmer regarded her adversary with a look of incredulity tinged with something between pity and contempt.

'This has never been about me, Nancy. Yes, I've belatedly played a leading role in exposing the wrongdoing at Meadow Lane and hopefully getting rid of those who were responsible, but that was never with the intention of me taking over,' continued Lawrie to his disbelieving audience of one.

'I've never actually wanted to be a Head, some of them are amongst the finest people I've ever come across but, to be brutally honest, far too many seem like a bunch of self important and self obsessed shits. Either way...' continued Lawrie, recognising that Nancy Palmer had played her last card, '...I've got a school to secure and we've got about three minutes to exit the building once I've set this alarm, so if you'd like to wait outside for a moment I'll be happy to walk you to your car.'

Just for once Nancy Palmer was completely lost for words.

1. People in positions of authority often seek to cover up examples of wrongdoing that may reflect badly upon them and institutions/authorities will stop at little to protect themselves.

2. People in positions of power are also all too often experts in the area of dishonest subterfuge. Given this apparent all too common occurrence amongst so many of our current leading politicians this should come as no great surprise but, when you find yourself right in the middle of it, somehow it still does.

3. There will come times when you have to fight 'fire with fire'.

4. Knowing one's strengths and weaknesses and ignoring ambition for its own sake can be both liberating and enormously empowering.

ELEVEN

CORRUPTION, COMPLICITY
AND COMPROMISE

Track 36. 'Don't Know Why'. Norah Jones.

Lawrie was to remain in post as Acting Head at Meadow Lane from September through to the following Easter.

Nicola Fullard remained on long term sick leave and few would ever know what the NAHT made of Bill Bagshaw's defence, but he was never to be seen within the vicinity of Meadow Lane ever again.

Alan Haynes had been true to his word, leading to the teaching staff being openly thanked in the council chamber for their 'public spirited' actions. Julie Cooper remained in position as the school secretary, basically because the Authority was reluctant to open yet another can of worms, and things ran remarkably smoothly with the school benefitting from regular assemblies for the first time in years and a Head teacher, albeit only of the 'acting' variety, who was actually on site most of the time.

Attendance at Heads' Meetings did little to dissuade Lawrie with regard to his opinion of that particular breed. A couple of the secondary Heads proved a helpful exception, along with Carmen Doyle, the recently appointed Head at St.

Anthonys, who Lawrie's wife, Lisa, spoke particularly highly of. By and large though, Lawrie was astonished at the amount of time wasted in Heads' meetings as in-jokes and back slapping complacency seemed to dominate proceedings and 'delegation' appeared to be as treasured a word as it was a much favoured strategy.

Lawrie wondered what the correct collective noun for a group of Head teachers might be, before finally concluding to himself that it was probably a *'conceit'*.

Curiously the most disruptive event of Lawrie's two term tenure was to arise from the opposite end of the personnel spectrum, with the prolonged absence of the school caretaker.

Caretakers are frequently a law unto themselves. They also however fulfil a number of particularly vital functions, as Lawrie would rapidly discover when the freshly appointed and somewhat morose example at Meadow Lane announced that he had been *signed off* for at least three weeks as a result of his notorious 'bad back'.

To what extent the condition was genuine, or an attempt at causing disruption, out of some sort of misplaced loyalty to Bill Bagshaw, would never be known. When Lawrie suddenly found himself having to open up early each day, remain on site each evening until the cleaners had finished, spend forty five minutes first thing each morning running checks for Legionnaire's disease, assume responsibility for a cumbersome bunch of about forty horribly identical looking keys and regularly climb on to the school's roof to retrieve misdirected balls, he rapidly developed a greater respect for the responsibilities of caretaking than he perhaps displayed towards his more illustrious, albeit only temporary, professional peers.

It was then with neither any great reluctance, nor immense feeling of relief, that Lawrie relinquished his responsibility as Head of Meadow Lane by the time of the Easter break. Nothing dreadful had happened. Lawrie and Molly had effectively shared the previously contentious position of responsibility for Child Protection. No pupils had been lost, no staff had threatened resignation and the books had balanced at the end of the financial year, a feat which Lawrie considered to be possibly his most surprising achievement given the situation he'd inherited six months earlier.

There had been four candidates for the job of full time Head and Lawrie was particularly pleased that it had eventually gone to the one he would have chosen on the evidence he had garnered whilst conducting the traditional tour of the school.

Phil Kershaw was a couple of years younger than Lawrie, which was to be a first in terms of having a younger boss. Curiously, as these things so often are, Phil had grown up in the same Lancashire mill town, although where Lawrie had found himself going down the Grammar school route, Phil was a product of the local 'Technical College'.

'Our teachers used to tell us we'd have done just as well as you lot if we'd written on't' same fancy paper,' joked Phil who, still having family in the town, had retained more of the rolling rhoticity of his native Lancastrian accent.

'Aye lad...and just look at thee now,' replied Lawrie, laughing. 'Yon

Techie's only gone and become t'bloomin' mill owner!'

Lawrie and Phil hit it off together really well. As a newcomer, to both the city as well as the school, there were numerous occasions when Lawrie, given his infinitely greater knowledge of the pupils, their backgrounds and the neighbourhoods they came from, had to act as a guide for his new boss.

On the other hand Phil was clearly light years ahead of Lawrie as far as both preparing the school for future inspection and the whole process of 'networking', in order to raise funds and build contacts from which the school would go on to benefit, were concerned.

Within months a new enclosed games area had been created in the playground, creating a safer area for those who didn't enjoy the *survival of the fittest* mentality of break time ball games. It was all done through sponsorship, which didn't cost the school a penny, and Phil had also given up the comparative luxury of his office to move into a smaller room, allowing the former Head teacher's office to be used as a much needed meeting room.

For the two Lancastrians it was a relationship built on mutual respect. They formed a good team, seeing completely eye to eye in terms of both what the aims of the school should be and what their expectations of the pupils were. Phil made no secret of the fact that he wanted Lawrie to formally apply for the post of Deputy Head, but the shadow of Bill Bagshaw was to once more cast a long shadow over Meadow Lane.

THE SPECTRE AT THE FEAST

It was mid September, and approaching a year since anything had been heard of Bill Bagshaw, when Megan and Molly took a seat either side of Lawrie one morning in an otherwise largely empty staffroom.

'You're not gonna believe this!' announced Molly.

'Believe what? What are you talking about Mol?' asked a puzzled Lawrie.

'Bill bloody Bagshaw!' declared Molly, thrusting some papers into Lawrie's hand.

'They've only gone and let him become a damned Ofsted Inspector!' explained Megan.

'Give over...that can't be right, he's a discredited Head...they're not going to let him join Ofsted,' said an astonished Lawrie.

'Read it,' shrugged Molly. 'Certainly seems like he's been welcomed with open arms to me.'

Molly and Megan were right, and there in front of Lawrie was the evidence. A report from a secondary school in Nottingham, describing the makeup of the Inspection team including a certain Bill Bagshaw, who boasted of 'twenty one years experience of Headship', and who appeared to be largely responsible for inspecting the Geography department.

'Geography! He's never taught a lesson of geography in his fucking life,' said a shocked Lawrie, suddenly realising the need to moderate both his language and its volume as the staffroom began to fill up.

'Never mind that,' said Molly, resorting to an untypical whisper, 'It's not what he's inspecting but the fact that he's bloody inspecting at all that matters! So what are we going to do about it?'

Track 37. 'Wake Me Up When September Ends'. Green Day.

Gloria Carney had completed her four year spell as a teacher governor by the end of the previous school year. She'd had more than enough of Governors' Meetings and, given his performance during the original crisis (together with the fact that absolutely no one else wanted to accept the role) the teaching staff had asked Lawrie to take over.

Although aware that Nicola Fullard's future was still to be

properly resolved, Lawrie had never expected the issue of his former Headmaster to resurface and felt thoroughly despondent at the prospect of dragging all this up again with the new Governors and, in all probability, the Local Authority.

The teaching staff, this time openly supported by many of the TA's, were outraged at the news and utterly adamant that something had to be done.

Phil Kershaw though wasn't best pleased. As far as he was concerned this was a distraction from the past and something both he and Meadow Lane could well do without. The last thing he wanted was his teaching staff, and more especially his second in command, sidetracked by something like this, and yet he recognised the extent to which Lawrie and the rest of the staff felt aggrieved and that his passive support for their actions was, in the circumstances, to be both a practical and a moral requirement.

Lawrie's first task was to compose a letter, again to be approved and signed by the whole staff, outlining their concerns. The letter centred around three questions.

1. *How can someone who has acted in such a way and brought our profession into such disrepute now be empowered to sit in judgement over other honest, decent and committed professionals?*

2. *How did someone who left their employment in such circumstances gain a reference allowing them to join the Ofsted inspectorate?*

3. *Should it not be recognised, that by enlisting such a wrongdoer into a body which represents the supposed watchdogs and guardians of the education system, that the whole integrity and credibility of that system is now being brought into question?*

Copies of the letter were then sent to Phil, Alan Haynes, the Director of Education, and Jack Beckett, while both

Lawrie and Esther ensured that the matter appeared on the agenda of the first Governor's meeting of the new school year.

Both the new Chair of Governors and the even more recently appointed Head of the school appeared sympathetically, if somewhat reservedly, supportive of the staff's actions. Neither had any knowledge of the individuals involved, nor any firsthand experience of what the teaching staff had gone through. They were both, understandably, far more concerned with moving the school forward, but equally they fully recognised the staff concerns and the depth of feeling that the recent revelations had provoked.

A stony faced Nancy Palmer, who Lawrie was somewhat surprised to find in attendance at the first Governor's Meeting of the year, was not so even handed.

Following the retirement and departure of Simon Wolf, *NaPalm* was now in the position of Acting Deputy Director and the last thing she needed was yet another uprising from the troublesome staff at Meadow Lane.

'As you will recognise, I've invited a representative of the LEA to attend this evening in order to address the issues in item 3 on the agenda,' began Alan Haynes.

'I'd suggest, in order to save Mrs. Palmer's doubtless precious time, that we move straight to that item now in order that we may detain her for no longer than absolutely necessary...Lawrie, may I ask you to explain the situation so that the rest of the governors are fully conversant with the staff concerns.'

Taken a little by surprise, Lawrie rapidly shuffled the paperwork work in front of him and described how the details of Bill Bagshaw's appointment had come to light, before reading out the more salient details from the letter and describing the shock and concern that had been caused.

Esther had nodded approvingly throughout Lawrie's description and summing up of the situation, but it appeared that his carefully chosen words had not gone down at all well with the potential Deputy Director.

'Firstly I have to say that I'm both surprised and disappointed to find the staff still preoccupied with a matter that, as far as this school is concerned, was concluded almost a year ago,' began Nancy Palmer.

'In the intervening period this school has benefitted from a huge amount of support from the LEA and it really is no business of either the staff or the Governors at Meadow Lane to now concern themselves with what an ex employee has since chosen to do,' continued Nancy placing great emphasis on the prefix '*ex*'.

'So...erm... where did his reference come from?' asked Esther hesitantly, untypically picking up the gauntlet and simultaneously earning Lawrie's approval.

'I have absolutely no idea Mrs...erm...'

'Jacobs...and it's Miss,' answered Esther, '...and I'm only asking because, seeing as Mr. Bagshaw has worked here for about the last twenty five years, it's hard to understand where a reference could have come from if it wasn't from Area Office.'

'Yes well...' began a clearly flustered Nancy Palmer who, like Lawrie, had only anticipated one likely avenue of attack. 'However, as I was saying, I have no idea where Mr. Bagshaw obtained his reference from. It most certainly wasn't from me and frankly it's no business of either yours or mine'.

'So you're saying the LEA should accept no responsibility when known wrongdoers and former employees manage to infiltrate their way into positions of responsibility for which they are wholly unsuited?' interrupted Lawrie, suspecting correctly that Esther's most welcome, if surprisingly unguarded, intervention had probably run its course.

'I'm not saying any such thing!' responded Nancy angrily. 'What I am saying is that there is no proof that Mr. Bagshaw was, as you repeatedly and tiresomely describe him, a '*wrong-*

doer', and that it is none of your business, or for that matter anyone else's at Meadow Lane, how he chooses to earn his living as he no longer has any connection with this school.'

'Furthermore,' announced the Deputy Director, now fully living up to her nickname as she crescendoed her way to the denouement of her delivery, 'I would remind you all, as employees of this Authority, that...just like Mr. Bagshaw himself...you are bound by the conditions of the compromise agreement and that this must be an end of the matter!'

'Compromise agreement?' queried a puzzled Alan Haynes.

'Indeed, Mr. Chairman,' answered a temporarily more deferential Nancy Palmer.

'I knew nothing of this.'

'With respect, why would you?' responded Nancy. 'Strictly speaking, Mr. Bagshaw had left the school before you joined the Governors. The compromise agreement was something arrived at between the Director, Human Resources, Simon Wolf and Mr. Bagshaw himself.'

'Oh great!' announced Lawrie, his tone heavily laced with sarcasm. 'So...short of being a paedophile...a Headmaster breaks just about every rule in the book, but his mates in Area Office protect themselves by covering for him so that he's now allowed to sit in judgement on others with absolute impunity. Isn't that what you're really saying?'

'Mr. Utting! You simply cannot say things like that and I will not warn you again!' said the enraged Acting Deputy Director, a combination of indignation and shrieking stridency now threatening the classroom windows.

'Lawrie...' growled Phil Kershaw in a barely audible whisper, 'Tread carefully my friend, you're not going to win this one.'

'What I can say,' announced an almost schizophrenically transformed Nancy Palmer, 'Is that a resolution has now thankfully been reached regarding Mrs. Fullard's future.

There is no longer any possibility of her returning to Meadow Lane, and on that hopefully happier note...', she continued, with that apparently seamless mood change that only politicians and the emotionally sterile appear to have truly mastered, '...I believe my contribution to this meeting to be complete.'

RESOLUTION

Track 38. 'Killing the Blues' Robert Plant and Alison Krause.

The staff were not at all happy when Lawrie and Esther fed back to them about the conditions of the compromise agreement, which appeared to prohibit any one from making further public comments about all that had gone on without putting their job at risk.

They were however delighted to learn that there was no chance of Nicola Fullard returning, a view secretly shared by Julie Cooper.

The fact that Nicola went on to work at Area Office didn't go down well at Meadow Lane either, but at least she never set foot in the place again which was sufficient consolation for most.

Nancy Palmer was promoted to the position of Deputy Director of Education by the end of that October.

Michael Donovan, having again been found guilty, this time of fraud, forgery and conspiring to pervert the course of justice served another short jail term before disappearing off to his holiday home in Vaison-la-Romaine in the beautiful Vaucluse region of Provence, coincidentally close to Simon Wolf's lavish barn conversion on the outskirts of Carpentras.

Gloria, Molly and Lawrie all received phone calls from such local press publications as the Leicester Mercury, Nottingham Post and Birmingham Mail asking if they had any comment to make on the case of their former Head who was apparently now an Ofsted Inspector. All too aware of the compromise agreement, along with *NaPalm's* none too veiled threats and being conscious of the mouths to feed and the offspring to put through University, they all opted reluctantly to decline.

As for Bill Bagshaw, he took part in a further ten Ofsted inspections before a report appeared in the Times Educational Supplement asking how a 'failed Head' could be *'Unfit to lead but able to inspect?'*

No one knew the source of the information but it reported on 'out of date or missing documentation, chaotic finances and weak leadership while Mr. Bagshaw was head.' A spokeswoman for Ofsted went on to say that *'only individuals who are fit, proper, competent and effective may remain as an inspector'*. If only they'd known the whole truth!

Meadow Lane thrived under Phil Kershaw's leadership and, despite the belated efforts of the new Deputy Director, Lawrie was officially appointed to the position of Deputy Head and would go on to be described, in the school's next Ofsted inspection, as an *'excellent role model for staff and students alike'*.

Lawrie thoroughly enjoyed his time working alongside Phil Kershaw. His work in the areas of Residential Activities and the Youth Award Scheme went from strength to strength and he devised a popular 14-16 English curriculum around such texts as *'Danny the Champion of the World'*, *'Goodnight Mr. Tom'*, *'Oliver Twist'*, *'The Book Thief'*, *'Romeo and Juliet'*, *'Macbeth'* and, of course, *'A Kestrel for a Knave'*.

Winning non academic pupils over to the virtues of Shakespeare was never going to be easy, although designing schemes that involved Baz Luhrmann's Los Angeles based version of the battle between the Capulets and Montagues and Polanski's 'Macbeth', starring a very young Martin Shaw and a scantily clad Francesca Annis, hopefully helped.

It was however a sixteen year old, hard as nails, pupil called John Sims who would have the last word.

Even at that early stage in life John's future as a brick layer was virtually mapped out. The son of a builder, John cared for little else, other than football, fishing and Gabriella Carter, a sixteen year old classmate who he would eventually settle down and have three children with.

He was seldom a problem but it was as difficult to imagine John ever being won over by the delights of *'the bard'* as it was Lawrie ever producing a perfectly constructed brick wall. Indeed, in both cases, Einstein's advice about *'never judging a fish by its ability to climb a tree'* had seldom seemed more relevant.

As the group reached the conclusion of their topic on Macbeth, John Sims looked towards Lawrie and said, 'It's all about greed innit Sir? About never bein' 'appy with what you've got.'

'That's brilliant...absolutely spot on, John,' agreed the surprised and delighted teacher and, as Gabriella beamed her approval, Lawrie considered how John Sims might have taught a few adults at Meadow Lane a thing or two over recent years.

For Lawrie that brief appraisal from the would be teenage bricklayer meant more than any Ofsted report.

LESSONS 11

1. Never underestimate the value of a capable caretaker.
2. Those in power and authority often seek to hide the search for truth behind convenient legislation

and filibustering. Compromise and Non-Disclosure Agreements can be a good example of this.

3. Despite the accuracy of the statement immediately above, with determination and unity the 'truth will out'...sometimes. Without them it will remain forever hidden.

4. Try not to go it alone and remember that there are times when, as Ron Sherwood had wisely pointed out, discretion is indeed the better part of valour. Lawrie sometimes struggled with that last bit!

5. 'Out of the mouths of babes...'. Lawrie and John Sims seemed to understand more about greed and misplaced ambition than Macbeth, Nancy Palmer and Bill Bagshaw put together.

6. Truth is stranger than fiction. Or is it?

7. All it takes for wrongdoing to prosper is for good men, and women, to do nothing...but then you should have learned that already.

TWELVE

POSTSCRIPT

Track 39. 'Human'. The Killers.

Lawrie and Lisa had been together for well over forty years. By the time they retired they had over sixty five years of teaching experience between them and had brought up four children.

Lisa had been Lawrie's 'rock' throughout the difficult and frequently stressful years at Meadow Lane and their three sons had all witnessed and experienced enough to know that there had to be easier, and almost certainly more lucrative, ways of earning a living than teaching in the twenty first century.

Their daughter Zara however had, for reasons best known to herself, ignored all the evidence, and followed her parents' example.

Having qualified and completed her probationary year, Zara, showing far greater imagination and courage than either of her parents all those years ago, sought to put her newly acquired skills to good use in rediscovering the Italy she had grown to love during family holidays in North East

Italy and Tuscany, and spent four rewarding years working in two schools in Verona and Pisa.

Encouraged to return to England by a not so unusual combination of love, money and the need to pursue a more clearly defined career path, Zara hadn't followed the comparatively easy route presented by some of the employment opportunities available in the less challenging village schools.

Rather she had opted for the '*making a difference*' approach in poorer 'inner city' schools where neither Lawrie nor Lisa, for all their experience at the 'sharp end' of education, could fully comprehend some of the difficulties she now faced in the brave new educational world to be discovered some half a century on from her father's first tentative steps into Edgemoor Primary .

Thinking back to his own experience Lawrie could remember times when Meadow Lane had suddenly *acquired* dispossessed children from the aftermath of successive conflicts in the Balkans. Such unfortunate children had often been enormously damaged by either the way they had been treated or the atrocities they had no capacity to '*unsee*', and had arrived at the school both traumatised and with virtually nothing in terms of spoken English.

Such understandable limitations certainly made the practice of teaching harder but the school had benefited from the input provided by a Bosnian speaking youth worker and, to provide further perspective, at Meadow Lane such instances had been relatively few and far between. In comparison, at Zara's school, the pupil population was made up of children with no less than nineteen different home languages.

These of course may be best described as 'mother tongue' languages. Many of the children spoke better English than their parents, leading to the school having to introduce a 'translation team' of children to help settle in new entrants and communicate with parents. Even so, at the beginning of the school year in 2019 the school's crucial Y6 group had six pupils join with no English language skills at all and Lawrie and Lisa couldn't help but wonder how the advisors, politicians and inspectors would have dealt with that particular set of circumstances.

Lawrie could only concede that such a scenario would have been unimaginable during his fifty years of experience within the education system as either, pupil, student or teacher and he saw it is an enormous credit, to both pupils and teachers alike, that they had managed to create a positive out of such a potentially problematic situation.

Barry Hines wrote many years ago, *'Education reflects the system, rather than changes it. People say it's an instrument of social change; well if it is it's a bloody slow one. I think education reflects the class system, and the system has to change before education can.'*

Some things appeared to have changed beyond all recognition from the educational landscape that Lawrie had left behind and Zara had inherited. There is now obviously a much heavier reliance upon technology within the classroom and the LEA's input has been drastically reduced to the extent that over 75% of secondary schools and around 35% of primary schools are now run by Academy Trusts or the more grandly named, Multi Academy Trusts.

Yet despite all that, some things never change. The best thing about teaching for Zara would still be *'making a difference'*, particularly to those children who suffered the greatest levels of deprivation. The worst would remain the unhelpful interference from *'above'*, be that in the form of Government ministers, inspectors, advisors or sometimes parents, who would all happily identify faults but then offer little, if anything, in terms of resources, ideas or solutions regarding how to provide a remedy. Above all perhaps there still remains a system of knowledge and control which applies status and kudos to so called 'academic' knowledge but all too often places practical skills in the category of low brow 'also rans'.

Having inherited both her mother's work ethic and determination, along with Lawrie's stubborn inability to allow
bullying and wrongdoing to go unchallenged, Zara was never
going to be one to allow certain things to go unremarked
upon. In her first fifteen years of teaching she had come
across seven head teachers of which she only considered two,
her first and her most recent, to have been truly up to
the job.

Of the rest one appeared to have been hired, in a helpfully
named *'failing school'*, with the express aim of driving all the
existing staff away, one was a bully who was also suspected
of interfering with the SATS papers and the others were a
collection of often lovely people, who had performed well as
classroom teachers but appeared to have extraordinarily
limited ability as far as the business of actual school leadership was concerned.

These were the Heads, and indeed LEA officials who, in
Lawrie's opinion, appeared to have benefitted from *'The Peter
Principle'*, to have risen to what might best be described as
their 'level of incompetence' as a result of earning promotion
via an unhealthy combination of unbridled opportunist ambition and perceived success in roles that now required an
entirely different skill set.

Lawrie estimated that in the half century of his involvement in education he had come into contact with between
forty and fifty head teachers. It was a sad reflection of society
that in all that time only around a fifth had been women.

Of the Head teachers introduced during the course of this
book some, sadly a minority, should be seen as the very best
of role models and individuals whose qualities of compassion, commitment, acceptance of responsibility and leadership always shone through. They represent individuals who
would become mentors or friends, and in some cases both, to

Lawrie for life. The significance of such people, to all of those they come into contact with, cannot be overstated.

Of the others, few might have proved as corrupt and greedy as Bill Bagshaw, but too many would fit the description, which might not unreasonably be applied to the likes of 'Bendover' Bennett, Dr. Silk and Cliff Sullivan, of being self obsessed, narcissistic, egotistical, and possibly even sociopathic, bullies. Whether that remains the case where today's Executive Heads and vastly well remunerated Academy Trust CEO's are concerned may be for others to decide.

Let us then conclude by moving on from the fictional characters above, to brief consideration of the following three authentic and real life miscreants and lawbreakers.

Thirty years ago Colleen McCabe became Head teacher of St. John Rigby School in South East London, where she was praised for improving both discipline within the school and enhancing the facilities. Ten years later, at exactly the same time as the account of Bill Bagshaw's 'exposure' is set, she would be found guilty of six charges of deception and eleven charges of theft (totalling up to £500,000) from the school. She was sentenced to five years in prison.

More recently, as fans of the *Western* film genre may note, the entirely inappropriately named James Stewart, an 'Executive Principle' no less, of an Academy in Cambridgeshire, allegedly defrauded his school of £100,000 while turning his office into something described as a 'sex dungeon'. He hadn't been exposed by the LEA, but by a roofing contractor who reported seeing a large purple vibrator on the head teacher's desk through the office skylight. Mr. Stewart was eventually banned from teaching for life and jailed for four years.

Finally, let us turn our attention to Michelle Hollingsworth the Headteacher of Annie Lennard Primary

School in Birmingham who, along with her secretary, Deborah Jones, was described as fraudulently obtaining over £500,000 from her (unsurprisingly) deprived Primary school.

Both were sent to prison in late 2019 having been found guilty of fraud which involved, amongst other things, personal shopping sprees and 'kick-back' deals to tradesman and others including members of their families.

The Judge, at Wolverhampton Crown Court concluded,

'You had great responsibility at the school, were in a position of great trust and in charge of the finances to ensure best value for the school.'

'It wasn't your money and it had to be spent wisely, not generously on yourself.'

'You abused your position of power trust and responsibility to become the lynch pin of all this offending'

'You amassed a small network of people who each became involved in your dishonest scheme'.

'As a result the school is having to rebuild itself, not with bricks and mortar but with different financial procedures and other changes to raise morale from the parlous state caused by the two people running the school turning out to be criminals.'

It all sounded far too familiar to Lawrie. 'Oh well', he sighed, closing his lap-top and turning his attention to the view beyond his window and the sight of a solitary and resplendent Red Kite, a relatively new addition to the local ornithological landscape, soaring against the setting sun which illuminated the limestone walls and lush green hills of Derbyshire's White Peak. 'At least she didn't go on to work as an Ofsted Inspector. Just imagine if, with the full knowledge of the LEA, that could have ever been allowed to happen.'

About the Author

Martin Dale was born in North West England in the mid 1950's and grew up in a combination of Merionethshire, Lancashire and Oxford before moving to the Midlands where he taught for thirty years, a career which he loved and loathed in roughly equal measure.

On the subjects of loving and loathing, Martin's favourite places are Andalucia, Big Sur, Tremadog Bay and the Derbyshire Peak District, a place he has called home for the last four decades. Martin's other great loves are visiting the theatre, live music, whale watching, walking, rugby league, Test cricket and watching his grandchildren grow.

Of the things he loathes, sprouts, bullies and those who abuse their positions of personal, professional or political power feature particularly prominently.

The most important lesson he has learned in approaching seventy years is that...the only thing necessary for evil to triumph is for good men to do nothing.

Contact the author: accidentalheadteacher@gmail.com